A
MONK'S
CONFESSION

· hic liber est sce marie de sogento si qs eu abstulerit anathe ma sit
ac uere discretionis magistro NORBER
to fr Guibtus monachus nomine pec
cator opib; psps suis suoruq; gaudere 1103

SUCCES
SIBVSV

R
DVG
NI
MS
ET
MA
GIS

TRIS VETERIB; horresce in dm
psentis ppetie pelagus aggressur ad te liberalis
me doctor tanta audis causas tue conscii humi
lnatus inferim? Qui uerba excusationis n am
bigo qd modestia tua ta mte suscipiat, quia a
me intentione apud tuas sobrias aures promi
constat

A

A MONK'S CONFESSION

The Memoirs of Guibert of Nogent

Translated and
with an Introduction
by Paul J. Archambault

The Pennsylvania State University Press
University Park, Pennsylvania

Library of Congress Cataloging-in-Publication Data

Guibert, Abbot of Nogent-sous-Coucy, 1053–ca. 1124.
    [De vita sua. English]
    A monk's confession : the memoirs of Guibert of Nogent /
translated and with an introduction by Paul J. Archambault.
      p.   cm.
    Includes bibliographical references and index.
    ISBN 0-271-01481-4 (cloth)
    ISBN 0-271-01482-2 (paper)
    1. Guibert, Abbot of Nogent-sous-Coucy, 1053–ca. 1124.   2. Abbots—
France—Biography.   3. Benedictines—France—Biography.
I. Archambault, Paul J., 1937–   .   II. Title.
BX4705.G698A3   1995
271'.102—dc20
[B]   95–11479
                                          CIP

Third printing, 2004

It is the policy of The Pennsylvania State University Press to use acid-free paper
for the first printing of all clothbound books. Publications on uncoated stock
satisfy the minimum requirements of American National Standard for Information Sciences—Permanence of Paper for Printed Library Materials, ANSI
Z39.48–1984.

Frontispiece: Guibert presents to Christ his commentary on several Old Testament
books. Bibliothèque Nationale, lat. 2502, fol. 1.

For Marianna

CONTENTS

LIST OF ILLUSTRATIONS

ACKNOWLEDGMENTS

I must first acknowledge the debt I owe to the work of the late John F. Benton. The excellent historical scholarship and the continuing success of Professor Benton's translation of Abbot Guibert's memoirs (*Self and Society in Medieval France*) would seem to make my own superfluous. In section five of my Introduction, I set forth in detail my reasons for publishing a new translation of Guibert's *Monodiae*. I also am deeply indebted to the translation of the late Edmond-René Labande, *Guibert de Nogent: Autobiographie,* which appeared in Paris in 1981

My notes, which I recommend to the reader, owe much to the research of both Benton and Labande. Many of these notes provide the explicit source for Guibert's frequent quotations from, or allusions to, the Bible. The Latin text of Scripture, or Vulgate, was deeply imbedded in Guibert's mind, and he usually quotes it from memory. Guibert's explicit quotations from Scripture, or references to specific authors or books, have been footnoted. When a reference to Scripture is alluded to rather than explicitly quoted I have bracketed the reference. The English Revised Standard Version (RSV) has been used whenever I believe it provides the most appropriate translation of Guibert's Latin text.

Several colleagues at Syracuse University have provided me with invaluable help. I thank Wolfgang Müller, then a doctoral student, now an Assistent at the University of Augsburg, Germany, for reading and criticizing an earlier version of this translation; James Powell, for his advice with historical detail in the Introduction; Jaklin Kornfilt, for precious assistance with computer problems; Harold Jones, chair of the Department of Languages, Literatures, and Linguistics, for his encouragement; Benjamin Ware, vice-president for Research and Computing, for a grant-in-aid that enabled me to work at the Archives départementales de l'Aisne and at the Laon cathedral during the summer of 1994.

Without the refining editorial pen of Peter J. Potter, of the Penn State University Press, the present translation would be far more imperfect than it is now. I am alone responsible for any mistranslations or awkward renditions the reader may yet detect. I also am grateful to Nancy Cleaver of Pennsylvania Calligraphy for designing the map and chronological table.

I am, finally, deeply grateful to my wife, Marianna M. Archambault, professor of French at Bucknell University and prize-winning photographer, for encouraging me to undertake this new translation and for convincing me it was needed. If I am ultimately hesitant in recommending my translation, I am enthusiastic in recommending her photographs contained herein, which were taken from the towers of the Laon cathedral, or in the fields of Nogent-sous-Coucy. Had Abbot Guibert seen these pictures he might have repeated his favorite expression: "Why say more?"

Translator's Introduction

Guibert of Nogent as Witness of His Times

Guibert lived his entire life in northern France. He was born at Clermont, in Picardy, just a few miles east of Compiègne, probably in the year 1055.[1] He came from a family of minor nobility: his father had fought at the battle of Mortemer in 1054, less than a year before Guibert's birth, in the army of King Henry I of France against Duke William of Normandy. Ordinarily Guibert would have entered the military, as did his brothers and other members of his clan. In one of the most dramatic chapters of the *Monodiae* (or *Solitary Songs*), his largely autobiographical work, Guibert explains why he was destined from the day of his birth to be a monk rather than to wield the sword and ride a horse, like his father and one of his older brothers. At a crucial moment of his delivery, Guibert, as he himself puts it, "turned around in her [his mother's] womb," and it looked as if both the child and the mother might die. Then,

> The family held an urgent meeting. They rushed to the altar of the Mother of God. To the one who was, and ever will be, the only Virgin ever to give birth, they made the following vow and left it as an offering at our Lady's altar: if the child were male, it would be consecrated a cleric in God's service and hers; if the

1. The controversy surrounding the exact date of Guibert's birth is well summarized in Edmond-René Labande, *Guibert de Nogent: Autobiographie* (Paris: Les Belles Lettres, 1981), ix–x. Labande's argument for placing the date of Guibert's birth on Holy Saturday 1055 seems the most compelling. John F. Benton's argument for the year 1064 (*Self and Society in Medieval France* [New York: Harper & Row, 1970; rpt. University of Toronto Press, 1984], 229–39) is unconvincing.

child were of the lesser sex, it would be given over to a corresponding religious vocation. (book 1, chapter 3)

Guibert's vocation to the monastic life was determined from the day
of his birth. His father, who had been captured at the battle of Mortemer, appears to have died about eight months after Guibert's birth.
His mother, who was the great and only love of his life, vowed never to
remarry and saw to it that he would be dressed as an oblate, educated by
a private tutor, and deprived of all playmates or companions in the family
castle at Clermont from the age of six onward.

Guibert complains of the uncompromising strictness of his early
schooling at the tutor's hands, of his inability to engage in any sort of
physical activity, and of the mediocre results produced by an intellectual
regime that is all work and no play. He makes pertinent observations
about the counterproductive effects of physical punishment and about
the need for the mind to engage in a variety of pursuits if it is to maintain
its alertness and edge (1.5). Thus, the oppressive education Guibert
received between the ages of six and twelve undoubtedly contributed
to his proneness to overanxiety, scrupulosity, and occasional depression
revealed in the *Monodiae*.

Guibert's personality was powerfully shaped by family influence, particularly by his unflinching admiration for his mother. While he was
under tutorship at home, Guibert tells of an attempt by one of his older
brothers, which proved unsuccessful, to procure an ecclesiastical office
for him (1.7). He speaks admiringly of his mother's resistance to new
suitors after his father's death and her vow to remain chaste and never
remarry (1.13). When he was about twelve years old (ca. 1067), his
mother, who by now had been widowed nearly a dozen years, withdrew
from the family castle at Clermont to a little house that she had ordered
built for her in the vicinity of the abbey of Saint-Germer de Fly (1.14).
There she spent her days in prayer, fasting, tears, and penance. Guibert's
tutor was to follow her shortly thereafter to Saint-Germer, where he too
became a monk.

Left at home, Guibert indulged in what he considered, in retrospect,
the most "sinful" period of his life. He began to mock the church, hate
school, imitate the rowdiness of his young cousins by indulging with
them in horsemanship, curse the signs of his clericature while promising
himself quick remission of his sins, and overindulge in sleep to such an
extent that his body became anemic (1.15). When his mother received

news of her son's behavior, she begged the abbot of Saint-Germer to receive him in the monastery. When Guibert arrived at Saint-Germer he conceived his first real longing for the monastic life and for the rule of Saint Benedict, which he was to live by for the rest of his life, not without many intermittent temptations to lead a worldly life (1.16).

Guibert seems to have spent most of the next thirty-eight years (1067–1105) at Saint-Germer, with his mother living in the little house nearby. It was there, he tells us, that he developed a true passion for literary studies, wrote his first works, occasionally even some poetry (which has been lost), and was ordained to the so-called "minor orders," by which one presumes he reached the ecclesiastical rank of subdeacon. Guibert's years at Saint-Germer seem to have witnessed alternating periods of studious serenity and great internal agitation. At least on one occasion he was tempted to leave the abbey only to be dissuaded from doing so by his mother's account of a dream she had had in which the Virgin appeared, telling her that her son was vowed to her forever (1.16). He seems to have been tempted on several occasions by offers of ecclesiastical benefices outside the monastery, and he does admit (1.19) that during those years at Saint-Germer he was beset as much by ambition as he was by carnal temptation.

Guibert does not explicitly tell us whether he was ordained to the priesthood, but the great promotion that changed his life could have taken place without his receiving holy orders. In 1104, when he was about fifty years old, he learned that he had been elected abbot of the monastery of Nogent, about sixty miles east of Saint-Germer, situated just south of the castle of Coucy, in the fertile, rolling country between the Oise and the Aisne rivers. This election, which he had not directly solicited, seems to have brought him enormous satisfaction (1.19). It provided a legal, morally acceptable satisfaction to his devouring ambition. It also provided him with his first real opportunity to leave a mother in whose close company he had lived the first half century of his life.

Guibert remained abbot of Nogent from 1104 until his death, which occurred some time after 1121 and before 1125,[2] when he was in his late sixties or early seventies. He does not seem to have traveled much beyond the Compiègne-Noyon-Nogent-Soissons "quadrangle" during the last sixteen years of his life, except for a trip to Langres for an audience with Pope Paschal II in early 1107 (3.4). It was soon after he was elected

---

2. Labande, *Guibert de Nogent*, xi.

abbot of Nogent that his mother died at Saint-Germer (3.4). It was also
at Nogent (around 1108) that he wrote his two longest and most famous
works: the *Gesta Dei per Francos,* an account of the First Crusade based
upon his reading of an earlier version of the Jerusalem Expedition, the
Gesta Francorum,[3] and the *Monodiae, or Solitary Songs.*

The *Monodiae* is divided into three parts. (Editors since the time of
Dom Luc Dachéry, who edited Guibert's complete works in 1651, have
referred to them as "books.") Readers looking for autobiographical detail usually consider the first book, which covers the years 1055–1104
and comprises about 42 percent of the total, the most fascinating. It is
in this first book that Guibert tells of the constraining circumstances
surrounding his birth and of the factors that led to his vocation to the
monastic life. The book also contains digressive chapters dealing with
monastic development and reform in northern and eastern France, as
well as many colorful anecdotes of demonic visions and carnal temptations. Book 3, which occupies about 45 percent of the whole, is a history
of the bishopric of Laon and contains a dramatic, colorful narrative of
the uprising of the Laon commune in 1112, an event that the politically
conservative Guibert abhorred. Modestly inserted between Books 1 and
3, the "slight" second book is a serene history of Guibert's abbey of
Nogent. Antiquarian and archaeological in tone, it delves into its most
ancient legend, that of King Quilius, who allegedly lived at the time of
Christ, traveled to Jerusalem where he met the Apostles and Mary herself, and converted to the Christian religion, after which he returned to
Nogent to transform the site from a pagan burial ground to a Christian
abbey (2.1).

Many great political and ecclesiastical events occurred during Guibert's lifetime. In the political realm, his life coincides roughly with the
reigns of two Capetian kings, Philip I (1060–1108), and Louis VI, also
known as Louis the Fat (1108–37). Some of the events narrated in the
Monodiae, however, such as the history of the earliest bishops of Laon
(3.1), occurred before Guibert was born, during the reigns of Robert II
the Pious (996–1031) and Henry I (1031–60).

In terms of ecclesiastical history, Guibert's life coincides with the
foundation of the Grande Chartreuse (1.10–11), and with the Investiture

3. See Abbé J. P. Migne, ed., *Patrologiae Cursus Completus. Series Latina* [hereafter
PL], 227 vols. (Paris: Ed. d'Amboise, 1864-84), 156.681.

Controversy, which swept over France especially during the pontificates from Leo IX (1046–53) to Pascal II (1099–1118). Guibert's birth is almost contemporaneous with a great ecclesiastical event that remained unknown to most Europeans for many years — the great Schism between Rome and the Eastern churches in 1054. Likewise, several important political and ecclesiastical events occurred during his lifetime. The papal reform under Gregory VII (1073–85) firmly reasserted papal authority in matters such as the buying and selling of ecclesiastical offices, the naming and investiture of bishops, the reassertion of clerical celibacy, and the reform of monasteries. Guibert was still a novice in the Picard monastery of Saint-Germer in 1077 when Pope Gregory VII excommunicated Emperor Henry IV of Germany during a dispute over the investiture of bishops, and subsequently humiliated him at Canossa, in northern Italy. In 1095, Pope Urban II excommunicated King Philip I of France after the king had repudiated his first wife, Berthe of Frisia, and entered into concubinage with Bertrade de Montfort. Other momentous events that occurred during Guibert's lifetime included the First Crusade to reconquer Jerusalem (1095–99); the councils of Reims (1119), Soissons (1121), and Lateran I (1123), among other councils.[4]

Guibert was aware of some of these national and international events, as he shows in his Gesta Dei per Francos, his highly patriotic account of the Jerusalem expedition, written around 1108.[5] Curiously, the Monodiae, written around 1115, gives no indication whatsoever that Guibert had a broad picture of national, international, or ecclesiastical occurrences on a large scale. Perhaps because he considered the Monodiae a more private work than the Gesta, Guibert's picture of the world, when it is not focused on himself, rarely extends beyond the region of northern France where he lived all his life. Limited largely to ecclesiastical gossip and terrifying anecdotes involving demonic presences, his testimony is all the more precious because it is so partial, local, and parochial. Were we to rely on the Monodiae alone we would never know whether Guibert was

4. See Georges Duby, The Knight, the Lady, and the Priest, trans. Barbara Bray (New York: Pantheon Books, 1983); Rev. Fernand Mourret, A History of the Catholic Church, vol. 4: Period of the Later Middle Ages, trans. Rev. Newton Thompson, S.T.D. (London: B. Herder, 1947), 4.140; Robert Fawtier, The Capetian Kings of France, trans. Lionel Butler and R. J. Adam (New York: St. Martin's Press, 1966); Elizabeth M. Hallam, Capetian France 987–1328 (New York: Longmans, 1980); John C. Dwyer, Twenty Centuries of Catholic Christianity (New York: Paulist Press, 1985).

5. PL 156.695–702.

aware of the Gregorian reform except insofar as it affected his corner of Picardy. The *Monodiae* contains no allusion to the humiliation of the German emperor at Canossa, or to German affairs in general. In spite of his predilection for sexually titillating anecdotes in monastic circles, Guibert does not mention the adulterous affair between King Philip and Bertrade, which must have been the talk of the French kingdom. He does indicate, however, in the *Gesta Dei* that he knew of the event.[6]

If Guibert is at all aware of events on a national or European scale, it is by repercussion, insofar as they affected local abbeys and dioceses near Nogent. He discusses simony (the illegal purchase of ecclesiastical benefits, offices, and prebends) on several occasions and calls it a great enemy of the true religious life (1.19), aware that members of his family have, in the past, attempted to extort ecclesiastical dignities for him. He explicitly mentions the deposition of Manasses, archbishop of Reims, in 1080, by Pope Gregory VII's legate, Hugh of Die (1.11). He speaks directly and eloquently to Pope Paschal II at Langres, in the winter of 1107, to convince the Pope to approve the nomination of the corrupt courtier Gaudry as bishop of Laon; but he seems unaware of the larger fact that the Pope's visit to France in that year was prompted by a need to enlist the alliance of the young king-designate, Louis VI, son of Philip I (who lay dying), in the Pope's continuing quarrel with Emperor Henry V of Germany over investitures.[7] Here is one of many instances where Guibert shows far more interest in local ecclesiastical intrigue than in the overall picture; and after the encounter with the Pope, he even admits, rather glibly for a monk who is avowedly scrupulous about matters of simony, to having accepted a bribe from Gaudry himself in order to convince those opposed to his nomination (2.4).

Guibert, in sum, might be described as a local witness to his times who occasionally made history but was unaware of the history that he was making. His best talent as a witness is perhaps demonstrated in his narration of the uprising of the Laon commune (3.8–9); but he was far too parochial in his views, far too conditioned by his lifelong association with churchmen in power, to see the revolt of the commune as anything more than the devastation wreaked by an unruly mob. As careful as he might be in his self-examination he was not nearly so careful in confirming the "facts" related of others. Never did he attempt truly to under-

6. Ibid., 698.
7. Labande, *Guibert de Nogent*, 286, 305.

stand the real causes underlying the revolt of the Laon burghers, especially their intense dissatisfaction with the social, economic, and ecclesiastical structures of that city (3.7). In the *Gesta Dei,* written eight years earlier, he could repeat the worst allegations about those not of the Latin Christian camp. All the imaginable Christian heresies and vices come from the Eastern churches, and the religion of "Mathomus" (Mohammed). An epileptic religious leader who had died while being devoured by pigs was, in Guibert's mind, merely receiving retribution for all the previous "erroneous doctrines of the Greeks."[8] In the *Monodiae,* however, Guibert reveals a greater sense of fairness as he deals with matters closer to home.

Guibert was an interesting, sometimes fascinating witness to his times; but he did not have the breadth of experience and vision to understand them, the way a Saint Bernard, for example, had a broad-ranging conception of European Christendom. But this shortcoming is also a source of strength for his writing: Guibert's chief contribution may lie in his keen introspection into the labyrinthine recesses of his own soul, which offers us the rare opportunity to witness the inner world of medieval monasticism.

Guibert and the Critics

Guibert's *Monodiae* might arguably be considered his best-known work today, owing perhaps to the intense interest scholars have shown in medieval autobiography during the past thirty years. Nineteenth-century scholarship, however, seems to have had no special predilection for the *Monodiae,* setting it on very much the same level as Guibert's other works. Guizot translated and published the *Gesta Dei per Francos* before the *Monodiae* in his 1825 collection of the *Memoires relatifs à l'histoire de France;* and in his Preface to the *Gesta* he seems to give the work on the First Crusade pride of place over the autobiographical text.[9] In his his-

---

8. *PL* 156.687-91.

9. François M. Guizot, *Collection des Mémoires pour servir à l'histoire de France,* Vol. 9: *Histoire des croisades, par Guibert de Nogent — Vie de Guibert de Nogent, par lui-même* (Paris: J.L.G. Brière, 1825), x.

tory of the communal uprisings of the twelfth century in northern France, Augustin Thierry, perhaps the most politically liberal and methodologically scientific historian of the French Restoration period, paid exclusive attention to Book 3 of the *Monodiae*, arguing with fervor that the uprising of the Laon commune was one of the early medieval revolutions that led to the great revolution of 1789.[10] In 1896, the rationalist critic Abel Lefranc was especially impressed by Guibert's treatise on relics, the *De pignoribus sanctorum*, calling it an "absolutely unique" treatise because of its "rationalistic" approach to the cult of the saints. Lefranc, who was to engage three decades later in a famous polemic with Lucien Febvre over the question of Rabelais's "atheism," compared Guibert with other forerunners of the Enlightenment such as Rabelais, Calvin, and Voltaire.[11]

Around the turn of the century the young Bernard Monod, in a series of studies that preceded his premature death at the age of twenty-four, waxed lyrical about Guibert's approach to historiography, especially in the *Gesta Dei per Francos*, whose author he called "the most intellectual man of his century."[12] Monod was also impressed by Guibert's sense of patriotism in the *Gesta Dei*, calling him the first of a long line of French historians who have been convinced that France has a divine calling to lead the rest of the world to higher things.[13] Monod argued that the idea of a French nation and of a French patriotic sense arose during the reign of King Philip (1060–1108), and that it was no coincidence that the first *Chansons de geste* and Guibert's epically-entitled history of the First Crusade were contemporaneous with King Philip's reign.[14]

Guibert did not become a controversial figure until the 1970s, with the publication of the first critical English-language translation of the *Monodiae*, John Benton's *Self and Society in Medieval France*. Benton attempts a modest psychoanalytical reading of Guibert using Freudian

10. In his letter 16 of the *Lettres sur l'histoire de France*, Thierry writes: "Cette marche [the successive phases of the Laon uprising] qui est, nous le savons par expérience, celle des grandes révolutions, se retrouve d'une manière aussi précise dans le soulevement d'une simple ville que dans celui d'une nation entiére." See Augustin Thierry, *Lettres sur l'histoire de France* (Paris: Garnier, 1828), 218–313.

11. Benton, *Self and Society*, 8.

12. Bernard Monod, *Le Moine Guibert et son temps (1053–1124)* (Paris: Hachette, 1905), 256.

13. Monod, *Le Moine Guibert*, 229; Benton, *Self and Society*, 8.

14. Monod, *Le Moine Guibert*, 237–38.

analysis. He is cautious, however, about superimposing the grid of a reductionist, narrowly Freudian reading upon a religious figure living in a time so far removed and so distant:

> Guibert's fear of mutilation requires special attention because it raises the question of whether his relationship to his mother and his fears together fit the Freudian model of a castration complex. While the evidence available is insufficient to warrant any unqualified application of psychoanalytic theory to the culture of medieval Europe, the concurrence of circumstances in this particular case is striking.[15]

While Benton's approach is cautious and tentative, Jonathan Kantor's study, published in 1976, is more aggressively clinical in its search for unconscious causes of behavior. To "scratch" this historian, argues Kantor, is to discover "a guilt-ridden cleric, haunted by vivid sexual reminiscences of his mother and by the terrible chastening reality of the Virgin Mary."[16] No psychological analysis of Guibert's personality is possible without a consideration of the role of his mother, continues Kantor, who seems unable to accept at face value Guibert's characterization of his mother as "beautiful yet chaste." He concludes inexplicably that this "schizoid" woman had "something of both the saint and the whore in her."[17] Secure in "know[ing]" that the woman was the possible cause for her husband's impotence for many years before Guibert's birth," Kantor is also sure that the mother's sexual repression translated into Guibert's "abhorrence of all things sexual," while there probably remained in his adulthood "an intransigent substrate of erotic feelings in his unconscious that persisted from his oedipal stage."[18] Invoking the authority of Freud's *Outline of Psychoanalysis*, Kantor explains why Guibert's superego development proceeded "along matriarchal lines," and why "the erotic wishes of the son [were] sublimated in the veneration of the Virgin." He concludes that Guibert's case is a classic instance of displacement and sublimation of his sexual desires and pronounces the "fair" judgment

15. Benton, *Self and Society*, 26.
16. Jonathan Kantor, "A Psychological Source: *The Memoirs* of Abbot Guibert of Nogent," *Journal of Medieval History* 2 (1976): 281.
17. Kantor, "A Psychological Source," 285.
18. Ibid., 288.

"that Guibert dealt with his unconscious phallic aggression by forming a matriarchal superego on the paradigm of the Virgin."[19]

Freud's chief objection to religion, and to Christianity in particular, is well known: religion is a neurotic form of behavior that prevents the individual from attaining the true maturity of adulthood by feeding upon the reassuring delusions of childhood. In a well-known passage from *The Future of an Illusion* he wrote of religious ideas:

> These [ideas] which are given out as teachings, are not precipitates of experience or end-results of thinking: they are illusions, fulfillments of the oldest, strongest and most urgent wishes of mankind. The secret of their strength lies in the strength of those wishes. As we already know, the terrifying impression of helplessness in childhood aroused the need for protection — for protection through love — which was provided by the father; and the recognition that this helplessness lasts through life made it necessary to cling to the existence of a father, but this time a more powerful one. Thus the benevolent rule of a divine Providence allays our fear of the dangers of life; the establishment of a moral world-order ensures the fulfillment of the demands of justice, which have so often remained unfulfilled in human civilization; and the prolongation of earthly existence in a future life provides the local and temporal framework in which these wish-fulfillments shall take place.[20]

In recent years, Freudian-style readings of Guibert seem somewhat rarer in historical criticism; and when attempts at psychocriticism are made they tend to be holistic and open-ended. One such holistic approach antedates Jonathan Kantor's study by several years. In his monumental *Geschichte der Autobiographie*, written over a period of a half-century or more, Georg Misch (1878–1965), a student of Dilthey, provided a comprehensive, phenomenological approach to Guibert that accepts Guibert's religious experience on its own terms, without resorting to reductionist or pathological explanations.[21] Without pretending to rank

19. Ibid., 289.
20. Sigmund Freud, *The Future of an Illusion*, trans. James Strachey (New York: W. W. Norton, 1961), 30.
21. Georg Misch, *Geschichte der Autobiographie: Das Mittelalter* (Frankfurt am Main: G. Schulte-Bulmke, 1959), 108–62.

Guibert with his Augustinian model, Misch nonetheless claimed for Guibert's *Monodiae* the distinction of being the first "comprehensive" autobiography ("die erste umfassende Autobiographie") to come out of medieval literature, "comprehensive, in the sense that Guibert is the first medieval autobiographer to treat the course of his life in its broad temporal course from genealogy and birth onwards."[22]

The holistic methodology of the French *Annales* historians has also provided objective, sympathetic investigations of the mentality of distant persons or epochs. A humane, sympathetic view of Guibert and his *Solitary Songs* is provided by Georges Duby, who considers Guibert a sensitive, precious witness to an age when the ecclesiastical orders within the Roman church were reasserting a monastically-directed and monogamous conception of marriage over an older, feudal, polygamous conception. Plunging headlong and intuitively into the spirit of Guibert's age, Duby credits Guibert with a sensitivity of his own and clearly distinguishes a "mother fixation" from a young man's sincere cult of the Virgin. "Guibert," writes Duby, "was exceptionally intelligent and sensitive. I see him as typical of all the late-born sons of couples like his parents. What we are able to glimpse of his childhood shows him rejected — because of the lack of a father and his mother's adoption of the illegitimate child to redeem her husband's sin." From Duby's treatment of Guibert emerges an inclusive psychological portrait, enriched by considerations of family, class, and time and in keeping with the mental framework of Guibert's time:

> His isolation and resentment made him cling to his mother and regard her with morbid reverence. She was beautiful, modest, and above all chaste. She at least, amid the brutishness and violence of the knightly race around her, despised the flesh and shut her ears to obscene stories. Guibert clung to her apron strings: the first time he was separated from her was when he was made abbot of Nogent; he was then over fifty. A similar bond joined him to the Virgin Mary, to whom he had been dedicated even before he was born. . . . For him she was the lady par excellence, the mother who was inaccessible and — unlike his earthly one — undefiled.[23]

22. Misch, *Geschichte der Autobiographie*, 109.
23. Duby, *The Knight, the Lady, and the Priest*, 146.

Duby's reading of Guibert combines psychoanalytical insight with the most enlightening historical erudition. Guibert's fear of emasculation is rightly "linked to horror of women," but Duby adds that it is "a fear that was reinforced within religious houses by the tales told by inmates who had taken the habit late, and were not virgins, to others like Guibert, who had no direct experience of such things."[24] Characteristic of *Annales* historical writing, Duby's reading of Guibert is conscious of, but not subservient to, the criticism of religious experience provided by the nineteenth-century "philosophies of suspicion," Nietzschean and Freudian in particular. It is an attempt to examine the mentalities of Guibert's own time with a sympathetic eye, rather than to prove that Guibert's time was immature in comparison with our own. It is this type of reading, both sympathetic and deeply historical, that we must deepen if we are to achieve any understanding of Guibert's personality.

Guibert and Christian Contempt of Self

Even in an age when it was common to present a dramatically heightened picture of one's sinfulness, Guibert seems harsh on himself compared to famous contemporaries like Bernard of Clairvaux, Abbot Suger, Anselm of Canterbury, or Abelard. These religious personalities might have discerned in his hyperbolic professions of abjectness a subtle, familiar form of monastic hubris. What is unmistakable about Guibert's confession is that, whatever else his early life might have taught him, it never taught him to love himself. What is endearing about him is that he managed to rise above a psychic frailty that could have led others to self-destruction. The redeeming counterpoise to his weakness, so far as he was concerned, was the grace of Christ, in which he never lost faith.

Guibert shares with some of the greatest ecclesiastical writers of his age an intense preoccupation with the sinfulness of his soul. A common theme of much twelfth-century monastic literature was a discourse of self-contempt, or self-depreciation. In prayers that have struck some of his critics as the "products of supreme genius" but might seem to other

24. Ibid., 147.

readers to be exercises in self-depreciation, Saint Anselm of Canterbury (1033–1109) describes the horror of self-examination as worse than anything save the "damnation" of self-avoidance: "If I look within myself, I cannot bear myself; if I do not look within myself, I do not know myself."[25] In his "Prayer to Saint Peter," Anselm describes his soul as "bound by the chains of sin, / weighed down by a burden of vices, / stinking and dirty with misdeeds, / torn by the wounds of devils, / festering and filthy with the ulcers of crimes."[26] In his "Prayer to Saint Paul," Anselm considers himself both "my own accuser and judge."[27] The contemporary writer John of Fécamp asks God to "make my heart contrite and a fount of tears that I may weep for the wounds of my soul day and night until the accepted time, until the day of salvation."[28]

In the context of such a tradition, Guibert's own profession of iniquity does not seem exceptional. It is entirely natural for him to decry the "filth and misery of my own heart," and the "layers of accumulated filth" under which he buries the "qualities you had endowed me with" (2.3). After retiring to Saint-Germer de Fly, Guibert's mother confesses her former sins almost every day, "for she had learned that this is where all goodness begins." Her spirit is "ever preoccupied with an examination of her past actions." Everything she has ever done, thought, or said, as a young girl, as a married woman, or as a widow with a wider range of possibilities, is "unceasingly summoned to the trial of reason. She prays with "passionate outcries," and "eats away at herself with . . . anxiety of spirit" ("cum tantis videres . . . orare stridoribus, tanta spiritus anxietate tabescere"), yet no amount of penance can bring her peace and confidence of heart (1.14). Her anxiety seems to feed upon itself.

Many monastic writings of Guibert's time delight in repeating just how corrupt and perverse the human heart is if only one takes a close look at it. Historians of literature might easily be tempted to point to Augustine's *Confessions* as the work most responsible for introducing this "sense of guilt" into the literature of introspection. Whether the *Confessions* produces a sense of guilt or the same sense of liberation that it seems to have produced in its author ultimately depends upon the reader's own state of mind. But that is a minor matter. Like Augustine's,

25. Sister Benedicta Ward, *The Prayers and Meditations of Saint Anselm* (Harmondsworth: Penguin Books, 1973), 130.

26. Ward, *Prayers and Meditations of Saint Anselm*, 135.

27. Ibid., 143.

28. Ibid., 48.

Guibert's belief in the corruption of the soul is matched by his over-whelming confidence in Christ's infinite mercy. Temperamental and intel-lectual differences separate Augustine from Guibert, to be sure. August-ine was conversant with the major philosophical systems of Antiquity, while Guibert seems, at best, to have an uneasy grasp of the logical distinctions of his master, Anselm of Laon (1.17) and seems far more interested in monastic politics than in philosophy. The aberrations of Augustine's youth darkened his view of human sexuality and convinced him that our vulnerability to "concupiscence" is the clearest sign of our fallen nature.

But Augustine is never morbid the way Guibert can be, with an inten-sity all the greater because Guibert never quite reveals the nature of his "vices" to the reader. Though he condemns the witchcraft that pre-vented his father and mother from consummating "a natural and legiti-mate bond," he applauds his mother's attempt, once widowed, "to look as if she had reached the decline of life, with an old woman's wrinkles" (1.13). His mother has a vision of her dead husband issuing from a pit: a laceration in his side signifies that he has perverted his marriage bond with a prostitute; a wailing child in his arms signifies the damnation of the child conceived in sin (1.18). Guibert admits that his taste for poetry makes him "prone to immodest sexual behavior" (1.17), though he is characteristically vague about the "misfortunes" that his mother had warned him about and that have now befallen him (1.19). A monk is in the grip of "abominable vices," which no surveillance by anyone could keep him from (1.24). A nun from the Women's Abbey at Caen falls "into awful sins" and "cannot be persuaded by any admonition to make her confession" (2.5). As John Benton suggests, Guibert's fear of sexual contact only seems to intensify his sense of guilt for sexual "sins."[29]

Some allowance must be made here for historical factors. Guibert belongs to an age that holds very rigid distinctions of licit and illicit, pure and impure sexual behavior, even within married life. By Guibert's day, sexual morality is largely dictated by the church's codification. The sexual activity of married couples is as regulated by the liturgical cycles as is the life of the monk. Like the liturgy, married sexuality is sur-rounded with conditions and interdictions and is subject to the rhythms of the liturgical cycles. As there are days set aside for feasting and embracing, so are there days set aside for fasting and for refraining

29. Benton, *Self and Society*, 26–27.

from embracing. According to Jean-Louis Flandrin's remarkable study of penance manuals compiled between the sixth and the eleventh century, sexual intercourse is proscribed on certain days of the week and during the three Lenten periods of the year. Even within marriage, sexual activity bears the mark of impurity: "No sexual pleasure is free of fault, even in legitimate sexual union," writes Pope Gregory the Great to Augustine of Canterbury, echoing Saint Jerome (and, incidentally, Stoic thinkers as well).[30] As in Antiquity and in Old Testament days, women's biological functions are subject to ritual purification: women are not admitted to communion during their menstrual cycles, or during the period following childbirth and preceding purification. In keeping with a Pauline attitude of tolerance toward a way of life considered inferior to the Christian ideal of monastic celibacy, sexuality within marriage is an activity tolerated rather than condoned, and strictly ordained toward the procreation of children. The more often one abstains the closer one approaches the Christian ideal.[31]

Guibert is writing, then, at a time when sexuality within marriage is subject to nearly as much regulation as the life of the monk. According to Duby, it was during this time — the early twelfth century — that an ecclesiastical model of marriage was gaining the upper hand over an earlier, "disorderly" aristocratic model.[32] Perhaps, then, Guibert's views of sexuality and marriage are largely reflective of his age. He seems genuinely saddened in telling of the suffering of both his parents who,

30. "Nec haec dicentes culpam deputamus esse coniugium. Sed quia ipsa licita admixtio coniugis sine voluptate carnis fieri non potest, a sacri loci ingressu abstinendum est, quia voluptas ipse esse sine culpa nullatenus est" (Jean-Louis Flandrin, *Un Temps pour embrasser. Aux origines de la morale sexuelle occidentale. VIe–XIe siècle* [Paris: Seuil, 1983], 223n.50). I owe this entire development to Flandrin, 73–127.

31. Flandrin adds: "During this period not only did monks multiply, they became the conscience of the Church, its spearhead, and soon its doctrine-makers and administrators, since most of the great bishops were chosen among them. Now these men, who had chosen continence and celibacy because they considered them a necessary means of salvation, did everything they could — instinctively, no doubt, and out of scruple rather than prejudice or consciousness of innovation — to diminish the occasions that the members of the laity had for sexual union. One has only to consider the multiplication of obstacles that were placed before marriage, in particular the absolutely insane extension of interdictions due to family relatedness; the ease with which annulments, divorces, and separations were granted those wishing to lead a monastic life, and, for the others, the multiplication of periods of continence linked to feast-days and fast-days" (*Un Temps pour embrasser*, 126–27).

32. Duby, *The Knight, the Lady, and the Priest*, 17–18.

under some evil spell cast over them by a relative, were unable to consummate their own marriage for seven years. He reports his mother's "vision" of her dead husband's intense sufferings in Purgatory for having consorted with prostitutes and sired an illegitimate child during that same period. In keeping with orthodox Catholic theology Guibert considers sexuality as restricted to marriage, and the breaking of the marriage bond, whatever the attenuating circumstances, as subject to intense though temporary sufferings in purgatorial fires (1.18).

His real curiosity, however, is arrested by sexual aberrations and what contemporary manuals of confession might have termed "unnatural" sins. Monks and nuns are, like himself, often given to "monstrous" vices from which no form of human surveillance can keep them. The sexual anecdote he recounts at greatest length and with the most obvious relish involves an almost dismaying accretion of "unnatural" vices: devil worship, sperm libation, intercourse of a monk with a nun, and a public abjuring of the faith (1.26). Of this incident Guibert writes:

> Proh scelus! Proh pudor! Et is a quo haec exigebantur erat presbyter! Et haec ad tui ordinis et tuae benedictae hostiae sacrilegam ignominiam fecit tuus antiquus hostis, Domine. Ne sileas, neque compescaris a vindicta, Deus! Quid dicam? Como dicam? Fecit quod petebatur infoelix, quem tu, o utinam ad tempus, deserueras.

> [What a crime! What a shameful act! And it was being demanded of a priest! This is what your enemy of old does, O Lord, to blaspheme and dishonor your priesthood and your sacred host! "Do not be silent," O God, and do not put off your vengeance! What can I say? How shall I speak? The wretched monk whom you had abandoned (O let it be for a time only!) did what was asked of him.]

Even in this extreme instance, however, Guibert's dramatic expression of disapproval is very much in keeping with the language of his age. In the *Liber Gomorrhianus*, written between 1048 and 1054 and dedicated to the reformer Pope Leo IX, Peter Damian, a key figure in the mid-eleventh-century reform of clerical abuses, wrote quite as dramatically, in a "tearful lamentation" over the soul fallen into "unnatural" vices:

Ego, ego te, infelix anima defleo, atque ex intimo pectore de tuae perditionis sorte suspiro. Defleo te, inquam, miserabilis anima immunditiae sordibus dedita, toto nimirum lacrymarum fonte lugenda. Proh dolor! Quis dabit capiti meo aquam et oculis meis fontem lacrymarum?

[It is I, unhappy soul, who weep for you, and from the depths of my heart I bemoan the perdition toward which you are headed. I lament over you, I say, unhappy soul, fallen into the most sordid vices, and indeed you are to be pitied with all the tears that can spring from me. What shame! Who shall pour water over my head? Who will provide a font of tears for my eyes?][33]

Guibert seems to have thought of his own age as particularly immodest. The modesty of his mother's youth—the mid-eleventh century—has now given way, he laments, to the unbridled immodesty and levity of his day. "Alas," he complains, writing in or about the year 1115, "what a wretched and progressive decline since that time until our own in the sense of modesty and honor that was once thought characteristic of virginity!" He then adds a colorful picture of what he perceives as "present" womanly behavior·

Among married women the reality, and even the appearance, of reserve have disappeared. In their conduct they display nothing but coarse humor: nothing but jokes, winks of the eye, wagging of the tongue. They walk provocatively and show only silliness in their behavior. Their way of dressing couldn't be further removed from old-fashioned simplicity: their broad sleeves, their skin-tight tunics, the curling toes of their Cordovan shoes—in every detail they proclaim that they have cast all modesty to the winds. Any one of them would imagine she has reached the rock bottom of misery if she is presumed to be without a lover. Nobility and worldly glory are directly related to the number of suitors who follow in her footsteps. (1.12)

Like Augustine in the *Confessions,* Guibert goes beyond confession of sin. More than a mere *confessio peccati,* his *Solitary Songs* are also a con-

---

33. See Jer. 9, *PL* 145.178; my translation.

fessio laudis. The deeper Guibert's experience of despair, the more open he is to the breath of new life God's redeeming grace brings him. There is something moving about his recurring confidence, his spiraling emergence from the depths of despair, his ultimate victory over the forces that might have crushed such a fragile but sensitive psyche. Guibert emerges as a personality capable of growth toward maturity.

Another side of Guibert emerges when one examines the "neutral" portions of his narrative. The opening passage of the second book of the *Monodiae* reveals a curious, articulate archaeologist, a scientific man deeply conscious of the rich stratifications of the place where he lives:

> The place is called Nogent. Its use as a monastery is very recent, but its use for worship by worldly society is very old. Even if no written sources were available to sustain this conjecture, the uncustomary and, in my opinion, non-Christian arrangement of the tombs that have been discovered there would suffice to do so. Around and within the abbey church, a large number of tombs has accumulated since ancient times; the countless number of bodies buried in such a crowded spot testifies to the great reputation that was enjoyed by a place that so many people flocked to. The tombs are not arranged the way ours usually are, but are grouped in a circle around one of them. Vases have been discovered in these tombs the likes of which are unknown to Christian times. I can therefore find no other explanation except to think either that these were pagan tombs or very ancient Christian tombs arranged according to pagan custom. (2.1)

Masterly passages of reporting, such as Guibert's confrontation at Langres, in 1107, with Pope Pascal II over the appointment of Bishop Gaudry in Laon reveal a personality that is able to overcome personal inhibition and answer questions with a mixture of wit and political cunning:

> The pope began by asking us why we had elected someone we did not previously know. Since none of the priests was answering—some of them hardly knew the rudiments of grammar—he turned toward the abbots. I was sitting between the other two abbots, both of whom kept silent but began urging me to speak.

Being so young I felt shy, and I feared I would be thought rash
for daring to speak in such a place and about a matter such as
this. In fact I was so shy I hardly dared open my mouth. The
discussion was being conducted not in our native French tongue
but in Latin. Finally I spoke up, giving full expression to what
was on the tip of my tongue and in my mind. I gave fitting
answers to the pope's questions, speaking in carefully weighed
and well-phrased sentences not veering too far from the truth.
(3.4)

There can be no final, conclusive evaluation of Guibert's personality.
No amount of psychologizing can exhaust him, though it can certainly
enrich our reading of him. One is annoyed, then moved, by an extraordinarily vulnerable man who seems to be entirely too self-critical. Much of
Guibert's pessimism is the product, surely, of his own highly sensitive,
highly scrupulous, and frequently morbid psychic states, but Guibert
does not stop with self-abasement. He is also confident in the soul's
capacity to rise from its own depths and function with maturity, even
with joy. Guibert's confession of sinfulness may be an Augustinian vision
of the soul in even darker hues; but it is an Augustinian, not a Manichean view, in that it never considers the sexual body as evil in itself or
as the creation of an evil divinity. Evil, to Guibert, may be deeply imbedded within the soul's substance, but it is imbedded like a foreign accretion. Evil is a force distinct from the soul's fabric, weighing it down and
causing it at times to appear dead. It may be deeply rooted in the soul's
substance, but if Guibert dwells so much on the depth of its rootedness
it is only to show the incommensurate love of Christ, who has rescued
him time and again from such depths. His sickness is not that "sickness
unto death" which refuses even the possibility of redemption from despair and which medieval spirituality considered the only unpardonable
sin; it is, rather, the ultimately joyful account of an infinite number of
divine rescue operations:

I confess to your majesty, O God, the innumerable times I
strayed from your paths, and the innumerable times you inspired
me to return to you. I confess the iniquity of my childhood and
of my youth, still boiling within me as an adult. I confess my
deep-seated penchant for depravity, which has not ceased in
spite of my declining strength. (1.1)

Far from being the history of a self-destructive personality, the *Monodiae* describes a recurring struggle with the forces of death within the soul, and this may be the ultimate meaning of Guibert's "demons." With Guibert, as with Augustine, evil is closely linked to sexual inclination; but it is not coextensive with it. Evil is a force distinct from his sexuality, but it makes its way into the soul largely through its intermediacy.

The distinctness of evil from his soul's fabric, its otherness in relation to the soul's substance, is fundamental to any consideration of Guibert's frequent vision of demons, or of the Devil in person. It may seem natural to reduce such experiences to their clinical equivalents, but such an approach fails to deal with the reality of the raw experience. Guibert's visionary gift may have been linked to a corresponding vulnerability. One might have a psychic makeup both highly neurotic and richly visionary. The pertinent point to be made about demons and visions is Guibert's conviction that they are foreign to his soul's substance and must somehow be chased away, which they usually are, with the help of a superior force. Demons are foreign to the soul's substance, constantly besieging but never defeating it.

Guibert's Language

Guibert was a self-conscious stylist whose reflections on writing are spelled out most extensively in the preface to the *Gesta Dei per Francos*, his major work before the *Monodiae*.[34] In his dedicatory letter to Lysiard, bishop of Soissons, to whom Guibert describes himself as "indebted for his constant liberality [perpetuo suae liberalitati debitor]," Guibert is already aware of having a literary reputation. His readers are aware of previous works of his, he says, referring no doubt to two works which we know were written before the *Gesta*: the *Liber quo ordine sermo fieri debeat* and the *Moralia in Genesim* (both written before 1084, while Guibert was still at Saint-Germer). "If," Guibert tells his episcopal benefactor, "you find me drifting away in the present work from vulgar grammatical usage [a vulgari grammatica peregrinari], I am doing it to

34. *PL* 156.679–83.

correct the vices, I might say the creeping, ground-level rhetoric of the previous history [illud humi serpens eloquium praecedentis corrigebam historiae]". Fully aware that his history of the First Crusade represents a considerable improvement over the anonymous text on which he was basing his account, Guibert, very much the modernist in his attitude toward the past, waxes eloquent over the cultural superiority of his own age to previous ones:

> I have seen country villages, towns and castles turn with fervor to the study of grammar. Therefore I do not wish to stay at too great a distance from the older historians [a veteribus historicis] if my talent allows it. Consider that in the midst of my daily activities and the frequent audition of court cases, I kept being consumed with the intention of dictating, and, more importantly, transcribing; and while being forced to listen to importuning trifles on the outside, I had to retain firmly within me the order of things I had undertaken to recount. Let no one be surprised, then, that I am resorting to a style far different from the one I used in the Exposition on Genesis [Moralia in Genesim] or other minor works. It is right and proper to adorn history with a studied and elegant manner of writing [licet . . . prorsus operosa historiam verborum elegantia coornari], while treating the mysteries of sacred subjects not with poetic garrulity but with ecclesiastical simplicity.[35]

There is no reason to believe that Guibert meant to devalue the *poetica garrulitas* in favor of the *ecclesiastica simplicitas* of his minor works. He simply is distinguishing between levels of style, and there is no doubt that the *Gesta* must be treated in something approaching a "high" style. "I could not help believing," Guibert repeats in his Preface to the *Gesta*, "that [God] would grant me the truth about the things that had transpired, as He thought best, nor would He deny me the elegance of language appropriate to the subject I was recounting [nec negaret competentium ordini ornamenta dictorum]." The style of the writer or of the speaker must adapt itself to its subject, writes Guibert, echoing Horace, Cicero, and other classical theorists: "facts of war must be related in a verbally aggressive style [verborum acrimonia bellica facta ferantur],

35. Ibid., 679–80.

and what pertains to divine things must be said in a more tempered style [gradu temperatiore ducantur]."

Guibert is very conscious of belonging to a sophisticated, highly critical age of literary culture. Writing the history of a Crusade, he argues in his preface to the *Gesta Dei*, means adopting a style befitting Mars, while writing about divine things means attempting to satisfy Mercury, the god of seriousness. Guibert doubts that his own writing style is up to such a double challenge:

> Quae gemina, si facultas mihi suppeteret forma, in hujus stadio operis excurisse debueram, ut et facinorum suorum insignia nequaquam verbis recitata disparibus insolens Gradivus agnosceret, et nunquam gravitatis sibi inditae tonum, cum de pietate res agitur modestia Mercurialis excederet.

> [If my ability were in keeping with my will, I should in this work have satisfied both conditions, so that the insolent Gradivus (Mars) would find in my words nothing unworthy of his great deeds; and when pious matters are in question, Mercury in his modesty would find everything in keeping with the seriousness of tone that behooves such matters.][36]

Even in the human sphere there are the human critics, the readers, harsh in their judgments, especially at a time when people everywhere are feverishly studying grammar, and the increasing number of schools makes even the crudest people seek access to this discipline. "Having seen the Lord perform the most marvelous deeds in any century, I have thought it my duty," he says, "to extract these precious stones from the dust, and to rescue, with the best writing I could muster, these riches more precious than gold from the neglectful state in which they had been cast [curavi quibus potui eloquiis, id omni charius auro, quod neglectui tradebatur, absolvere]."[37]

Written seven years after the *Gesta*, the *Monodiae* is a mixture, in style and tone, of the *poetica garrulitas* of the epic historical work and of the *ecclesiastica simplicitas* of Guibert's minor works.[38] The opening passage

36. Ibid., 681.
37. Ibid., 682.
38. I cannot agree with Georg Misch who, without any detailed analysis, treats the *Monodiae* as a mere "opusculum," inferior in literary form to Guibert's *Gesta* and his

of the *Monodiae,* for example, is clearly reminiscent of the opening of Augustine's *Confessions* in language and emotional intensity; but it is an Augustinian style become manneristic, as Guibert transforms intensity into anxiety with repeated use of superlative adjectives, rhetorical questions, and like-sounding antonyms within symmetrical syntactical constructions:

> Confiteor amplitudini tuae, Deus, infinitum errorum meorum decursus et creberrimos ad te miserationis internae, quos tamen inspirasti, recursus. Confiteor pueritiae ac juventutis meae mala, adhuc etiam in matura hac aetate aestuantia, et inveterata pravi tatum studia, necdum sub defatigati corporis torpore cessantia. (1.1)

There can be no doubt that the *Monodiae,* like the earlier *Gesta Dei,* was the work of a fairly sophisticated stylist. Guibert can be tender and coy, as when he tells the Virgin, using the familiar form of the vocative, that she cannot neglect taking care of him, given the vassalic tie that binds him to her ("tu meis necessitatibus, si dicere audeam, ex debito deesse non possis" [1.3]). He can indulge in word play, as when he says of one of his intriguing cousins that, "though not canonically appointed, he demanded of the canons that they respect the canons [et canones a canonicis non canonicus exigebat]" (1.7). And he is perhaps most touchingly vulnerable when, at the end of a series of rhetorical questions phrased in an Augustinian manner, almost as if to indicate his sense of exhaustion or self-disgust in his quest for an elusive perfection, he ends the series with an image both Pauline and rustic in character:

> Non te miserante abutor, quotiens per peccandi necessitatem peccare compellor; verum profana nimis esset abusio, si quia perfacilis post peccatum est ad te reditus, semper me peccandi delectet excessus. Pecco siquidem, sed, ratione recepta, in affectum cordis transisse me poenitet, tamque stercorosis cophinis mens graviter invita succumbit. (1.1)

---

theological commentaries and moral tractates: "Die Autobiographie tritt zwar nicht mit dem literarischen Anspruch auf wie seine [Guibert's] Geschichte des Kreuzzugs und die theologischen Kommentare und moralischen Traktate, die er verfasst hat; sie gibt sich als blosses 'opusculum' " (*Geschichte der Autobiographie,* 115).

[Every time I succumb to the compulsion to sin I do not abuse
your mercy; but I would abuse it sacrilegiously, if assuming that
nothing is easier than turning back to you after sinning, I were
to delight in sinning even more. I do sin, of course, but when I
recover my senses it pains me to have given in to my heart's
inclinations. It is entirely in spite of myself that my spirit beds
itself in baskets full of manure.]

Dom Mabillon described Guibert's language as "not unlearned but
rough [non inerudite sed scabroso stilo]."[39] Labande, on the other hand,
described it as "refined in form, almost to the point of preciosity and
hermeticism . . . almost pedantic . . . more elegant and recherché . . .
than that of many contemporary prose writers."[40] Guibert's was not the
powerfully, nearly classical prose and crystalline thought of Abelard, nor
did he have the gentle suavity and color of an Abbot Suger or the
stripped-down syntactical austerity of Saint Bernard. His language does
have a roughness about it, but it is a powerful roughness. His language
is very much his own, and he would be far less endearing had he attempted to write like any other contemporary.

Editions and Translations

The first edition of the complete Latin text of Guibert was done by the
Benedictine monk Dom Luc Dachéry in 1651. True to fashion, the Abbé
Migne pirated the Dachéry text and notes in his transcription of the
complete works of Guibert.[41] For the Latin text I have made use especially of Edmond-René Labande's Latin text with facing French translation. Labande occasionally improves upon the excellent Bougin Latin

---

39. Benton, Self and Society, 2.
40. Labande, Guibert de Nogent, xx.
41. PL 156.1018–1202. For an entertaining account of Migne's pirating practices,
see R. Howard Bloch, God's Plagarist: Being and Account of the Fabulous Industry and
Irregular Commerce of the Abbé Migne (Chicago: University of Chicago Press, 1994),
esp. 58–77.

edition of 1907, which is increasingly difficult to locate. For references to the *Gesta Dei per Francos* I have referred to Migne.[42]

The *Monodiae*, like the *Gesta Dei per Francos*, was first translated into French by Guizot in his 1825 *Mémoires relatifs à l'histoire de France*.[43] Guizot, who worked with a team of collaborators, provided an elegant, readable, frequently cavalier translation of both works; but his French translation is still precious, especially in attempting to understand some of the difficult passages—and there are many—of the *Gesta Dei*. Labande's French translation, the first since Guizot's, is far more literally precise and faithful to Guibert's text.

I am not the first to attempt an English translation of Guibert. Indeed if I am to justify a fresh English translation of Guibert's *Monodiae* I must acknowledge the excellent contribution and continuing success of the late John F. Benton's, known under the title *Self and Society in Medieval France*. To assert the merits of one's own translation in the face of Benton's is to acknowledge the debt one owes a revered late colleague with whom one occasionally differs but does not wish to quarrel.

First published in 1970, Benton's translation was the final phase of a touched-up version of C. C. Swinton Bland's translation of 1925, which had been emended earlier by Michael Alexander and Andrew C. Kimmens. According to Benton himself, Bland had shown "a cavalier disregard for names (Rouen is rendered as Rome and Fly is consistently called Ely), made serious errors of translation, and sought to create a feeling of archaism by preserving much of Guibert's confusing sentence structure."[44] Benton's "fundamental revision" of Bland's work was enriched by painstaking historical research as evidenced by footnotes, by a highly competent introduction, and by informative appendices.

The chief weakness of the Benton translation is that it retained far too much of the archaic flavor of Bland's translation (especially the sustained use of Thee's and Thou's), and had glaring inaccuracies of its own. My growing awareness of the insufficiencies of the Benton translation convinced me of the necessity of producing a new translation of Guibert. One of several possible examples of such inaccuracies occurs in Book 1, chapter 8, when Guibert is discussing the decline of several monasteries in Gaul. Guibert writes:

42. *PL* 156.681–838.
43. See Guizot, *Collection des Mémoires*, vols. 9 and 10.
44. Benton, *Self and Society*, 1.

Inter quae profecto quaedam speciali pollentia districtione fuerunt, quae nonnulla, in quibus fervor ordinis tepuerat, monasteria saepe nobiliter innormarunt; ut fuit aliquando Luxovium in Gallia, quaedam etiam in Neustria, quae nunc appellatur Northmannia. . . . Et licet tum minus apud eos religio curaretur, ex sua siquidem fiebant raritate ipsi monachi cariores.

Benton translates:

Among these, some were certainly harmed to a certain degree by their power; some monasteries, in which the zeal of the brotherhood fell away, often grew immense in a notable fashion, as at one time did Luxeuil in Gaul, and some places, too, in Neustria, which is now called Normandy. . . . And as among them there was little concern for religion, because of its rarity even fewer became monks.[45]

A more accurate translation reads:

Among them some stood out who were exceptional in the rigor of their discipline [speciali pollentia districtione] and who managed, quite remarkably, to restore zeal for the rule [innormarunt] in several monasteries where it had grown lukewarm. This was the case, once upon a time, at Luxeuil, in Gaul, etc. And yet, however little these monks observed the religious life, the very scarcity of their numbers made them even more precious.

One could cite other mistranslations in the Benton text. For example, Guibert speaks of his parents' inability to consummate the sexual act from the very start of their legitimate union ("efficientia conjugalis . . . in ipso . . . exordio, solveretur") but Benton's translation states, quite ambiguously, that "conjugal intercourse was made ineffective," implying that the key problem was the parents' inability to have children rather than their ability to have intercourse (1.12).

In the same chapter Guibert describes the attempt by Guibert's father's clan to hound his mother persistently so as to make her leave of her own volition:

45. Ibid., 53–54.

Verum postquam haec eorum suggestio nihil evaluit [to make my father repudiate my mother and take the monastic habit], puellam crebris coeperunt urgere latratibus, ut videlicet, a suis longe posita, dum externorum oppressionibus pulsaretur, sine ullo repudio, per se, injuriis fatigata, discederet.

Benton's translation takes no account of the persistence of the houndings ("crebris latratibus"), misleads the reader into thinking that the "externorum oppressionibus" is not just the "violence of strangers," but the "pressures of those external to her own family," and mistranslates "repudio" by "divorce."

My purpose here is not to discredit Benton. I would be churlish, moreover, were I to fail to acknowledge the debt I owe Benton's historical research. My goal in this book is simply to provide an idiomatic, precise, readable translation of Guibert that builds upon previous ones but makes Guibert more accessible to a contemporary English and American reading public. As a scholar living in the late twentieth century I cannot ignore the life and language of my own time. We cannot translate Guibert in the 1990s the way he might have been translated by a Renaissance or Victorian humanist, a French historian of the 1820s, or an English gentleman of the 1920s. Without indulging in popularization or vulgarization, I have attempted to provide a lively, readable, sometimes colloquial translation of Guibert's difficult Latin which might be useful to undergraduate and graduate readers of medieval literature and history, and to cultivated readers with a taste for autobiography. Furthermore, I am certain there is some justification for a better translation, and for scholarly notes that take into account a work that was still unfinished in Benton's lifetime, Edmond-René Labande's bilingual translation/edition of 1981. Labande's meticulous, at times almost literal rendering of Guibert into French avoids the elegant inaccuracies of Guizot's 1825 translation and builds upon more than three centuries of French paleographic expertise with the Latin text.[46] In doing my translation I have consulted these editions as well as the Baluze 42 ms., the only complete manuscript of the *Monodiae*, at the Bibliothèque Nationale in Paris.

The Benton and Labande translations are already available to scholars with access to a sizable university library. I believe this translation might

46. Dachéry, 1651: rpt. *PL* 146.837–962; also, Georges Bourgin, *Guibert de Nogent. Histoire de sa vie (1053–1124)* (Paris: A Picard et fils, 1907).

serve the need of making available, in both a physical and a linguistic sense, a work that the French historian Auguste Molinier called "one of the most precious of the Middle Ages."[47]

Chronology of Editions and Translations

1651   The Maurist Benedictine Dom Luc Dachéry edits complete works of Guibert.

1825   Guizot translates Guibert's *Gesta Dei per Francos* and *Monodiae* into French for the collection *Mémoires relatifs à l'histoire de France.*

1827   Augustin Thierry's *Lettres sur l'histoire de France* reveals Guibert's *Monodiae* as an important source for history of the communes in northern France.

1853   Abbé J. Migne reprints the Dachéry edition of Guibert's works in his *Patrologia Latina,* vol. 156.

1907   First critical edition of *Monodiae* (entitled *De vita sua*) by Georges Bourgin appears.

1925   First English translation of *Monodiae* by C. C. Swinton Bland (Broadway Translations) is published.

1970   Revised English translation of *Monodiae* by John F. Benton, with extensive new historical research and an excellent introduction, is published.

1981   Edmond-René Labande publishes critical bilingual edition (Latin/French) of *Monodiae* based on all previous scholarship.

47. Labande, *Guibert de Nogent,* xxii.

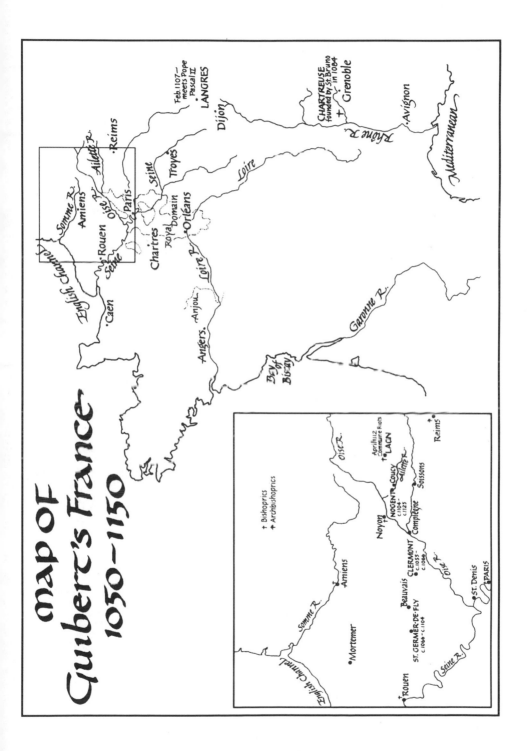

Map of
Guibert's France
1050–1150

English Channel

Somme R.
Amiens
Oise R.
Ailetti R.
Reims
Paris
Seine
Rouen
Caen

Chartres
Royal Domain
Orléans
Loire R.

Troyes
Seine
Dijon
Loire
LANGRES
Feb. 1107—
meets Pope
Pascal II

CHARTREUSE
founded by St. Bruno
in 1084
Grenoble
Avignon
Rhône R.
Mediterranean

Anjou
Angers

Bay of
Biscay
Garonne R.

English Channel
Mortemer
Somme R.
Amiens
Oise R.
Noyon
NOGENT
c.1104–
c.1125
Compiègne
Soissons
Ailetti R.
LAON
COUCY
April 1112
Commune Riots
Reims

Rouen
ST. GERMER-DE-FLY
c.1060–c.1104
Beauvais
CLERMONT
c.1055–
c.1060
Oise R.
St. Denis
PARIS
Seine R.

† Bishoprics
✝ Archbishoprics

Chronological Table

996–1031	Reign of Robert II the Pious of France
1031–1060	Reign of Henri I of France
1033	Saint Anselm, future archbishop of Canterbury, born at Aosta
1046–1053	Pontificate of Pope Leo IX
1053–1059	Pontificate of Pope Nicholas II
1054	Guibert's father captured at the battle of Mortemer, about 60 mi. W. of Clermont
1055	(Holy Saturday, mid-April) Guibert born at Clermont
1056	Guibert's father dies
1060	Philip I succeeds Henri I as king of France
c.1061–c.1066	Guibert educated at home by tutor
1067	Guibert's mother withdraws to the Abbey of Saint-Germer-de-Fly, about 20 mi. W. of Clermont; Guibert soon follows her
c.1067–c.1104	Guibert a novice at Saint-Germer; receives minor orders and is ordained to the priesthood
1073–1085	Pontificate of Pope Gregory VII (Gregorian Reform)
1075	In his Papal Dictates, Pope Gregory VII forbids married priests to celebrate Mass and reaffirms clerical celibacy and papal authority over emperors and kings regarding nomination and investiture of bishops
1077	Pope Gregory VII excommunicates German Emperor Henry IV after quarrel over investitures; Henry IV requests papal absolution at Canossa (northern Italy) and is absolved (28 January)
1079	Peter Abelard born at Pallet (Brittany)
1081	Suger, future abbot of Saint-Denis and great promoter of Gothic art ("Ars nova"), born at Saint-Denis or Argenteuil
1088–1099	Pontificate of Pope Urban II
1090	Saint Bernard of Clairvaux, future reformer of Benedictine order (Cistercian Reform), born at Fontaines-lès-Dijon

# of Guibert's Time

The
Memoirs of
Guibert Of
Nogent

BOOK ONE

My Early Life

1

Invocation

I confess to your majesty, O God,[1] the innumerable times I strayed from your paths, and the innumerable times you inspired me to return to you. I confess the iniquity of my childhood and of my youth, still boiling within me as an adult. I confess my deep-seated penchant for depravity, which has not ceased in spite of my declining strength. Lord, every time I recall my great persistence in self-defilement and remember how you have always given me the means of regretting it, I can only marvel at your infinite patience. It truly defies the imagination. If repentance and the urge to pray never occur without the outpouring of your spirit, how do you manage to fill the hearts

---

1. Guibert himself refers to his work as the *Liber monodiarum mearum;* see Abbé J. P. Migne, ed., *Patrologiae Cursus Completus. Series Latina* [hereafter *PL*], 227 vols. (Paris: Ed. d'Amboise, 1864–84), 156.622B. In his *Etymologiae* (6.19.6), Isidore of Seville defines *monodia* as a song "sung by one person": "Cum autem unus canit, Graece monodia, Latine sincinnium dicitur; cum vero duo canunt, bicinium appellatur: cum multi, chorus" (*PL* 82.252).

of sinners so liberally and to grant so many graces to those who have turned from you and who even provoke you?

O great Father, you know how we harden our hearts against those who have offended us, and how difficult it is for us to forgive those who have offended us by a look or by a word. But you are not only good, you are goodness itself, the source of all goodness. You who reach out to everyone in general, might you not be able to bring aid to each in particular? Why not? When the world lay in ignorance of God, shrouded in darkness and the shadow of death, while night pursued its course and silence covered all, whose was the merit, whose the all-powerful voice, that convinced you to leave your royal seat? If the indifference of all humanity could not deter you from showing mercy, it is no wonder that your compassion overflows toward a single sinner, however great. I cannot say that you are more ready to show mercy to one than to all, for your ease in granting mercy does not appear to err either way. Besides, in you there is nothing requiring greater effort for one thing than for anything else. Since you are the fount, and since what you pour forth is meant for all, clearly you exclude no one from what is meant for all.

So I am always sinning, and always returning to you from the midst of my sin. When I flee from piety or desert it, does piety lose any of its essence? Though choked by so many offenses, will it prove to be any different? Is it not said of you that in your anger you will not withhold your mercies?[2] And these mercies, the psalmist says, remain not only now but forever. You know that I do not sin because I see you as merciful; rather I proclaim you merciful with full confidence because you are available to all who implore your forgiveness. Every time I succumb to the compulsion to sin I do not abuse your mercy; but I would abuse it sacrilegiously, if assuming that nothing is easier than turning back to you after sinning, I were to delight in sinning even more. I do sin, of course, but when I recover my senses it pains me to have given in to my heart's inclinations. It is entirely in spite of itself that my spirit beds itself into baskets full of manure.[3]

In the midst of these daily miseries, what must I do when I recover from some lapse or other? Isn't it far more sensible to long for you for a while,

---

2. Guibert is quoting Ps. 76.10, with a slight modification: "aut continebit in ira tua misericordias tuas?"

3. No doubt Guibert means baskets containing manure used for fertilization of gardens and crops. In the agrarian culture of early twelfth-century France, Guibert's excrementitious imagery would not have seemed as "singular" as it does to Labande. Cf. Edmond-René Labande, *Guibert de Nogent: Autobiographie* (Paris: Les Belles Lettres, 1981), 6n.1.

to rest in you even for a moment, rather than to forget the remedy outright and to despair of your grace? And what is despair if it isn't casting oneself deliberately into the swamp of every crime? Whenever the spirit no longer resists the flesh, the substance of the unhappy soul is eaten and wasted away by pleasure. A man who finds himself engulfed by raging waters is soon pulled to the bottom: so is one's judgment sucked down from the mouth of the well into the abyss of perversion.

O good God, when I come back to you after my binges of inner drunkenness,[4] I don't turn back from knowledge of myself, even though I don't otherwise make any progress either. If I am blind in knowing myself, how could I possibly have any spark of knowledge for you? If, as Jeremiah says, "I am the man who has seen affliction" [Lam. 3.1], it follows that I must look very carefully for the things that compensate for that poverty. To put it differently, if I don't know what is good, how am I to know what is bad, let alone hateful? Unless I know what beauty is I can never loathe what is ugly. It follows from this that I try to know you insofar as I know myself; and enjoying the knowledge of you does not mean that I lack self-knowledge. It is a good thing, then, and singularly beneficial for my soul, that confessions of this sort[5] allow my persistent search for your light to dispel the darkness of my reason. With steady lighting my reason will no longer be in the dark about itself.

2

My mother's beauty and chastity

First I should confess to you the benefits you have conferred upon me,[6] so that faithful followers of yours who will read this book might know

4. Literally the "inebriations of the inner man" ("has interioris mei hominis temulentias"), an expression that Guibert could have borrowed from Saint Paul (Rom. 7.22): "condelector enim legi Dei secundum interiorem hominem." Cf. Eph. 3.16: "ut det vobis . . . virtute corroborari per spiritum eius in interiore homine."

5. Guibert's use of the term "confessiones" seems to hint at an Augustinian influence. Of the three explicit references to Augustine in the Monodiae, none is to the Confessions. Guibert surely knew Augustine's work, but not well enough to quote it from memory.

6. "Est itaque primum confiteri tibi, quae mihi contuleris beneficia." Cf. Augustine, Confessions 9.6: "Munera tua tibi confiteor, domine deus meus, creator omnium et multum potens formare nostra deformia."

how cruel my ingratitude is. Even if what you have given me is no different from what you have given others, does it not exceed anything I have
deserved? To this you added many things that are to your credit alone,
not mine, and others still that I choose to pass over. For if noble birth,
wealth, and beauty, not to speak of other gifts, are from you, O Lord,
good people whom you have so blessed should not boast of them unless
some rule of moderation protects them; or unless they openly despise
these things because they are fleeting. What do I care for things whose
very name or appearance turns them into an excuse for lust or arrogance? They are so ambiguous that one's very frame of mind can turn
them to good or evil purposes. The more fleeting they are, the more
their very transitoriness makes them suspect. If one can find no other
argument to despise them, it is enough to point out that one's genealogy,
or physical appearance, are not of one's choosing. In these particular
matters we only have what we have been given.

Other things can sometimes be acquired through effort: wealth, for
example, or talent. As Solomon puts it: "When the iron has been dulled
it can be rehoned only at great cost."[7] But the truth of my assertion here
is only relative. If the light, which "enlightens the way for every man
coming into the world" [John 1.9] fails to enlighten reason—and if
Christ, the key to all science, fails to open the doors of right doctrine—
then, surely, teachers are fighting a losing battle against clogged ears.
Any careful person, then, is unwise to lay claim to anything except sin.
But let me drop this and get on with my subject.

Dear God, I have already stated that I am thankful to you for your
gifts. I thank you, first and foremost, for having given me a mother who
is beautiful yet chaste and modest and filled with the fear of the Lord.[8]
Mentioning her beauty alone would be profane and foolish if I didn't add
(to show the vanity of the word "beauty"), that the severity of her look
was sure proof of her chastity. For poverty-ridden people, who have no
choice about their food, fasting is really a form of torture and is therefore less praiseworthy; whereas if rich people abstain from food their
merit is derived from its abundance. So it is with beauty, which is all the
more praiseworthy if it resists flattery while knowing itself to be desirable.

---

7. "Ferrum . . . cum retusum fuerit, multo labore exacuetur." Cf. Eccles. 10.10: "Si
retunsum fuerit ferrum et hoc non ut prius sed hebetatum erit multo labore exacuatur."

8. The phrase "pulchram, sed castam, modestam mihi matrem timoratissimamque"
summarizes Guibert's view of ethical womanly conduct.

Sallust was able to consider beauty praiseworthy independent of moral considerations. Otherwise he never would have said about Aurelia Orestilla that "good men never praised anything in her except her beauty."[9] Sallust seems to have meant that Aurelia's beauty, considered in isolation, could still be praised by good people, while admitting how corrupt she was in everything else. Speaking for Sallust, I think he might just as well have said that Aurelia deserved to be praised for a natural, God-given gift, defiled though she was by all the other impurities that made up her being. Likewise a statue can be praised for the harmony of its parts, no matter what material it is made of. Saint Paul may call an idol "unreal" from the point of view of faith,[10] and indeed nothing is more profane than an idol, but one can still admire the harmony of its limbs.

The instability within our very blood makes ephemeral beauty a changeable thing, to be sure; but considering the good Image-Maker's design, one has to admit it is good. If everything that has been designed in the eternal plan of God is good, every particular instance of beauty in the temporal order is, one might say, a mirror of that eternal beauty. "It is created things that make the eternal things of God intelligible," says Saint Paul.[11] Angels themselves have appeared to people in the most beautiful disguises. As Manoah's wife puts it: "I saw a man of God coming toward me with the face of an angel."[12] On the other hand, devils who, as Saint Peter puts it, "are to be kept in darkness until the day of the Last Judgment,"[13] usually appear with the most hideous faces; sometimes, of course, they "disguise themselves as angels of light" [2 Cor. 11.14], which is not entirely unjust since they once rejected the glorious condition of their noble compatriots in heaven.

It is written in this regard that our bodies, too, will be glorified like

9. " 'In qua,' ait, 'praeter formam nihil unquam bonus laudavit.' " Cf. Sallust, *The War with Catiline*, trans. J. C. Rolfe (New York: G. B. Putnam's Sons, 1920), 15.2, 27. Here Sallust describes Catiline as being "seized with a passion for Aurelia Orestilla, in whom no good man ever commended anything save her beauty."

10. Guibert writes: "et licet idolum ab Apostolo quantum spectat ad fidem, nihil appelletur." Cf. 1 Cor. 8.4: "scimus quia nihil est idolum in mundo."

11. Guibert is quoting almost verbatim from Rom. 1.20: "invisibilia enim ipsius a creatura mundi / per ea quae facta sunt intellecta conspiciuntur."

12. Guibert's text reads: "Venit . . . vir Dei ad me, angelicum habens vultum." Cf. Judg. 13.16: "Vir Dei venit ad me habens vultum angelicum terribilis nimis."

13. Guibert writes: "daemones qui, juxta primi Petri vocem, sub caligine ad diem magni judicii reservantur." Cf. 2 Pet. 2.17: "hii sunt fontes sine aqua / et nebulae turbinibus exagitatae / quibus caligo tenebrarum reservatur."

Christ's glorious body [Phil. 3.21] and that any ugliness they might have contracted by accident, or through natural corruption, will be corrected according to the model of the transfigured Son of God on the mountain. If, then, internal replications are beautiful and good if they conform to the image of the model, it is enough for them, provided they do not break the model's harmony, to be beautiful in order to be good. In his book entitled *On Christian Doctrine* (if I am not mistaken), I recall that Saint Augustine wrote something like this: "A person with a beautiful body and a corrupt soul is more to be pitied than one whose body is also ugly."[14] If, therefore, we lament beauty that is blemished, it is unquestionably a good thing when beauty, though depraved, is improved through perseverance in goodness.

Thank you, God, for instilling virtue into my mother's beauty. The seriousness of her whole bearing was enough to show her contempt for all vanity. A sober look, measured words, modest facial expressions hardly lend encouragement to the gaze of would-be suitors. O God of power, you know what fear your name had inspired in her from her earliest years, and how she rebelled against every form of allurement. Incidentally, one rarely, if ever, finds comparable self-control among women of her social rank, or a comparable reluctance to denigrate those who lack self-control. Whenever anyone, whether from within or outside her household, began this sort of gossip, she would turn away and go, looking as irritated as if she were the one being attacked. What compels me to relate these things, O God of truth, is not a private affection, even for my mother, but the facts themselves, which are far more eloquent than my words could ever be. Besides, the rest of my family are fierce, brutish warriors and murderers. They have no idea of God and would surely live far from your sight unless you were to show them your boundless mercy as you so often do.[15]

14. "Is qui pulchrum habet corpus et turpem animam magis lugendus est, quam si foedium haberet et corpus." Guibert's phrasing is similar to that of Augustine in *De doctrina christiana* 4.28: "Sicut autem cuius pulchrum corpus et deformis est animus, magis dolendus est, quam si deforme habent et corpus, ita qui eloquenter ea, quae falsa sunt, dicunt, magis miserandi quam si talia deformiter dicerent" (The relation of eloquence to falsehood is the same as the relation of physical body to a corrupt mind). See *De doctrina christiana*, ed. J. Martin, in *Corpus Christianorum. Series Latina* [hereafter *CCSL*] (Turnholt: Brepols, 1972), 32.165.

15. "Certe cum caeteros generis mei aut animales et Dei ignaros, aut efferos armis et caedium reos." Guibert's judgment on his clan was not exaggerated judging by the conduct he alleges of them further on in the text: brutishness, ignorance of God, war,

Perhaps I will find a more opportune place to talk about her life in the course of this book. For the time being let me get on with my own life.

3
Circumstances surrounding my birth

You granted, then, that I, the worst of her offspring, should be born of this woman who—it is my belief and my hope—was perfectly honest.[16] In two senses of the word I was the *last* of her children. Several of my siblings, who promised better things than I for the future, have died so that I alone am left, and I am really a desperate case. Evildoers like myself can only place their entire hope of salvation in their own mother's merits, after Jesus, his mother and the saints. I know, and I find it impossible not to believe, that just as she held me dearly and spoiled me after bringing me into the world (aren't mothers usually more affectionate with their last-born?) she is not forgetting me now that she is in God's presence. Since her youth she had been "filled with the fire of God in Sion";[17] deep down she worried about me when she was asleep, and even more when she was awake. Now that she is dead, the wall of her flesh having crumbled, I know that the fire of her love is alive for me in Jerusalem, with a flame more fervid than one can express. From her place in heaven, in full enjoyment of God, she knows the troubles I am entangled in; and although she is in bliss, she sighs and groans when I stray from the path, her sighs being commensurate with my disregard of her repeated warnings, her conduct, and her example.

O Lord God and Father, evil as I am, you gave me the privilege of

---

rapine, and murder for gain were, indeed, routine occupations and attributes for many feudal lords around the year 1100.

16. Guibert's penchant for positive and negative superlatives may be attributed in part to his feeling of total inadequacy in trying to measure up to a "perfect" mother: "Ex hac . . . *verissima* mihi, omnium, quos genuit ipsa *deterrimo*, tribuisti nasci" (emphasis mine).

17. Guibert: "Ignis plena Dei ea a juventute fuerat in Sion." Cf. Isa. 31.9: "dixit Dominus cuius ignis est in Sion et caminus eius in Hierusalem."

being born of a mother with a real, not artificial, goodness. Thanks to her merits you also granted me a hope that I would never dare entertain by myself unless I could relinquish my fear of sin and learn to relax in your presence. This hope, or semblance of hope, that you instilled in my wretched heart is also due to your allowing me to be born, and reborn, on that holiest of days, the most important and most eagerly awaited by all Christians.

As she approached the end of her pregnancy my mother had been in the most intense pain throughout the season of Lent. How often she reproached me in later years for those pangs of childbirth when she saw me straying and following the slippery downhill path! Finally Holy Saturday, the solemn vigil of Easter, dawned. My mother was wracked with continuous pain. As the hour of delivery approached, the pains increased, but they were presumed to lead to a natural delivery. Then I turned around in her womb, with my head upward. My father, his friends, members of the family, all feared for both our lives. The child, they thought, was hastening the mother's death; and the offspring's exit from the world at the very moment he was being denied an entrance into it added to their sense of pity.[18] On that day, except for the solemn liturgy that is celebrated at a certain hour, the offices usually sung for members of the household were not scheduled. The family held an urgent meeting. They rushed to the altar of the Mother of God. To the one who was, and ever will be, the only Virgin ever to give birth, they made the following vow and left it as an offering at our Lady's altar: if the child were male, it would be consecrated a cleric in God's service and hers; if the child were of the lesser sex,[19] it would be given over to a corresponding religious vocation.

At that moment a frail little thing came forth, looking almost like an aborted fetus, except that it was born at term. It looked like a most miserable being, and the only reason for rejoicing was that the mother had been saved. This tiny human being that had just seen the light was so lamentably frail that it looked like the corpse of a stillborn baby. The little reeds that sprout in mid-April in this part of the country are fuller

18. Guibert's text reads: "prolis similiter exitium, dum ei negatur exitus." I have tried to render Guibert's pun on *exitium, exitus,* with the antithesis "exit . . . entrance."

19. In the Latin text, *masculum* is opposed to *deterior*: "si partus ille cessisset in masculum, Deo et sibi obsecuturus clericatui traderetur; sin deterior, professioni congruae mandaretur."

by comparison than were my little fingers.[20] On the same day, as I was brought to the baptismal font—this was often related to me as a joke when I was a child, and even during my adolescence—a woman kept rolling me over from one hand to the other and saying: "Do you think this little creature's going to live? I guess Mother Nature never quite finished this one. She gave him an outline more than a body." All these things foreshadowed the way I am living now. Has any faithful service ever been found in me? In serving you I have shown no firmness, no constancy. Whenever I have produced some kind of good work, my lukewarm intention has too often turned it into something insignificant.[21] I have already said, O God of supreme goodness, that you gave me hope, or some small facsimile of hope by granting that I be born, and reborn, on the vigil of such a joyous day, and that I be offered to Her who is, after God, Queen of the universe. And yet, Lord God, have you not given me enough reason to realize that the day of one's birth brings nothing more useful to those who live unprofitably than the day of one's death? If it is obvious and irrefutable that one's merits cannot precede the day of one's birth, they can, nevertheless, precede the day of one's death; but if one's life is spent without doing good, then I think it makes no difference whether the day of one's birth, or death, was glorious or not.

It is true that "He made me, not that I made myself" [Ps. 100.3], and that I did not determine the day of my birth or deserve that it should occur at that moment. But this God-given birthday brings me neither hope nor honor, unless my life bears out the religious significance that this day symbolizes.[22] Our birthdays would bathe in the glow of the feast it commemorates if we were bent on achieving by our actions the virtue we strive for. The glory that has been given people on the day they enter

20. Benton mistranslates "iduato ferme aprili junci" as "it being then the middle of April." Cf. John F. Benton, *Self and Society in Medieval France* (New York: Harper & Row, 1970; rpt. Toronto: University of Toronto Press, 1984), 42.

21. Guibert's constant sense of unworthiness and his penchant for self-depreciation were no doubt shaped by the circumstances surrounding his birth, especially if his mother kept reminding him of her birth pangs whenever he allowed himself to follow the "slippery path" ("lubrica"): "quos . . . angores mihi devio, et lubrica consectanti, totiens improperare solebat."

22. The allusion is to Guibert's natural birth, and his rebirth through baptism. He accuses himself constantly of not living up to the lofty symbolism of Easter by living in the "death" of sin.

into the world would seem all the more deserved if their souls could persevere in virtue to the point of making the day of their exit glorious. Whether my name is Peter, Paul, Remigius, or Nicholas, this name, "bequeathed by the great Julius," if I may quote the poet,[23] will be of no use to me unless I reproduce with meticulous care the models of those whose name Providence (or Fortune)[24] has given me. See, O God, how everything that swells up in my soul ends up deflated! How everything that seemed about to develop my prestige vanishes into nothing!

As for you, O sovereign Lady who rules heaven and earth after your only Son, how well they were inspired, those who dedicated me to you in that moment of great urgency. I would have listened so much better if, once an adult, I had based my life on that same vow! Of course I will admit that I was offered to you as a special gift; but I cannot deny that I often pulled away from your path, knowingly and sacrilegiously. Was I not pulling away from you when I preferred my stinking desires to the sweet perfume of your will?[25] And yet I may repeatedly and perversely have escaped from you, but I hastened back to you with even more confidence, and through your intercession to your only Son, the only Son of God the Father, remembering that I had been offered to you. I may have eaten away at myself for sins a thousand times repeated, yet I felt my confidence renewed by your inexhaustible tenderness. The gift of your former mercies led me to hope. But why do I call them "former" mercies? I have experienced the constancy of your mercies so many

---

23. Guibert writes: "a magno dimissum nomen Iulo." Cf. Vergil, Aeneid, trans. H. Rushton Fairclough (Cambridge, Mass.: Harvard University Press, 1966), 1.288: "Iulius, a magno demissum nomen Iulo." Guibert's nearly verbatim rendering of Vergil is ironic. In the Vergilian context, Jupiter is loftily prophesying to Venus how illustrious her son Aeneas's lineage will be, as it will include Julius Caesar, who will take his name from the great Iulius. Guibert, however, is saying that it is pointless to have a great name unless one can live up to a great model.

24. Like Boethius, Guibert was sufficiently read in the classics to use both a pagan and a Christian symbol interchangeably. In De consolatione philosophiae, Fortune upbraids Boethius for his complaints with the same authority as Jehovah upbraiding Job: "Quid tu homo ream me cotidianis agis queribus? Quam tibi fecimus iniuriam?" See Boethius, The Consolation of Philosophy, trans. H. F. Stewart (Cambridge, Mass.: Harvard University Press, 1966), chap. 1.

25. "Qui voluntates faetidas tuo odori praetuli." Guibert often refers to his sinfulness in olfactory terms. Cf. the "stercorosis cophinis" (note 3, above), and the cousin who bore his sexual misdemeanors about him like a bad smell: "cum faetido passim pro talibus spargeretur odore."

times! In fact, with your help I have so often escaped the captivity of my sin that it would perhaps be better not to speak of my "former" enslavements when there have been so many deliveries from captivity. When repeated sinning produces a cruel hardening of my heart, an immediate, almost instinctive return to you mollifies me; and when I consider the misery within me and am about to sink into despair, I feel in my unhappy soul, whether I like it or not, a renewed assurance that I will be drawn toward you. Thus I am convinced that whatever bad things I am involved in, you owe it to me, if I dare say so, not to fail me if I am in need. I have been cast into your arms since I left my mother's womb: if you were not to come after me when I turn away, if you were to reject me when I come back to you, you would be the one I would justly blame for my perdition. But since it suffices for you to will something to obtain it, and since it is well known that the Son's power reverberates in the Mother, from whom could I better solicit my salvation than from you? Sharing the condition of servant with you, I can cry out: "I am thine!" [Ps. 119.94].[26]

I would be quite willing to reason with you about these matters at some other time. For the time being, let me move on to other things.

4

My early education

I was hardly born, I had scarcely learned to grasp my rattles,[27] when you made me an orphan, dear God, you who were my Father-to-be. Yes, I

26. Georg Misch (*Geschichte der Autobiographie. Das Mittelalter* [Frankfurt am Main: G. Schulte-Bulmke, 1959], 3.2, 119) and E. R. Labande (*Guibert de Nogent,* 24n.1) have both noted the feudal character of this passage. As vassal, Guibert is bound to his Lady ("domina") by contract, and she owes it to him ("ex debito") to come to his aid in case of need ("ex necessitatibus") no matter how many his aberrations ("peccatorum iterationes"). Guibert almost coyly addresses the Virgin as an errant son would a forgiving mother who is under obligation to take him back lest she be blamed for his aberrations: "si aversum non revisas, si reversum minime recipias, perditionis meae justas in te utique conferam causas." Misch insists on the formal, reciprocal nature of the feudal contract.

27. Guibert's expression is "fovere crepundia," *fovere* having both a physical and a derivative meaning (to warm, to look warmly upon).

was just eight months old when my physical father died: thank you so much for having permitted this man to die in a Christian state of mind. Had he lived he unquestionably would have tried to block the providential design you had for me. My physical build, coupled with an alacrity of spirit quite natural for my age, seemed, in fact, to direct me toward a worldly vocation; so nobody doubted that my father would break the vow he had made when it came time for me to begin my education.[28] O good Provider, you managed a resolution that worked for the well-being of both of us: I was in no way deprived of the rudiments of your teachings, and he never broke the oath he had made to you.

I was raised in the loving care of your faithful widow, my mother. When the time came to send me to school, she decided to do so on the feast of Saint Gregory.[29] She had heard that that famous servant of yours had had a brilliant intelligence, and that a boundless wisdom had flourished in him. With abundant donations to the poor she strove to obtain your confessor's intercession, so that he, who had received wisdom, might grant me a taste for intellectual things.

I began to study Latin. Some of the basics I learned as best I could, but I could hardly make sense of it. My dear mother, who really wanted me to be a scholar, decided to turn me over to a private tutor.[30] In the recent past, and even partly during my childhood, there had been such a shortage of teachers that you could find hardly any in the towns and rarely any in the cities. When one did happen to find some, they knew so little that they couldn't even be compared to the wandering scholars

28. Literally the text reads "cum literis ediscendis habile tempus adesset," that is, around the age of seven. At birth Guibert seemed destined to remain in frail health, therefore to be more fit for the monastic life than for the rugged activities of the warrior, like other members of his family. By the time he was seven, his handsome looks, strong physique and alacrity of spirit would have given his father—had he been alive—second thoughts about the vow he had made at the time of Guibert's christening.

29. Guibert means the feast of Saint Gregory the Great (Pope Gregory I), which falls on 12 March. Pope Gregory I reigned from 590 to 604.

30. A *grammaticus,* that is, one who would teach him the science of speaking correctly and would introduce him to the texts of great poets. Quintilian had defined *grammatica,* the first of the liberal arts, "recte loquendi scientia et poetarum enarratio" (*Institutio oratoria* 1.iv). Guibert's description of his *saevus grammaticus* seems in direct opposition to Quintilian's description of the skillful teacher, "dicendi peritus" described in *Institutio oratoria* 1.iii–iv. We have no evidence, however, that Guibert knew of Quintilian's treatise. See *Institutio oratoria,* trans. H. E. Butler (New York: G. B. Putnam's Sons, 1933).

of the present day. The man my mother decided to send me to had begun studying grammar late in life, and he was all the more incompetent in his art for having absorbed so little of it in his youth. He was a very modest man, though, and he made up in honesty for what he lacked in literary knowledge.

My mother sought the confidential opinion of those clerics named "chaplains" who celebrate the Divine Office in her household.[31] With their recommendation she made this teacher an offer. He had already been assigned as tutor to a little cousin of mine and was very close to this cousin's parents, who gave him room and board at their court. He was impressed, however, by the urgency of my mother's approach and liked her honesty and forthrightness. And so, though he was afraid of offending those other relatives, he decided to accept my mother's hospitality. What confirmed his decision was this dream:

One night, as he slept in his room—I can see it still, it was the room where the whole cycle of "liberal arts studies" was taught in our town[32]—he dreamed he saw a venerable-looking, white-haired old man leading me by the hand to his door. He stopped there while I stared inside, then he pointed to the bed and said: "Go up to this man. He will take a great liking to you." Then he let go of my hand, which until then he had been holding. I ran up to the man and began smothering his face with kisses. He woke up. He was so taken with affection for me that, without further delay, spurning any fear of my relatives (though he depended on them for his, as well as his family's, entire subsistence), he consented to come and live at my mother's residence.

The boy for whom until that moment he had been responsible was handsome and aristocratic-looking,[33] but allergic to the liberal arts, recalcitrant to any form of discipline, and for his age quite a liar and a stealer. He could put up with no form of supervision, seldom came to school, and could be found hiding in the vineyard just about every day.

31. Guibert's mother belonged to a sufficiently high level of feudal nobility to permit her to house several chaplains in her home to conduct the divine services.

32. Having already deplored the almost total dearth of teachers in the towns of his youth, Guibert is no doubt being ironic in calling his tutor's "cubiculum," the place where the "studium generale," the whole cycle of studies extending from grammar to theology, was dispensed.

33. "Erat autem puer . . . pulcher quidem et nobilis." Guibert's sensitivity to physical beauty is evident here as elsewhere. Was his persistent sense of sinfulness derived in part from a feeling of guilt in finding the human body attractive?

Our tutor was getting tired of the boy's ways, and my mother's offer of friendship appealed to him at the right time, so what he saw in the dream I have already mentioned gave him the courage he needed. He gave up tutoring the child at the same time he left the service of his masters. He could hardly have done this with impunity had he not been protected by my mother's power and prestige.

5

Reflections on the education of children

I was placed under this master's authority. So sternly did he raise me and so diligently did he shelter me from the high jinx that are natural at that age that I wasn't even allowed to play the usual games. I couldn't go anywhere without his permission, couldn't eat outside the house, couldn't accept a gift from anybody without his consent. I couldn't do anything "intemperate," whether in thought, word, or deed. He seemed to expect me to behave more like a monk than a cleric. The other boys of my age could come and go as they pleased and, at times, with no constraints at all. I, on the other hand, was scrupulously guarded from such behavior. I would sit in my cleric's garb and watch the squads of players like a trained animal.[34] Even on Sundays and saints' feasts I had to put up with the constraints of this scholastic system. There was not a day, not a moment, when I was allowed a holiday. It was study, study, study all the time. Besides, when he had accepted my tutorship, my master was not allowed to take on any other student.

Because he worked me so hard everybody who watched us was convinced that with so much perseverance he would considerably sharpen my fledgling mind. Alas! This didn't happen. My master was totally ignorant of the techniques of composition or metrics. Meanwhile I was deluged everyday with a hail of blows and whippings. This man was trying to force me to learn what he couldn't teach![35]

34. Benton's translation, "like of beast awaiting sacrifice" (*Self and Society*, 46), mistranslates "quasi peritum animal." The image is closer to that of a dog trained to do tricks (Labande, *Guibert de Nogent*, 31n.3).

35. Once again Guibert exhibits his taste for word play: "ipse me cogeret *discere*, quae *docere* nequiverat" (emphasis mine).

I spent a good six years wrestling with him, but the result of my effort was simply not worth the amount of time I wasted. On the other hand, as far as learning the basics of proper behavior there is nothing he didn't teach me. Everything pertaining to modesty, chastity, and good manners he taught me with consummate loyalty and affection. But I painfully discovered, at my own expense, how inconsiderate and lacking in moderation he was. Although pretending to instruct me, what he did was goad me like a taskmaster, unremittingly. Any person's nature, let alone a child's, ends up being blunted if it has to submit to too much intellectual work. The more a mind is fired up by extended study, the more the spirit cools as the energies become overexerted. Energy dissolves into apathy.

It is very important, then, to treat the mind with moderation while it is still weighted down by the trappings of the body. If, as Scripture puts it, "there was silence in heaven for half an hour,"[36] even the gift of contemplation cannot be sustained unceasingly. It is the same thing for any activity of the mind: it cannot be maintained without interruption. It is my belief, then, that any mind concentrating on a specific object should use varying degrees of attention. Alternately thinking about one thing, then another, we should then be able to come back to the one that our mind is most interested in, as if renewed by the recreation we had given ourselves. Nature, too, tends to get tired and should find its remedy in a variety of activities. We must remember that God did not create a uniform world but allowed us to enjoy time changes—days and nights, spring and summer, autumn and winter. People who call themselves schoolteachers should find ways of varying the education of children and young people. Even students who have the seriousness of old people about them should not be treated any differently, in my opinion.[37]

The love this man bore for me was cruel. His punishments were unfair

36. Guibert: "quia, si silentium hora media fit in caelo." Cf. Rev. 8.1: "Et cum aperuisset sigillum septimum, factum est silentium in coelo, quasi media hora." Benton's translation (*Self and Society,* 47) needlessly complicates the obvious point Guibert is making, that even in heaven there is need for relief from the sustained effort of the contemplative life.

37. Guibert is stating the soundest pedagogical principles here: variety, change of pace, exercise, and so on, are necessary ingredients in the education of the young. Auguste Mollard has argued that Guibert's picture of his overly severe schoolmaster was intended to contrast with the model teacher in Quintilian, *Institutio oratoria* 1.12.1. Guibert is perhaps less indebted to Quintilian for these ideas than to painful reminiscence of his own education. He speaks with conviction and uncharacteristic assertiveness.

and excessively severe; and yet he followed the rules in the minutest detail. Clearly I did not deserve the blows he gave me, for, if he had been an expert teacher as he had boasted, I was perfectly able, despite being a child, to understand what he was saying if he had said it correctly. But he could hardly ever express a complete sentence, since what he was straining to express wasn't at all clear in his mind. When he spoke he wandered in a banal but not very obvious circle,[38] and he could never quite conceptualize, even less render intelligible, what he was saying. As I have already stated, he was so uneducated that what he had once badly assimilated as an adult he never bothered to correct. And if he uttered something that can only be termed stupid, since he thought all his opinions irrefutable, he would maintain and defend them with blows.[39] I think, however, that he would have abstained from doing anything that reprehensible; for, as a learned man has said, before nature has really absorbed knowledge, it is no less glorious to refrain from saying what one does not know than to say what one knows.

While my master was taking it out on me for not knowing what he himself did not know, he might have been well advised to consider the harm he had done in squeezing out of my frail little head what he had never put there in the first place. Lunatics' words can barely be understood by the sane, if at all; similarly the utterances of people who are ignorant but pretend to know something, and who pass on their "knowledge" to others, become even murkier when they attempt to explain what they are saying. There is nothing harder than trying to hold forth about something you yourself don't understand. It is obscure for the speaker,

38. "Ut circa vilem, sed non patulum, qui colligi ab eo non poterat, nedum intelligi faceret, orbem." Guibert is here closely paraphrasing Horace, in *Ars poetica*: "Publica materies privati juris erit, si / Nec circa vilem patulumque moraberis orbem" (*Satires, Epistles, and Ars Poetica*, trans. H. Rushton Fairclough [Cambridge, Mass.: Harvard University Press, 1961], 131–32). Horace encourages the poet to make even the well-known epic field ("publica materies") his own through originality of handling, not slavish translation. The "vilem patulumque . . . orbem" is that of repetition and imitation.

39. Guibert seems to be paraphrasing Sidonius Apollinaris's "Sayings of the Wise Men" (*Poems and Letters*, trans. W. B. Anderson [Cambridge, Mass.: Harvard University Press, 1936], 1.7.9, 5) relating what was said of Pythagoras, that he "taught [his pupils] the lesson of patient silence before he taught them the lore of speaking, and that all the novices endured five years of dumbness among the chairs where their fellow disciples sat at their discussions, so that even the quicker minds were not allowed to gain a word of praise before it was proper for them to be recognized."

and even more so for the hearer; it is really as if both were being turned into stone. I'm saying this, O Lord, not because I want to stigmatize this man who, all things considered, was a good friend, but in order to let the readers know, whoever they might be, that we must not think we are entitled to teach as truth anything that crosses our minds. Let us not lose other people in the clouds of our own theories.

I have tried to spice my present subject matter with reason, however poor it might be. Even if ultimately the subject is considered to be of little value, and perhaps rightly so, at least the presence of reason will add some merit to these pages.

6
Difficult relations with my tutor

However oppressive he was, my master made it clear to me in all kinds of ways that he loved me no less than he loved himself. He watched over me with great diligence; he looked after my well-being with care, fearing the ill intentions some people had toward me; he warned me urgently to guard against the corruption of some people who had their eyes on me; he cautioned my mother against dressing me too elegantly; in a word he seemed more a parent than a tutor, more my soul's caretaker than my body's. As for me, though I was somewhat clumsy and shy for my age, I had such a liking for him—striped as my poor little skin might have been by his many whiplashes—that I obeyed him, not out of fear (as would generally be the case in relationships like these) but out of some curious feeling of love, which overwhelmed my whole being and made me forget all his harshness.

When my mother and my tutor saw that I was paying both of them their due respect, they put me to the test several times to see which of the two I would give my preference to in a specific circumstance. One time the experiment was attempted without the slightest ambiguity, without either of them telling me what to do. One day I had been beaten in school—the school being nothing more than a dining hall in our house — [40] my tutor having had to relinquish teaching other boys when he accepted to take me on. My mother had very wisely demanded this of him in exchange for increased wages and better status. At the time of vespers, having finished some school task or other, I had come to sit at my mother's feet. I had just received a worse beating than I deserved. She started asking me, as she usually did, whether I had been beaten that day. So as not to appear to denounce my tutor, I said no outright. Without asking my permission, my mother took off my undergarment. (Some call it a tunic, others an undershirt.) She saw that my little arms were black and blue, and that the skin on my poor back was swollen all over from the canings I had received. My mother groaned when she saw how cruelly I had been treated at such a tender age. She was disturbed and quite agitated, and her eyes filled with tears as she said: "If that's the way it's going to be, you will not become a cleric! You will not put up with this kind of punishment just to learn Latin!" I looked at her, summoning up as much indignation as I could, and cried out: "Even if I die, I will not give up my lessons! And I will be a cleric!" I should add here that she had already promised me, when I came of age, to provide me with arms and equipment if I wanted to be knighted.[41]

I rejected every one of her offers, not without some measure of contempt. My mother (your servant, Lord) was so pleased, so elated by my contemptuous rejection of her proposal that she repeated my reply to my tutor. Both rejoiced to see that what I seemed to want most corresponded to the vow that my father had made. I was quick to pursue my lessons, however badly they were taught; and I did not shun my churchly duties. On the contrary, when came time for them, or when some obligation came up, there was nothing I preferred to these duties, not even meals. That is how it was then. But alas! dear Lord, you know how much I shunned such duties later on, and how reluctantly I would go about the Divine Office! There came a time when even the compulsion of blows could hardly get me to perform them. Clearly my earlier motivation had

---

40. Guibert uses "triclinium" here, as he used "cubiculum" earlier, to designate the room where the "studium generale" of the town was held. Was it also, as Benton suggests, the "dining hall" of the residence? Cf. Benton, *Self and Society,* 49.

41. Guibert's mother seems willing to renege on the vow that was made on the day of her delivery that Guibert should enter the religious life, if becoming a cleric means his being treated inhumanely. Her piety is neither rigid nor unconditional. The phrase "apparatum se mihi militiae et arma daturam" should not be interpreted to mean that Guibert's mother intended to dub him knight (Labande, *Guibert de Nogent,* 40n.3).

not been religious. It was not a product of mature thought but of childish impulse. But when adolescence came and my instinctive perversity bloomed,[42] I began to reject every outward form of restraint, and all my earlier devotion vanished. Oh my God! For a time there had been goodwill, or some semblance of goodwill, aglow within me, but soon it was snuffed out by a black deluge of perverse fantasies.

7
My family's search for a church prebend

My mother was determined to obtain for me some ecclesiastical title, whatever the cost. The first opportunity proved not only bad but harmful. It involved one of my adolescent brothers, who was a young knight living in the town of Clermont (that is, the one situated between Compiègne and Beauvais). He was expecting some money from the lord of this place—whether it was a loan or some kind of feudal obligation I don't know. When the lord proved slow in repaying his debt (from lack of funds, presumably), one of my relatives suggested he give me a canonicate, or, as they call it, a "prebend," in the church of that town. (Contrary to all church regulations, this church was under his authority.) In exchange for this prebend my brother would cease pestering him about repayment.

At that time the Holy See had initiated a new attack against married clerics.[43] Consequently some zealots began railing against these clerics,

42. Literally: "my adolescence, soon exhausted by my ingrained perversity" ("adolescentia, ingenitae nequitiae jam effocata"). The reader is left wondering what Guibert really meant by his "ingenita nequitia."

43. At the Lateran Council of 1059, Pope Nicholas II, strongly urged by Peter Damian, took strong measures to curb the marriage of clerics. He "deprived married priests, even in the external forum, of the right to perform liturgical acts of worship, and they were forbidden to live in the *presbyterium* of the churches. They were also denied all further rights to ecclesiastical prebends. To further his effort, the Pope tried to enlist the support of the laity by prohibiting them to attend Mass offered by a married priest or by one who lived in concubinage. Many laymen, indeed, were gravely scandalized by clerical immorality and supported the program of papal reform" (*New Catholic Encyclopedia* [Washington, D.C.: Catholic University of America, 1967]), 3.372–73).

claiming that they should either be deprived of ecclesiastical prebends or forced to abstain from priestly functions.[44] It just so happened that one of these zealots was a certain nephew of my father. This man, who was more powerful and cunning than his peers, would indulge in sex like such an animal that he never put off having a woman when he wanted one,[45] and yet to hear him rail against clerics regarding this particular canon, one would have thought he was motivated by a singular modesty and distaste for such things. As a layman he was unable to conform to the laws governing his own state in life. The more liberal the laws the more easily he transgressed them. He could never be chained to a woman through marriage, for he never intended to be shackled by such bonds. Everywhere he went, a stinking odor followed him; but his worldly fortune protected him, and he never ceased loudly reproaching the clergy for its "impurity."

Finding a pretense by which I might benefit at the expense of a certain well-placed priest, he began pressing the lord of the castle (over whom he had gained much influence by making himself indispensable) to call me and to confer upon me this ecclesiastical benefice in the absence of the other priest, and without his consent. For, contrary to every law, human and divine, this man had been authorized by the bishop to be the abbot of that very church. Thus, even though he himself had not been canonically appointed, he was demanding of the canons that they respect the canons![46]

At this time it was not only considered a serious offense for members of the higher orders and canons to be married, but it was also considered a crime to purchase those ecclesiastical offices involving no pastoral care, such as prebends, chantries, provostships, and others of this sort, not to mention the dignities that are called upon to deal with internal matters of the church. Those who took the side of the cleric deprived of his prebend, as well as many contemporaries of mine, started murmuring

44. This passage shows that the reforms of Pope Gregory VII, especially concerning married clergy, had strong support among lay Catholics who were "zealous about their clergy" ("vulgi clericos zelantis").

45. Benton's translation, "that he had no respect for any woman's conjugalities," is an inaccurate rendering of "ut cujuspiam necessitudini feminarum in nullo deferret" (*Self and Society*, 51).

46. "Canones a canonicis non canonicus exigebat." Guibert's fondness for word play has already been noticed. Guibert had earlier described members of his extended family as "animales et Dei ignaros."

openly about simony as well as about the excommunications that had recently proliferated.

Even though he was a married priest, this man could not be forced to part with his wife through the suspension of his office; but he had given up celebrating Mass. Having given the divine mysteries less importance than his own body, he justly received the punishment that he thought he had escaped by renouncing the sacrifice. Once he was stripped of his canonical office, there being nothing left to deter him, he began publicly celebrating Mass again while keeping his wife. Then a rumor spread that, in the course of these ceremonies, he pronounced excommunication on my mother and her family and repeated it several days in a row. My mother, who was always fearful about divine matters, feared the punishment of her sins and the scandal that might erupt. She surrendered the prebend that had been illicitly granted and secured another one for me from the lord of the castle in anticipation of some other cleric's death. Thus do we "flee the weapons of iron, only to fall under the shafts of a bronze bow."[47] To grant something in anticipation of someone else's death is hardly more than issuing a daily incentive to murder.[48]

O Lord my God, at that time I was all wrapped up in these wretched hopes. I was in no way interested in waiting for your gifts, which I had not yet come to know. This lady of yours, my mother, had not yet understood what hope, what security, she would find when you became my Provider, nor could she recognize the benefits with which you had already endowed me. Being still caught up in the affairs of the world she felt things for a certain time the way the world feels them; she sought things for me that she had seen fit to seek for herself, thinking me ready to seek the things of the world.

Later on, however, she became aware of the peril her own soul was in; and having searched every corner of her heart she ended up deploring her past life, as if she had said, "I will not do unto others what I would not like done unto me" [Tob. 4.16]. She decided it was the height of madness to try to obtain for others what she refused to obtain for herself. She thought it pernicious, and harmful to the other person, to desire for that person what she had ceased being personally ambitious about. For

47. Guibert: "Fugimus itaque arma ferrea, et incidimus in arcum aereum." This is an almost verbatim quotation of Job 20.24: "He will flee from an iron weapon; a bronze arrow will strike him through."

48. In late 1114, the Council of Beauvais had declared it anathema to grant prebends to a "successor" while the incumbent was still alive.

many people it is the other way around: they renounce their own possessions in a show of poverty; yet they preoccupy themselves greatly with
things acquired not only by their own family members (which is bad
enough) but by strangers (which is worse).

8

The decline of monasticism in the present day

In keeping with what I have been saying about our own time, I would
like to talk more about the condition of religious life and the conversions
we have witnessed. We might thereby understand where [my mother and
many others]⁴⁹ drew their examples for a happy transformation of their
lives. We have an abundant literature relating how the monastic state
flourished in ancient times. Leaving aside foreign countries, we know that
under certain kings of France the rules of this way of life were observed
in various places, under different founders. In some of these places the
sheer numbers of men who came to live the pious life together were so
great that we wonder how they could manage within such limited space.
Among them, some stood out who were exceptional in the rigor of their
discipline and who managed, quite remarkably, to restore zeal for the
rule in several monasteries where it had grown lukewarm. This was the
case, once upon a time, at Luxeuil, in Gaul, as well as some places in
Neustria, which is today called Normandy. But, as the poet so aptly puts
it, "great things don't last forever,"⁵⁰ and (which is even truer) the world
is declining, led by the bridle of iniquity, and the love of holiness is
growing cold [Matt. 24.12]; so some of these churches gradually lost
their material prosperity. Hence, with growing contempt for manual labor, men of a holy life became rarer and rarer.

49. There is a lacuna of a few words in the text at this point.
50. Guibert's phrase "summis negatum est stare diu" is taken from the Prologue of
Lucan's *Pharsalia* 1.70–71, wherein Lucan describes the fall of Rome into civil war:
"inuida fatorum series summisque negatum / stare diu nimioque graves sub pondere
lapsus" ("standing for long on the heights of success forbidden; the massive collapse
of too much weight"). See Lucan, *Pharsalia*, trans. Jane Wilson Joyce (Ithaca: Cornell
University Press, 1993), 6.

In our own time, some very old monasteries have seen dwindling numbers even though they have enjoyed an abundance of goods donated in former times. They have been content to set up small communities in which there were very few monks who had rejected the world out of scorn for sin. These churches were populated mostly by monks brought there in early life through the piety of their kin. The less these monks feared their own sins (which they imagined they had never committed), the more callously they went about their business inside the monastery walls. Whenever some administrative charge or duty, undertaken out of necessity or in response to their abbot's wishes, sent them outside the monastery, they always found an easy opportunity to squander their monastery's funds with indiscriminate spending. This was because they were anxious to follow their own inclinations and because they were inexperienced with the freedom of the outside world. And yet, however little these monks observed the religious life, the very scarcity of their numbers made them even more precious.[51]

9

Great monastic vocations of old

This, then, is how they were conducting themselves. Hardly anyone of any worth was joining their ranks. Then a certain count of the castle of Breteuil, which is situated on the border between the Amiens and Beauvais region, appeared, and his example stirred the hearts of many. He was in the prime of life, a most pleasingly elegant man. His family was noteworthy for its old nobility. He himself was conspicuous for his out-

51. Given his interest in the reinvigoration of monasticism in the first quarter of his century it seems only natural that Guibert should give so much attention to earlier, more vigorous days of monasticism in northern France. Benton (*Self and Society,* 54) translates "Et licet tum minus apus eos religio curaretur, ex sua siquidem fiebant raritate ipsi monachi cariores" as "And as among them there was then little concern for religion, because of its rarity even fewer became monks." Like Labande (*Guibert de Nogent,* 52), I believe "ipsi monachi cariores" refers to those exceptional monks mentioned earlier who lived according to a very strict rule ("speciali pollentia districtione") and constituted that minority of good monks ("bene conversantium . . . raritas").

standing qualities. He owed his renown to the possession of other castles and of every kind of wealth. At the height of his pride, however, the man came to his senses, and by dint of self-scrutiny he became aware of the horrid vices that he had begun to cling to in the world. Once he realized that he was miserable and that he was doing nothing else in the world except damning and being damned, polluting and being polluted, he began discussing at length with a few friends whom he had confidentially informed of his yearning what way of life he should take up. His name was Evrard,[52] and he was known all around as one of France's greatest men.

At last he decided to execute what he had been meditating on for so long. Without telling anyone, he fled to foreign parts where his name was unknown and where he could live as he pleased. Accompanying him were those he had approached secretly to enlist them to the religious life. To make a living he spent his time making charcoal and selling it throughout the villages and towns. It was then he realized for the first time that he had gained the supreme riches, and he understood what it was like to contemplate all the glories of the king's daughter from within.[53]

Now I should mention the model from whom Evrard had drawn his inspiration. Thibaud, whom everyone today recognizes as a saint—many churches bearing his name proclaim it far and wide—was before the time I speak of, a youth of noble birth. In the midst of his training for knighthood he gave up the military life, fled his friends with bare feet, and took up the same aforementioned trade. For a long time he lived a life of poverty, for which he had not been prepared. This, I say, was the example that stirred Evrard, who resolved he would make his living from this same humble occupation.[54]

---

52. Evrard of Breteuil, viscount of Chartres, retired from the world in 1073 and later entered the Benedictine Abbey of Marmoutier near Tours. He died sometime after 1095. The subsequent examples of conversion to the monastic life will follow the same pattern: noble origins, life in the world, disgust with the *seculum,* withdrawal to a solitary life, and entrance into, or creation of, a monastic order.

53. Guibert: "et erat considerare omnes et intus filiae regis glorias." The allusion is to Ps. 44.14: "Omnis gloria ejus filiae regis ab intus in fimbris aureis circumamicta varietatibus."

54. Saint Thibaud, who came from a noble family of Champagne, entered the religious life in 1044 and died a hermit at Vicenza in 1066. In some parts of northern France he is considered the patron saint of coal miners.

There is nothing good, however, that does not occasionally provide some cause for wickedness. One day, while Evrard was in a village to carry out some mission or other, a man stood before him dressed in a scarlet cloak. His silk stockings contrasted sharply with his torn foot-wear, and his hair was parted like a woman's—in the front and sweeping down to his shoulders. In short he looked more like a gigolo than a man in exile.[55] Evrard, with perfect ingenuousness, asked him who he was; the other man raised his eyebrows and looked sideways, most immodestly, and refrained from answering. The more he kept silent, the more Evrard was curious and urged him to speak. Finally, as if overcome by Evrard's persistence, the stranger burst out: "I beg you not to tell anyone, but I am Evrard. I used to be count of Breteuil, and I was once rich in France, as you know. I sent myself into exile to do voluntary atonement for my sins." In speaking thus this striking man astounded his questioner by revealing this borrowed personality to him. Evrard marveled at the incredible impudence of this perverse man and, spurning any further dialogue with this replica of himself (one might say), he turned to his friends and said: "You should know, my friends, that this way of life may be useful for us, but it is pernicious for most other people. For what you have just heard from this man's mouth, you can imagine that you might have heard it from many others. If, then, we wish to be fully pleasing to God we must avoid what provides others an occasion for scandal, or even falsehood. Let us move to some permanent place, where we might abandon the name of exile that we suffer for the love of God, and remove from others any reason for impersonating us." After he had spoken, they took their new resolution and headed for Marmoutier where, taking the monastic habit, they observed that way of life forever.

While he lived a secular life, one is told, Evrard had been second to none among his rich peers in his concern for wearing sumptuous clothes. Moreover he was so habitually ill-tempered that it was difficult for anyone to cross swords with him, even verbally. Later we saw this man, once become a monk, treat his body with such contempt that, seeing his frumpy clothes, his shy demeanor, and his frail body, one would have said he was not a count but a little peasant.[56] And when his abbot ordered

---

55. For a man to wear his hair shoulder-length was, obviously, an ambiguous social sign: it could just as well signify the adoption of a dandy's ways as the rejection of social conventions.

56. Guibert: "non fuisse comitem, sed agrestem rusticulum." Here again Guibert

him to go through cities and towns he never could manage of his own volition to enter even once into towns he had once relinquished. The things I have just related about him he told me himself, for he had great respect for me even when I was a youth and considered me a member of his family. I was in a special way the object of his affection.

One of his most charming habits was this: if he happened to meet people whom he knew to be famous scholars, he would coerce them into writing something, in prose or in verse, for his benefit in a little book he often carried with him for that purpose. When he had collected the sayings of those who were reputed in the literary field, he would weigh the meaning of each of their sayings. Even if he did not discern the meaning himself he would soon obtain from those to whom he had given these maxims an unequivocal opinion as to which of these sayings were the most pertinent, either in their meaning or in the way they were turned.

I have now said enough about this man, who was once noble and whose holy death made him nobler still: a man, I would say, who stands out among those we have known by the glowing example of his conversion.[57]

10
Other great monks of former days

But God, who fashioned Paul for himself through Stephen's prayer,[58] spread the example of conversion more broadly and with even more felicitous results with a yet more powerful man. A certain Simon, son of Count Raoul, enriched the religious life of our time with a conversion as marvelous as it was unexpected.[59] Many are still alive who remember his

indicates that a frail physical build seems to set one apart as a monk or peasant, while a solid physique is the mark of a feudal warrior.

57. *Conversio*, in Guibert's time, meant a "turning" from the secular to the religious life.

58. The allusion is to the prayer of Stephen for Saul's conversion (as later recounted by Paul) in Acts 22.20: "And when the blood of Stephen thy witness was shed . . . he said to me, 'Depart, for I will send you far away to the Gentiles.' "

59. Simon, count of Valois, succeeded his father, Raoul III, in 1074. He entered the monastery of Saint-Claude, in the Jura mountains in 1077, and died in 1082.

great deeds and can testify to the power for which he was famous throughout France—the cities he invaded and the fortified towns he attacked and conquered with remarkable skill. How great he was might be inferred from this alone, namely that he married the wife of King Henry (who was also mother of King Philip) after her husband's death.

At his father's death the young Simon had the honor of inheriting his counties for a short time. It is said that the cause of his hasty conversion was the following: his father's remains had been buried in a fortified town that he had obtained more through usurpation than heredity. Fearing that this might harm his father's soul, he intended to transfer the body to a town that belonged to him by right. Before the body was removed, it was first uncovered, and the son was able to see it naked with his own eyes. As he gazed on the rotting corpse of what once had been his most powerful and most daring father he began to meditate on the wretchedness of his own condition. From that day onward whatever had appealed to him in the way of glory and high rank became tedious to him. He conceived a new plan, his desire for it grew and he brought forth what he had conceived. He fled his homeland and his friends, left the borders of France and made his way to Burgundy, at Saint-Oyen, in the territory of the Jura. I have even heard it said that he was engaged to a young woman of the highest rank. When she learned that this young man, who loved her so much, had forsaken her and the world she could not bear the thought of seeming inferior to him: determined to remain a virgin herself, she joined the ranks of virgins who serve God.

Some time after he had taken the monastic habit he returned to France. The purity of his words and the humility of his spirit, which he bore on his face, inspired so many men and women that innumerable legions of both sexes rose up to follow in his footsteps during his lifetime. From every side there were many who found the force of his example convincing. The man's zeal attracted a great swarm of men from the knightly ranks.

11

Manasses, Bruno, and the founding of the Grande Chartreuse

It was appropriate that one of the learned should, in the very same spirit, draw behind him a crowd of those in holy orders. Indeed there was around this time in the city of Reims a man named Bruno, trained in the liberal arts and director of higher studies.[60] He is said to have taken his cue for conversion from the following occasion. After the death of Gervais, a very famous archbishop, a certain Manasses took over the government of Reims by using simony. He was a nobleman, to be sure, but he had none of that serenity of temper one associates with noble birth. His new position made him so egotistical that he seemed to be imitating the royal ways of foreign rulers, and even their barbaric manners. I have said "foreign rulers," for among French kings there is such a natural sobriety that they have, even unawares, borne out the words of the Sage: "They have made you a Prince; but be among them like one of them."[61]

This Manasses, then, who enjoyed the company of knights but neglected that of clerics, is quoted as having said on one occasion: The archbishopric of Reims would be a fine thing if it didn't mean having to sing Mass. The man's morals, not to mention his shameless and stupid behavior, had begun to horrify all decent people. Bruno, who enjoyed an excellent reputation among the churches in Gaul at this time, left Reims out of hatred for this wretched man. Several of the most noteworthy figures of the clergy of that city followed him. Some time later Hugo of Die, archbishop of Lyon and legate of the Apostolic See, a man known for his spirit of justice, issued repeated anathemas against Manasses. When the latter tried to rob the church of its treasures by force of arms, the nobles, clergy, and burghers chased him from the See that he had so

60. Saint Bruno the Carthusian, described here as "magnorum studiorum rector," was born at Cologne around 1030. He was chancellor of the Reims cathedral in 1076. Forsaking a life of ease in the world, he left this prestigious position to found the Grande Chartreuse in a mountainous region in present-day Savoy in 1084. For six years he lived like a hermit with a few clerics and laymen in this small valley, 3,500 feet above sea level. The site of the Grande Chartreuse was "surrounded by rugged mountains and possessed of severe climate—a site well suited to guarantee silence, poverty, and small numbers." In 1090, Pope Urban II unexpectedly called Bruno to his side in Rome, which was then occupied by the Normans. That summer both men were obliged to flee Rome for southern Italy. Saint Bruno founded the hermitage of Santa Maria de La Torre. He died 6 October 1101 and was buried in the hermitage (*New Catholic Encyclopedia* 2.836–37).

61. Guibert is here alluding to the Book of Sirach (Vulgate, *Liber Iesu Filii Sirach*), 32.1: "rectorem te posuerunt noli extolli esto in illis quasi unus ex ipsis." Guibert's chauvinism is entirely understandable. The "naturalis modestia" of the French kings to which he refers here designates not merely the sobriety of their ways but the relative modesty of their official titles. This "modesty" remained characteristic of the French monarchy until the Renaissance.

wickedly occupied. Manasses was sent into perpetual exile. Being excommunicated, he joined Emperor Henry, who was himself excommunicated at the time. Then he wandered in different places, and he finally died without the last rites.

One thing is very much worth recording, which happened in the city under Manasses's wicked rule. Among the church treasures he had doled out to the soldiers who upheld his tyranny was a gold chalice. For two reasons it was considered quite valuable: because it was very large, and because a bit of gold—I am uncertain as to its size—that had been offered the Lord by the Magi, had allegedly been melted in it. Manasses ordered the chalice to be cut up with large scissors and planned to distribute the pieces to his men. But nobody was willing to accept any part of an object so sacred. Finally an impious knight, who was as bad as his benefactor, dared to accept the object; or rather, he seized it with a total disregard for the sacrament's majesty. He went mad on the spot. Far from enjoying the benefits of the gift he had so presumptuously accepted, he immediately paid the penalty for his rash deed.

As for Bruno, once he had left the city he decided to renounce the world. Fleeing all contact with his friends he made his way to the region of Grenoble. There he chose to live on the promontory of a steep and truly terrifying mountain that one could reach only by way of a rugged and rarely used path. Beneath this path opened the abyss of a deep valley. It was there that Bruno established the way of life that I am about to describe. His followers pursue it to this day.

The church is not far from the foot of the mountain, within a fold of its downward slope. Thirteen monks live there. They have a cloister that is well suited for the cenobitic life, but they do not live cloistered as do other monks. Rather, each has his own cell around the perimeter of the cloister, in which he works, sleeps, and eats. Every Sunday the cellarer provides each of them with food, namely, bread and vegetables; with this each makes for himself a kind of stew, which is always the same. As for water, whether for drinking or for domestic use, they draw it from a conduit, which leads from a spring and goes around all the cells and flows into each of these little houses through holes that have been drilled for that purpose. On Sundays and great feasts they have fish and cheese—fish, I might add, that they have not bought, but received through the generosity of a few devout people.

They take neither gold nor silver nor ornaments for their church from anyone. They have nothing with them but a silver chalice. They do not assemble in their church, as we do, at the usual hours, but at others. If I am not mistaken they hear Mass on Sundays and on solemn feasts. They hardly ever speak, and if they must ask for something they do it with a sign. If they happen to drink wine it is so diluted that it loses its strength and tastes little different from ordinary water. They wear hair shirts next to the skin: otherwise they wear few clothes. They are directed by a prior. The bishop of Grenoble, a very religious man, carries out the functions of abbot and treasurer. Though they live in the utmost poverty, they have built up a very rich library. The less they abound in bread of the material sort, the more they work at the sweat of their brow to acquire that food that does not perish but endures forever.

Let me show how jealously they guard their poverty. This very year the count of Nevers, a man whose piety is equal to his power, paid them a visit, driven by his own devoutness and their excellent reputation. He warned them repeatedly to guard against the accumulation of worldly goods. Once he returned home he thought anew about their poverty, which he had observed; but he did not heed his own warnings and sent them some silver vessels, such as cups and dishes of very great value. But they did not forget what he had told them; for once he made his intentions known he found himself fully refuted with his own words. "We have decided," they said, "to keep no riches that might come to us from outside, whether for our own upkeep or for furnishing our church; and if we are not to use them for either of these two purposes, what would it avail us to accept them?" Ashamed to have made a proposal that contradicted his own words, the count pretended not to have heard their refusal and sent instead a new offering of oxhides and parchments in abundance, for he knew that they would inevitably make use of these.

The place is named La Chartreuse. Only a small portion of the soil there is used for growing grain. They raise sheep in large numbers and use the fleece to procure whatever else they might need. There are also, at the foot of the mountain, little dwellings that house faithful laymen, more than twenty in number, who work under their supervision. As for the monks the fervor of habitual contemplation so sustains them that the passing of time cannot deter them from their rule; nor do they grow lukewarm, however long their way of living may last.[62]

---

62. Guibert's extraordinarily detailed description of life at the Grande Chartreuse, the mother house of the Carthusian order, situated beween Grenoble and Chambéry, is an invaluable document on the life of that order in the early twelfth century.

This wonderful man Bruno left the place, I forget on what occasion, having broadly inculcated in them by word and deed the rules of life we have just mentioned. He made his way to Apulia, I believe, or Calabria, and there instituted a similar manner of living. There he conducted himself in the most humble manner, providing examples of piety that shone all about him. The Apostolic See sought him out for the dignity of a bishopric and even offered it to him; but he fled, wary of the world and fearing to lose the taste of God that he had savored. It was the worldly, not the spiritual aspect of such an honor that he rejected.

These, I say, were the people who ushered in a new season of religious conversion. Crowds of men and women immediately joined them, from every rank of society. What can be said about ages when one saw little children of ten or eleven meditate like old men and mortify the flesh seemingly beyond the endurance of their tender years? These conversions allowed one to witness what used to be the habits of the martyrs of old; a livelier faith was to be found in weak and tender bodies than in those who had the vigor of years and the authority of knowledge.

Since there was no place to lodge the new monks except in very old monasteries, new places were begun everywhere, and a great deal of revenue was allocated for the feeding of people who were flocking in from all sides. When the means did not exist for building on a large enough scale, they arranged for room and board, some for two brothers, some for four, or for as many as they could provide. Thus one soon began to see, in villages, towns, cities, fortified castles and even in woods and plains, swarms of monks spreading out in all directions. Places that in former times had been the lairs of wild beasts or the dens of robbers were now devoted to the name of God and the worship of the saints.

With so many examples all around them, the nobles became attracted to voluntary poverty. They entered the monasteries and filled them with the things they had spurned, and their pious "hunting" unfailingly ended up drawing others to the same way of life. There were women no less illustrious who renounced the bond that tied them to husbands of renown, rid their pious hearts of the love they bore their children, surrendered their worldly goods, and dedicated themselves to ecclesiastical service. As for men and women who were unable to renounce their possessions fully, they supported those who had made a full renunciation with frequent gifts drawn from their own fortunes. They adorned churches and altars with many welcome gifts. Unable to imitate the prayers and embrace the pious way of life of the others, they attempted to provide the equivalent with material help whenever possible for those who did. And so the monasteries made great progress in those days through the great number of gifts and donors and by the zeal of those who entered the religious life or of those who supported the inhabitants of the churches with such generous gifts. With the increasing wickedness of modern times there seems to be a corresponding decline in the conditions that flourished then. Alas! today the fathers' original intentions have been perverted in every way by their sons, who either reclaim completely what their parents had given to these holy places with a pure heart, or repeatedly ask to buy them back.[63]

12

My parents' unconsummated marriage

After these digressions I return to you, O my God, to talk about the conversion of that good woman, my mother. When she was barely of marriageable age, my grandfather gave her to my father, who was himself just an adolescent. She was blessed with a lovely face and a naturally and most becomingly sober demeanor, but since her earliest childhood the fear of God's name had been nurtured in her. In fact she had learned so well to detest sin (not out of experience but out of some instinctive fear of God) that her mind was flooded with great fear of sudden death (as she often told me). Thus, when she was older she lamented that her mature mind no longer felt the sting of that same beneficent fear she had felt at a tender and ignorant age.

It so happened that from the very start of their legitimate union, my parents were prevented from consummating the conjugal act by an evil spell cast over them by certain persons. It is said that their marriage had

---

63. Guibert seems to consider the "present" (ca. 1115) as a period of religious and moral decline compared to the previous century. The decline in the number of new monks is one indication of that decline. His remarks foreshadow those he is about to make in the following chapter (1.12) about the decline of sexual modesty since his mother's time.

drawn upon them the envy of a stepmother, who had nieces both beautiful and well-born, and who would have liked to slip one of them into my
father's bed. When this attempt failed utterly, she is said to have resorted
to evil spells to prevent the consummation of the marriage. Thus my
mother preserved her virginity intact for seven full years. This great
misfortune[64] was kept secret for a long time, until my father finally revealed it when summoned to speak before his relatives. One can imagine
what means these relatives employed to get them to divorce, and how
sedulously they counseled my father, who was then young and inexperienced, to become a monk, though at that time they did not mention this
matter explicitly. They gave him this advice not to save his soul but
because they wanted to take possession of his lands. When they realized
that he was not taking their advice they began hounding the young girl
persistently. They imagined that being far from her own family she would
cave in under the pressure put upon her by strangers to her clan. She
would, they thought, be worn out by their attacks and leave of her own
volition, without waiting for a divorce. But with serenity she patiently
endured the abuse they heaped upon her and pretended to be unaware
of the violent arguments that resulted.

To add to this, a few very rich men, seeing how she was inexperienced
in conjugal matters, began to lay siege to the young girl's heart. But you,
Lord, the builder of inner chastity, inspired in her a modesty that neither
her nature nor her youth could have maintained. It is because of you that
she did not burn, though placed in the midst of fire. It is thanks to you
that, in spite of her tender age, she was not morally corrupted by the evil
talk that surrounded her, even though oil may have been poured on the
fire. Even though temptations from the outside mixed with inner impulses
that are common to human nature, the soul of this young girl was always
in control. She never allowed any temptation to lead her astray. Surely
this was your work and yours alone, Lord. For while she was in the prime
of her life and constantly engaged in conjugal duties, you kept her seven

64. Guibert's description of this seven-year period of sexual nonconsummation as
"tantum infortunium" shows that he had a perhaps healthier conception of sexuality
within marriage than he has been given credit for. His use of "septennio" need not be
taken literally, but rather in its biblical sense of a long period of trial. In view of the
alleged "evil spells" cast over Guibert's young parents by an envious stepmother, Benton's judgment that Guibert had a "censorious mother who had nearly destroyed the
potency of her husband" (Self and Society, 13) seems a bit harsh.

full years in such a state of continence that, in the words of a certain wise man, "even rumor did not dare lie in her behalf."[65]

You know, Lord, how difficult, maybe even impossible, it is to find such chastity in women today, whereas in those days modesty was so great that no marriage was ever tarnished by any public rumor. Alas! what a wretched and progressive decline we have seen since that time in modesty and honor, which was once thought characteristic of virginity! Among married women the reality, and even the appearance, of reserve have disappeared. In their conduct they display nothing but coarse humor: nothing but jokes, winks of the eye, wagging of the tongue. They walk provocatively and show only silliness in their behavior. Their way of dressing couldn't be further removed from old-fashioned simplicity: their broad sleeves, their skin-tight tunics, the curling toes of their Cordovan shoes—in every detail they proclaim that they have cast all modesty to the winds. Any one of them would imagine she has reached the rock bottom of misery if she is presumed to be without a lover. Nobility and worldly glory are directly related to the number of suitors who follow in her footsteps.

In those days, I swear to God, there was far greater modesty in men who took wives (so much so that they blushed to be seen among women) than there is today in brides themselves: indeed, shameful conduct makes women more boastful today and more willing to exhibit themselves in public. How can one explain this, O Lord my God, if not that no one today is ashamed of levity and immodesty, seeing as how everyone behaves the same way? And when one is about to behave the way everyone else does, why should one be ashamed to desire passionately what everybody else seems to desire with equal passion? But why do I even talk about shame when the only thing one is ashamed of these days is to be counted among those who least exhibit their debaucheries? The secret pride a man takes in having a number of love affairs, or in seducing a particularly beautiful woman, is no source of reproach to him. Nobody is despised for flaunting love affairs before your face; rather one enjoys an extraordinary favor that only serves to increase the general corruption. People cheer when things that should be kept modestly silent and

65. The saying is attributed to Bias of Priene, one of the seven sages of ancient Greece, who describes the chaste woman as "she about whom scandal fears to lie" (according to Ausonius, *Septem sapientum sententiae,* trans. Hugh G. Evelyn White [New York: G. B. Putnam's Sons, 1919], 2.272).

completely hidden, things that anyone conscious of the decline of chastity should condemn, are wildly and impudently broadcast in all direction rather than consigned, as they should be, to eternal silence. In this and in other similar ways, the modern world corrupts and is corrupted, pouring its evil ideas upon some, while the filth spreads to infinity like a hideous epidemic. O holy God, these things were unheard of in the days when your servant, my mother, behaved as I have described. Then shameful things were concealed under the cloak of sacred modesty, and honorable behavior was rewarded.[66]

In those seven years, Lord, that virginity, which you miraculously prolonged in her, was severely tested under countless pressures, as frequently they threatened to dissolve her marriage to my father and hand her over to another husband or send her to live with relatives far away. Against such insistent pressures she struggled bitterly; yet against the tinglings of her own flesh, against the attempts of others to seduce her, she strove with an admirable self-control. Still, Lord, she owed it all to you. I am not saying, O Lord of goodness, that she acted out of virtue but that the virtue was yours alone. For how can one speak of virtue if one acts, not because of a conscious choice of spirit over flesh, not out of a pious inclination toward God, but solely to maintain appearances or to avoid dishonor? It is useful, of course, to resist imminent sin out of shame, if nothing else. But if shame is useful before a sin is committed, it is damnable afterward. For that which instills modesty in the soul so as to dissuade it from committing sin is useful at that moment. The fear of God can, indeed, add a divine seasoning to a rather bland modesty and endow an act that had a merely limited and secular utility with an eternal value. That is the sort of shame that one can be proud of. But after an act is committed shame is harmful because it leads to obstinacy, which is an obstacle to the true remedy — a holy confession.[67]

66. While Guibert is no doubt sincere in thinking that the sexual morality of his time is more licentious than that of his mother's youth, his condemnation of the behavior of the *modernum seculum* as compared with that of a simpler, more modest past is a well-known literary trope. Cf. Seneca's *Letters to Lucilius* 90, describing the simple virtues of an earlier age when men actually enjoyed sharing nature's goods in common: "Quidquid natura protulerat, id non minus invenisse quam inventum mostrari voluptas erat" (Seneca, *Ad Lucilium epistulae morales,* trans. Richard M. Gummere [New York: G. B. Putnam's Sons, 1930], 2.424).

67. The passage shows that Guibert considers genuine chastity as rooted in strength, *virtus,* rather than in mere sexual repression. A sense of shame, *verecundia,* might act as a deterrent to sexual sin; but shame is pernicious once the fault is committed, "pernici-

O Lord my God, your servant, my mother, intended nothing that might contradict the customs of the world. Yet, in keeping with the writings of Saint Gregory, which she had never read nor heard read, she was led to abandon this intention, for soon she diverted all her desires to you alone. Nevertheless it was a good thing for her to have respected worldly conventions for a time.[68]

For seven years and more, the evil charms that prevented the consummation of a natural and legitimate bond did their work. It is easy enough to admit that if the sense of sight can be perturbed by sleight-of-hand tricks—some magicians make people see things where nothing exists, as it were, or make them take one thing for another—sexual energies and activities are incomparably easier to perturb. Indeed, these arts are frequently practiced among the people, and even the uneducated know about them. Finally an old woman put an end to these evil charms, and my mother submitted to the duties of the marriage bed as faithfully as she had kept her virginity, despite so many pressures to the contrary.

Maybe she had been better off in her previous condition! Her new state led her not only to misery but to wretchedness. For this good woman, who became even holier as time went on, gave birth to an evil being, myself, who grew progressively worse. You know, O Almighty One, how she raised me according to your holy ways. What pains she took to choose my nurses, tutors, and masters! My little body was not deprived of luxurious clothes when I was very young, so that I seemed as nobly dressed as a young prince or count. These tender feelings toward me, Lord, you did not sow in my mother's heart alone. Others, who were richer than she was, had them as well. They assured my nourishment and my comfort, not because blood ties made it necessary for them to do so but because you had assured me of a certain grace.

O God, you know what warnings she poured daily into my ears so that I might not listen to the voices of corruption. Whenever she managed some leisure time away from domestic chores she taught me how to pray, and for what intentions. You alone know what pains she took—comparable to those of childbirth—to prevent an unclean spirit from

---

osa post culpam," and merely acts as an obstruction to the true remedy of confession. Guibert's sense of sexual morality, far from being based on fear, incorporates many elements of Stoic ethics (cf. Michel de Montaigne, "Du repentir," in his *Essais* [Paris: Garnier, 1962], 2.232).

68. Guibert's mother remained chaste during the seven-year trial out of regard for worldly convention. After her husband's death, she would vow her chastity to God.

perverting the healthy and promising youth that I owed to your generosity. In answer to her prayers you had granted that I should burn for you alone, unceasingly, so that to my external appearance might be added inner virtue, or wisdom. Good Lord, my God! What would she have done had she been able to see in advance the heaps of filth[69] I would end up using to bury the qualities you had endowed me with? What would she have said? What hopeless lamentations she would have uttered! How torn her mind would have been! Thank you, sweet and temperate Creator, who "fashions the hearts of us all" [Ps. 33.15]! Surely, if her purest of eyes had penetrated to the depths of my soul (unworthy as it is of any pure scrutiny), I would be surprised if she had not died on the spot.

13

My father's death. My mother vows to remain a widow

Having said these things by the way, let me now come back to a few matters that were omitted earlier. As I have said, this woman, while serving in the world, always maintained a fear and reverence for the name of God; so much so that whether in respecting the churches, in helping the poor, or in her sacrificial offerings, she bore herself in a way that made everybody respect her. But I know fully well what great difficulties I face in making this testimony seem credible, and some will undoubtedly be suspicious of my praise in view of our close relationship. If praising my mother seems a clever and underhanded way of praising myself, I call you to be my witness, God, you who as tenant of her soul knew her so well, to ask you to confirm that she excelled in all things, as I have claimed. Since it is as clear as day that I have strayed from the path of goodness and that my real interests are an insult to all sensible people, what good is it for me to extol the name of my mother, or my father, or my grandfather, if in the end all this great effort does nothing more than reveal the wretchedness of their offspring? Shall I, who

---

69. "Quanto sordium cumulo obliteratus." On Guibert's fondness for images of filth, see note 3 above.

through lack of will and action fail to make their good deeds live again, heap infamy upon my head by claiming for myself the praise they deserve?

My mother was still a young newlywed when something occurred that considerably impelled her to amend her life. In the days of King Henry, the French were locked in bitter combat with the Normands and with their Count William, the one who was later to conquer the English and the Scots. In the course of an armed encounter between the two peoples my father was taken prisoner.[70] It was a habit with the count in question never to hold his prisoners for ransom but to put them in prison for the rest of their lives. When the news was brought to the prisoner's wife — I was not yet born, and so I am omitting the name of "mother," though I came into the world shortly after[71] — she felt a frightful pain and fainted. She then refused either to eat or to drink, and worry brought her to the brink of despair, which made sleeping even more difficult. Her grief was caused not by the enormity of the ransom but by the prospect of an unredeemable captivity.

In the dead of a dark night, as she lay awake in her bed filled with this unbearable anxiety, the Devil, whose custom it is to attack those who are weakened by grief, the Adversary himself, appeared all of a sudden and lay upon her, crushing her with his tremendous weight until she was almost dead. The pressure began to suffocate her, she was completely deprived of bodily movement, and her voice could not utter a single sound. Unable to speak but free of mind, she could only implore the help of God. And suddenly, from the head of her bed, a spirit, undoubtedly a benevolent one, began to cry out in a voice as affectionate as it was clear, "Holy Mary, help!" The spirit spoke this way for a few seconds, and she began to comprehend what he was saying. Intensely tormented as she was, she suddenly felt that this spirit had violently hurled himself against the foe, who then rose up. The other spirit faced him, took hold of him, and threw him to the floor with a fierce noise. Their impact shook the room violently, and the servants who were usu-

---

70. At the battle of Mortemer, in February 1054, Duke William of Normandy routed the army of the French king, Henry I. Guibert's father was later released from captivity.

71. Benton translates "nec longo post tempore fui" as "nor was I for a long time after," and postulates the date of Guibert's birth as April 1064 (Benton, *Self and Society,* 230–31). Labande (*Guibert de Nogent,* ix) suggests the far more likely date of April 1055, the year following the battle of Mortemer.

ally plunged into a deep sleep were unexpectedly awakened. When divine power had overcome the evil one, the pious spirit, who had cried out to Mary for help and had expelled the devil, turned to the woman he had freed and said to her, "See to it that you are a good woman!" The servant women, dumbstruck by this sudden commotion, rose from their beds to see what condition their mistress was in. They found her half dead, with her face drained of its blood and all the strength of her frail body gone. They asked her about the noise and immediately heard her tell her story; but even by their presence, their conversation, and the lighting of lamps they still had some difficulty in reviving her.

Those parting words of her deliverer, who was in fact your messenger, O Lord God, she kept engraved forever in her memory; and she stood ready to use them for the sake of a greater love, if ever you were later to give her the opportunity. Thus when my father passed away, my mother decided to remain a continent widow, however beautiful her face and complexion continued to be; and I, hardly six months old, became the sole object of her concern.[72]

The story I am about to relate now might give some idea of the determination with which she carried out her vow and of the proof she gave of her modesty. Some of my relatives, who were eager to own my father's lands and possessions, conspired to gain possession of everything by excluding my mother, so they set a day for bringing the case to court. The day came, and the judges sat to render a just decision. My mother, who knew everything about my relatives' consummate greed, had withdrawn to a church, where she stood before the image of the crucified Lord, knowing how urgent it was to pray. One of my relatives on my father's side, who had the same intention as the others, was delegated by them to invite her to come to the court to hear the decision of those who awaited her. She replied: "In these matters I shall do nothing except in the Lord's presence." "Whose Lord?" the relative asked. She extended her hand toward the image of the crucified and said: "This is my Lord. This is the legal counsel I shall submit my case to." When he heard this the relative flushed with anger; but since he was something of a rascal, he put on a forced smile to hide his evil intent and withdrew to tell the

72. Guibert's chronology is often unclear. Guibert's father was no doubt released from captivity some time after the battle of Mortemer (February 1054). Guibert says that his father was present at his birth (probably April 1055). His father must have died in late 1055.

other relatives what he had heard. They too were overcome by the reply she had given and, recognizing that in the face of her perfect honesty their cause was totally dishonest, they ceased pestering her.

Immediately after, one of my father's nephews, a leading figure in the area and in the whole region and a man whose greed was equal to his power, accosted her with the following words: "Lady, you have your youth and your beauty. Wouldn't it be best for you to remarry and enjoy life in the world? My uncle's children would be placed under my care and I would faithfully raise them. As to his possessions they would, as is customary, be legally transferred to me." My mother said: "You know that your uncle came from high aristocratic stock. Now that God has called him back, the rites of marriage will not be repeated for me, my Lord, unless I am offered the chance of marrying someone of much nobler rank." My mother, of course, being the clever woman she was, spoke of a "nobler" possibility knowing full well that this was hardly likely, if at all. The young man was annoyed by the word "nobler"; and she intended to keep refusing marriage proposals, whether from nobles or from commoners, so as to deprive them of the hope that she might marry a second time. But because the young man was accusing her of great arrogance for having used the word "nobler," she added: "Of course, I mean someone nobler, or no one at all." The young man finally understood what my mother meant to say, so he gave up his plan and never again asked her anything of the sort.

This prudent lady continued to protect us and our possessions, guided by a great fear of God and by a love no less great for her family and especially for the poor. And the fidelity she had shown her husband while he was alive she continued to show with double fervor to his soul. She did not destroy the former union of their bodies by entering into a new bond once he had departed. She also came to his aid almost every day through the offering of the Victim who brings salvation. She welcomed all the poor, whomever they were, but for some she showed a particular compassion, commensurate with her means, in a manner both generous and courteous. She was so tormented by the memory of her own sins that it was as if she had indulged in every form of iniquity and dreaded suffering the pains that are due for the sins of all humanity. It was impossible for her to live frugally, as fasting was neither called for, given her frail body, nor becoming, given what her social rank allowed. But in other ways she behaved most unconventionally. For I have seen with these very eyes and touched with these hands, a hairshirt she wore next to her skin, while outwardly she was dressed with a rather studied elegance. More than just wearing it during the day, she slept in it at night, which was a very harsh way of treating such a delicate body.[73]

She never, or almost never, missed the night office, and she regularly attended the holy offices prescribed for all of God's people. Thus the chaplains in her home were kept constantly busy, so that there was hardly a moment when the praise of God was not being sung. The name of her dead husband was always on her lips, so much so that she seemed to have nothing else on her mind. Whether she was praying, giving alms, or carrying out the most common occupations, she spoke of him constantly and was unable to do otherwise. When the heart is filled with love for someone, that person's name keeps coming back, whether one wants it to or not.

14
My mother's chastity. She retires to a monastery

Passing over those instances when she showed her goodness but not her most admirable qualities, I shall continue my narrative. I had been alive almost twelve years since my father's death (I was told) and she, as a widow, had been taking care of her household and her children in keeping with the conventions of the world, when she resolved to bring to fruition something she had been meditating on for a long time. While she was deliberating over her plan, speaking about it only to my tutor (the one about whom I spoke earlier), I heard some devil of a fellow, who ate regularly at her table, cry out under a demon's compulsion, after

---

73. The life of Guibert's mother after his father's death was in every detail in keeping with the prescriptions of the Church Fathers for continent Christian widowhood. Saint Augustine describes his mother Monica as having been the wife of one man ("fuerat enim unius viri uxor," [*Confessions* 9.9]), and adds that she rests in peace with her husband, "before, or after whom, she never had any other" ("ante quem nulli et post quem nulli nupta est" [9.13]). Christian teaching on the counsel of continent widowhood is based on 1 Cor. 7.39: "A wife is bound to her husband as long as he lives. If the husband dies, she is free to be married to whom she wishes, only in the Lord. But in my judgment she is happier if she remains as she is."

having barked out I don't know what else about her: "The priests have put a cross in her loins!" In fact nothing could have been truer, although at the time I had no way of knowing what he meant; for subsequently she endured not one but many crosses. In short, even though nobody knew of her intention except the man I have spoken of,[74] one of the stewards in her household (who would later follow her example by swiftly renouncing the world) had the following dream. He saw her taking a husband and celebrating her nuptials, an event that greatly surprised and shocked her children, her friends, and her relatives. The next day my mother took a walk in the country with my tutor and this very same steward, who then recounted what he had seen in his dream. My mother, who was most subtle in these matters, did not need an interpreter. Without speaking, she turned toward my tutor and let him know that the steward's dream was a portent of that love of God that they had spoken of together and that she desired to be God's bride. Finding it difficult to bear the fire that raged inside her, she accelerated her plans and took leave of the town that had been her home.

Upon leaving she stayed for a while in the episcopal estate belonging to the lord Bishop Guy of Beauvais, who had granted her permission to stay. Guy was a perfect courtier in his manner, of noble birth, and blessed with an outward demeanor that was well-suited for the office he held. After bestowing generous benefits on the church of Beauvais (among them his laying the first stone to a church of regular canons dedicated to Saint Quentin), the very men whom he had trained and promoted accused him of simony and other crimes before the papal legate, Archbishop Hugh of Lyon. Because he did not respond when summoned, he was condemned in absentia to be stripped of his bishopric. He was at Cluny when he heard of the sentence; it so terrified him that he converted then and there to the monastic state. He was very attached to my mother and my relatives; his affection for me was especially great, especially because he conferred on me all the church orders except that of the priesthood.[75] Thus, when some of my mother's closest relatives

74. Guibert's *grammaticus*, or tutor.

75. Guy became bishop of Beauvais in 1063 or early 1064. Guibert describes himself as having lived "about twelve years, some say," since his father's death. This would seem to confirm the time of his birth as occurring around 1055. Benton translates "omnia benedictionum sacramenta praeter sacerdotium" as "every sacrament of benediction except that of the priesthood," and argues that this includes Guibert's baptism, confirming that Guibert was baptized by Guy of Beauvais in 1064 (*Self and Society*, 74).

asked him to grant her permission to live in one of his houses next to the local church, he gladly consented. The name of this little village is Catenoy.[76] It is situated about two miles from our town.

After staying there a while she resolved to retire to the monastery of Fly.[77] She had a small dwelling built there, next to the church, following the instructions of my tutor (whom I have already mentioned) and finally left the small village in which she was residing. She knew that I would henceforth be an orphan and that I could no longer count on anybody's support. (In fact I had a plethora of relatives and friends, but no one was willing to give me the care a young boy needs at such an age.) Though I would not be in want of food and clothing, I would suffer from the lack of affection that is indispensable to children at that tender age and that only women can give. She knew, then, that I would be exposed to this neglect, but the fear and the love she bore for you, my God, gave her the resolve she needed. Still, when she was moving to the monastery, she passed by the town where I was living, and her heart was so torn that she was unable to bear the pain of looking at the house. She felt the most bitter pangs of melancholy when she thought of what she was leaving behind.

She must have felt as if her own limbs were being torn from her body. She considered herself, and heard others call her, a heartless, cruel woman. How could she lock such children out of her soul (they said) and leave them utterly without support? And so lovable at that! (My relatives adored me, and friends outside the family as well.) But you, O good and holy Lord, through your sweetness and love, strengthened her heart (which was, to be sure, the most compassionate in the world), so that her compassion might not work against her. For softness of heart would most certainly have been her ruin if she had put us ahead of her own salvation and, if neglecting God because of us, had turned her attention to worldly things. But her love for you was "strong as death" [Song

---

Labande (*Guibert de Nogent*, 100 n.2) interprets "sacramenta benedictionum" to mean minor orders, subdiaconate and diaconate. Had Guibert been baptized by Guy when the latter had just become bishop of Beauvais he certainly would have seen fit to mention it.

76. Guibert's town was presumably located near present-day Clermont, on the road from Compiègne to Beauvais.

77. Saint-Germer de Fly, about six miles west of Clermont. The monastery was founded by Saint Germer in the seventh century.

of Sol. 8.6], for the more intensely she loved you, the more firmly she broke with those things she had loved before.[78]

When she arrived at the monastery, she saw an old woman dressed in monastic habit whose appearance gave every evidence of piety. She coerced this woman into living with her, showing her the submission of disciple to master. I say "coerced" because once she had experienced the woman's character, she craved her company. Step by step, then, she began to imitate the austerity of that older woman; she took up the same frugality, settled for the simplest foods, did away with the luxurious mattresses to which she was accustomed and was content to sleep on a straw mat, covered with a simple sheet. Although she was still quite beautiful and showed no sign of aging, she made every attempt to look as if she had reached old age with an old woman's wrinkles. Her flowing hair, which usually is an essential component of feminine charm, succumbed under the scissors' repeated assault. A dark cloak with unusually broad folds, dappled with innumerable patches and repairs, served as proof, along with a small, undyed coat, and shoes with hopelessly irreparable soles, that the One whom she was endeavoring to please with such unassuming apparel was within her.

She confessed her former sins almost every day, for she had learned that this is where all goodness begins. Her mind was ever occupied with an examination of her past deeds, summoning relentlessly to the tribunal of reason what she had done, thought, or said, whether as a young girl, as a married woman, or as a widow with a wider possibility of action. She would bring the fruits of her examination to the priest, or rather to God through his intermediary. Thus one might have seen the woman praying with such sharp cries, consumed by such anguish of spirit that even while at her work she hardly ever stopped pouring out prayers of supplication, interrupted with the most terrifying sobs. She had learned the seven penitential psalms [Pss. 6, 31, 37, 50, 101,129, 142] with the old woman I have already mentioned, not by reading them but by listening. She ruminated on them, if I may say so, with such pleasure day and

---

78. Even her contemporaries, some of them at least, found Guibert's mother cruel and heartless to put God above the upbringing of her own children. Guibert, however, relates her decision with admiration, realizing that his mother is following an evangelical counsel to the letter. Her rejection of the *modernum seculum* follows a pattern similar to that of Thibaud, Evrard, Simon, and Bruno, in the previous chapters (see 1.9–11).

night that her chanting, which resonated so beautifully in your ears, O
Lord, was always accompanied with sighs and lamentations.

If ever some small encounters with people from outside the monastery
came to disturb the solitude she had embraced—for indeed all who had
known her before, especially men and women of the nobility, enjoyed her
conversation immensely and found her playful and restrained at the same
time—if after their departure she found that something untrue, futile, or
trivial had slipped into their conversation, one cannot imagine what torment she felt in her soul, until she had once again come to the waters of
compunction or penance.

But whatever effort and zeal she might put into such matters she never
succeeded in giving her spirit the confidence and peace of mind she was
seeking without having to continuously lament and question, through her
tears, if she could ever deserve pardon for her sins. You alone know, O
God, what sins were involved, we do not. Yet how great, Lord, compared
with hers, is the sum of other people's sins, who neither regret them nor
sigh over them. Insofar as I was able to guess what she was thinking in
her soul's depths I know that the fear of damnation and her love for you
never grew lukewarm.

15

Study and struggle with the Devil at Saint-Germer

Need I say more? When she had renounced the world, as I have just
said, I remained alone, without a mother, without a tutor, without a
master. For he who after my mother had so faithfully educated and instructed me, had in turn become a monk at Fly, inspired by my mother's
example, love, and counsel. I therefore took hold of my perverse freedom
and began, without restraint, to abuse my power, to deride the churches,
and to abhor the schools. I tried to gain the company of young lay
cousins of mine who were devoted to knightly pursuits by cursing the
outward sign of my clerical state, all the while telling myself that my sins
would be remitted. I began to oversleep (having been allowed so little
sleep beforehand) to such a point that excess of it made me waste away.
Meanwhile the renown of my activities reached my mother's ears, and

after what she heard she predicted my imminent ruin and nearly died. The fine clothes she had procured for me for church processions and to encourage me to enter the clerical state I used for frivolous purposes quite unbecoming my age. I was emulating the older boys in their impertinence. In short, I lost all moderation and discretion.[79]

Thus my behavior grew wild and destructive, especially if one contrasts it to the narrowly disciplined manner of my previous life.[80] My mother could no longer bear the reports she heard about me, so she went to the abbot and petitioned him and his brothers to allow my former tutor to take charge once again of my education. The abbot, who had been raised by my grandfather and was indebted to him for a benefice he had once received, willingly consented to my mother's request. My arrival pleased him, he received me warmly, and thereafter he treated me even more warmly. You are my witness, O Lord, you who had arranged all this ahead of time, that the moment I entered the church of that monastery and saw the monks sitting side by side, there welled up within me at the sight of this spectacle such a yearning for the monastic life that my fervor could not be abated nor my soul find its peace until its prayer was granted. Living with these monks within the same cloister I was able to admire their way of life as well as their whole condition; and as a flame is fanned by the wind, my spirit, which was always most eager to conform to theirs by watching what they did, found it impossible not to catch fire. Moreover the abbot of the monastery was urging me every day to become a monk; and though I passionately desired to do so, my tongue could not unloose itself to the point of making the promise, in spite of all the entreaties of those around me. And being the child I was I had no difficulty in silencing the great number of things that filled my

79. "Pensi et moderati omnino nihil habere." Guibert is fond of this expression, which he used earlier in relation to his schoolmaster ("parum pensi ac moderati in eo eum habuisse" [1.5]). It is borrowed from Sallust's *War with Catiline* 12.2. Cf. Labande, *Guibert de Nogent,* 33n.2.

80. Guibert's reported behavior hardly seems to justify the judgment "dissolutius, immo vesanius me haberem." Habits such as oversleeping, wearing fine clothes, seeking the company of fun-loving cousins, have hardly the "criminal" character that Guibert would like to imprint on them, considering especially that Guibert has yet taken no monastic vows. We should perhaps remember that this adolescent taste of freedom is his very first, and that his vivid imagination, coupled with a deeply-ingrained tendency to self-accusation, no doubt impel him to dramatize what was in fact a brief and innocuous identity crisis.

heart, something I find very difficult now that the years are weighing me down.

Finally I informed my mother; but she was afraid that my plan might be due to the fickleness of my years, and she spoke against it with such lengthy argumentation that I was more than a little sorry I had told her anything in the first place. Then I told my tutor about the same thing, and he dissuaded me even more. Much annoyed by this double setback, I resolved to apply my mind in other directions, and therefore I decided to behave as if I had never wanted any of these things. I put off any decision from the octave of Pentecost until Christmas, yet I continued to hope fervently that my project would go through. Finally I managed to break free from the reverence I had for my mother and the fear I had of my tutor, no longer being able, Lord, to resist your inner goading. So I went back to the abbot, who greatly wanted this to happen, and yet who in spite of so many entreaties had been unable to draw any promise out of my mouth. I fell at his feet and tearfully implored him to receive me, sinner that I was [Ps. 119.116]. He gladly granted my request and presented me as quickly as possible, the next day in fact, with the necessary habits; and as my mother looked on from a distance, in tears, he clothed me with them. Then he ordered that alms be offered that very day.

From that point on my former tutor, unable to teach me any further because of the restrictions of the rule, took pains to encourage me, at least, to study closely the holy books I was reading, to reflect upon lesser-known expressions with the aid of better known ones, and to compose little sequences of prose and verse; and he urged me to apply myself all the more to a self-instruction that seemed to preoccupy very few other people. O Lord, my true light, how well I remember the boundless generosity you showed me then. For scarcely had I put on your habit at your invitation when it seemed to me that the cloud that had obscured the face of my heart was removed, and things began to enter me that previously I had groped for like a blind beggar. Moreover I was soon inspired with such a great love of learning that I aspired to nothing else and considered any day wasted if I did not accomplish something related to learning. How often I was thought to be asleep and keeping my fragile body warm under its sheet when really I was concentrating on reciting texts or else, fearing the objections of others, reading under the blanket.

And you, dear Jesus, were not unaware of my intention as I did these things. I needed to garner as much praise as possible and to acquire the greatest possible honor in this world. My friends were clearly working against me then, for even though they offered sound advice, again and again they insinuated that my studies would bring me praise and acclaim, and by means of these, honorable positions and wealth.[81] Thus they poured into my shortsighted heart hopes far more noxious than adders' eggs [Isa. 59.5]; and since I thought I would immediately obtain everything they promised I was deceiving myself with the vainest expectations. What they predicted would happen in my maturity I obviously expected to occur in my adolescence and early youth. They kept pointing to my learning (which grew day by day under your guidance), my noble origin (as the world sees it), and my good looks. But they had not remembered your injunction against "going up by steps to your altar lest their nakedness be exposed" [Exod. 20.26]. Whoever goes up that other way is "a thief and a robber" [John 10.1], and therein lies one's corruption.

But these were my initial moments, Lord, and you were my inspiration. If my soul had known better it might have been better prepared for temptation. Indeed one might say that at that time my wisdom was something foolish.[82] Occasionally I experienced outpourings of joy and fits of anger such as a child experiences them; but O how I wish, Lord, that now I could fear your judgments and be horrified by my sins, including the great ones, the same way I was then horrified by the smallest sins, some of which were hardly sins at all! I dreamed (and with what passion) of being like those whom I saw deploring their evil deeds; my sight and my hearing delighted greatly in whatever came from you. Today I pore over the Scriptures for sheer display or to make speeches, going so far as to remember the disgraceful sayings of pagans to feed my chatter, whereas in those days I garnered from them reasons for tears or sorrow. I could never feel I had read unless I could gather from my reading something conducive to contemplation or compunction.[83] Thus I was behaving wisely without realizing it.

81. A learned cleric with noble origins and a handsome physique could aspire to high acclaim, a solid reputation, and considerable wealth. Cf. Abelard, *Historia calamitatum,* chap. 4: "Tanti quippe tunc nominis eram, et juventutis et gratia praeeminebam, ut quamcunque feminarum nostro dignarer amore, nullam vererer repulsam" (*PL* 178.127).

82. "Insipide sapiebam." On Guibert's taste for word play, see notes 35 and 46 above.

83. Monastic scrupulosity in the attainment of *compunctio* is considered a quality, rather than a fault, as it might be today, even in monastic orders. Speaking of Saint Anselm's prayers and meditations, Sister Benedicta Ward writes: "What Anselm attempted was, first of all, to stir up his own sense of honor, compunction, humiliation,

But our ancient Enemy,[84] whose long experience has taught him to adapt to every type of soul in every age, our Enemy, I repeat, had prepared to issue new challenges to my spirit and to my diminutive body. While I slept he would often introduce into my imagination the visible shapes of dead men, especially those I had seen being killed, by the sword or by some other means, or those whose death I had been told about. As I lay plunged in sleep my spirit was so terrified by these apparitions that there were nights when I could have neither remained in bed nor prevented myself from crying out had it not been for the vigilance of my tutor (whom I have already mentioned). I was hardly in control of my senses. Such a painful experience may seem childish and ridiculous to those who have not experienced it, but to anyone who has undergone it, it is a frightful calamity. The intense anxiety, which many people may think unfounded, can be diminished by no amount of reasoning or counseling. Try as one might to scorn what is making one suffer, no resolution of the mind can succeed in driving out those terrifying visions when sleep takes over. Deeply shaken by fear, the mind is even afraid to fall back asleep. It matters little whether we are alone or in company to fight such affliction. Company does not drive away the fear; and constant solitariness either increases it or maintains it at the same level.[85]

Lord God, I behaved far differently then from what I do now. I then lived with a truly great reverence for your law and with a boundless hatred for any kind of sin. I drank most avidly of everything that could be said and heard and thought of you. I know, heavenly Father, that such enthusiasm on the part of a young child must have greatly irritated the Devil; but later I would appease him by abandoning all religious fervor.

One night (in winter, I believe) I was awakened by an intense feeling of panic. I remained in my bed and felt reassured by the light of a lamp close by, which threw off a bright light. Suddenly I heard, not far above

---

and self-abasement at the recollection of his sins" (*The Prayers and Meditations of Saint Anselm* [Harmondsworth: Penguin Books, 1973], 48).

84. The Devil, "hostis ille antiquus," all the more dangerous because he is able to adapt himself to all types of soul-states and ages ("pro statibus animorum, pro qualitatibus aetatum se habere longaeva diuturnitate").

85. Guibert's description of the terror of nightmares, and the sense of helpless anxiety they awaken in their victims, has a remarkable ring of authenticity. Many who have experienced such terrors know that even a prolonged psychotherapy does not guarantee the prevention of such "visions."

me, the clamor of what seemed to me many voices coming out of the dark of night, voices without words. The violence of the clamor struck at my temples. I fell unconscious, as if in sleep, and I thought I saw appearing to me a dead man who (someone shouted) had died in the baths. Terrified by the specter I leapt out of the bed screaming, and as I did so I saw the lamp go out. Then I discerned in the darkness an enormous shadow, the very contour of the Devil standing near me. Such a terrifying vision might have been enough to drive me mad had not my tutor, who frequently stayed with me to calm these terrors, not appeased my distraught and troubled spirit. I was not unaware, O my God, that in my tender years, the good intentions that filled my fervid soul must have contributed immeasurably to the devil's inciting me toward evil. O my God, what victories I would have won, what crowns I would have deserved for these victories, if I had steadfastly stood firm in this combat!

Judging from the many things I have heard I am convinced that demons are more vehement in attacking recent converts or those who continually aspire to this holy way of life. I remember that in the time of Guy, bishop of Beauvais, whom I have previously mentioned, there was in his intimate company a young man of equestrian background, on whom the bishop bestowed an affection surpassing what he showed any of the boy's companions. This young man felt a persistently nagging sense of repentance for his sins and was attempting by every means to flee from life in the world. He was, in fact, being literally consumed by the persistent thought of such a conversion as he lay sleeping one night in the bishop's own bedchamber.[86] With him lay another equally pious man by the name of Yves, who came originally from Saint-Quentin, if I am not mistaken.[87] Yves was famous for his writings, excelling even more in the art of brilliant speech. He was a monk from Cluny, where, under the leadership of Abbot Hugo, of blessed memory, he had long held the function of prior. Other men lay sleeping in that same room near the bishop, distinguished by the nobility of their origins quite as much as by the sanctity of their lives. One man, a wise and very courtly person who came from the nobility of a nearby town, lay awake in the silence of night while the others slept. He was looking about the room letting his thoughts roam freely, when suddenly there appeared to him the figure of a chief devil with a small head and very broad shoulders, and it seemed to the man that as he advanced through the room on tiptoe he was

86. Sharing the bedchamber of a bishop or a king was a sign of privilege bestowed by the mighty on their familiars, while assuring their own protection.

87. Yves of Saint-Quentin, later prior of Cluny. He died some time around 1110.

looking at the beds one after another. When he came to the bed of the young man I have just mentioned, the one the bishop preferred to the others, the great deceiver stopped, looked at the young man as he slept, and said: "This one irritates me more than all the others who are sleeping here." Having said this he headed for the door of the latrines and went in. While this was happening the man who witnessed the scene felt such a weight upon him that he found it totally impossible to either speak or move. Once the Adversary had gone, both faculties returned to him. In the morning he related what he had seen to men of very sound mind; and having asked them about the identity and the spiritual state of the young man he discovered it was a soul particularly inclined toward the attainment of great holiness.

If "there will be more joy in heaven over one sinner who repents than over ninety-nine righteous persons who need no repentance" [Luke 15.7], it is also believable beyond a doubt that the enemies of humankind, who bitterly hate those who are changing for the better, are saddened when these escape their grasp. And just as I after a good start have continued walking like someone plague-ridden, the young man to whom the Devil had paid tribute slowly grew lukewarm, then cold, and finally returned to worldly pursuits. Still it is entirely believable that the hearts of devils are seriously stung by the sudden stirrings of our good intentions. That the Devil should be pained by our sudden, even ineffectual impulse toward repentance should not surprise us. Even the perfunctory humility of Ahab, the robber king, did not prevent God from looking kindly upon him even before people did. If I am not mistaken, God said to Elias: "Have you not seen Ahab, humiliating himself in my presence? Because he has humiliated himself for my sake I will not add evil to his days."[88]

16
My mother dissuades me from leaving Saint-Germer

While my little body grew my soul was titillated by my life in the world, itching to satisfy its share of lusts and other needs. Meanwhile my mind

88. III Kings 21.29 (Vulgate): "Nonne vidisti humilitatum Ahab coram me / Quia ergo humiliatus est mei causa non inferam malum in diebus illis." Guibert is once again quoting the Vulgate from memory and with slight modifications (ergo = igitur; inferam = inducam).

was swirling about while my memory reviewed everything that I might be in the world. As I juggled these thoughts about repeatedly in my mind, I often imagined far more than the truth would have justified. O dear God, who cares for all, you made these things clear to your servant, my mother. Whatever direction, sound or unsound, my fragile conscience turned, your judgment, O Lord, allowed her an immediate vision of its very state. And since dreams are known to "come with much business" [Eccles. 5.3], and nobody doubts this, my mother's dreams were elicited not by the effervescence of greed but by a genuine concern for my spiritual well-being. Whenever an unpleasant dream disturbed her most pious mind—and she was an extraordinarily subtle and perceptive interpreter in such cases—she would interpret the acute discomfort these dreams brought her as a sign. Then she would summon me and talk with me in private about my activities, what I was doing and how I was behaving. Since I was accustomed never to deny her the mutual understanding we shared, I would readily confess all the ways my spirit had grown sluggish, following the tenor of her dreams (as I understood them). Whenever she admonished me, I would immediately and sincerely promise to correct myself.[89]

O my God, how many times she revealed to me that she had been informed of this situation, which I still suffer from today, and through how many images! Anything that she instinctively thought I had done or would do, I daily experience in the depths of my heart as something that has occurred. Likewise my tutor, who also nurtured an indelible affection for me in his heart, was enlightened by many visions you revealed to him. He saw what was happening at that moment and he foresaw those things that were to follow. Thus, by God's special grace, both of them were able to prophesy my future sorrows and joys, terrifying me in one sense but comforting me in another. I was therefore spared that hidden evil that you miraculously revealed only to those who loved me, and I sometimes rejoiced at the prospect of living a better life.

At times a sense of overwhelming distress[90] would sweep over me, for

89. Guibert's mother seems to have had an immediate intuition of everything her son was thinking, whether she was near or far. An unpleasant dream was a sign, *portentum*, that Guibert was not living up his promise or her expectations and would precipitate a highly secret interview. Never was the symbiosis between mother and son ever closer than this.

90. The word "distress" is arguably an adequate rendition of Guibert's "spiritu accidiae," and another translator might prefer "sullenness," or "sloth." The latter

many of my superiors and my peers made me the object of their envy. In such moments I hoped to use the influence of my relatives to move to another monastery. In our own monastery, some had known me for a long time as their inferior in age, learning, ability, and understanding; and now that God, the key of all knowledge, had instilled in me a tremendous love for learning, through a gift all his own, they began to notice that I equaled them, or even, if I may say so, surpassed them. So they became so furiously, wickedly indignant with me that I became weary of incessant disputes and attacks; and more than once I regretted having ever become interested in learning or having acquired it. Indeed, my concentration was so perturbed by these discussions, and so many quarrels sprang up from the ceaseless questions related to that learning, that it seemed to me that my colleagues were determined only to detract my attention and to create obstacles for my mind. But just as when oil is poured on a fire it intensifies the flames it was supposed to extinguish, so also the more my enthusiasm was smothered in these difficult matters, the more it heated up as in an oven, and the better it functioned. Questions that were presumed to make my mind duller only served to sharpen it. Pitfalls contained in the objections forced me to ponder assiduously about hypotheses, and I perused volumes of all kinds to comprehend the multiple meanings of words and to find adequate answers. This behavior of mine made them dislike me even more, but you know, O Lord, that I did little if anything to reciprocate their hostility. Powerless as they were to stigmatize me, they compensated with slander,[91] accusing me of letting a little learning go to my head.

In the midst of these many vexations, which I had much trouble bearing up under, my soul lay exhausted and tormented under the burden. But even though overall they revealed themselves to be beneficent trials, neither my heart's terrors nor the state of weakness to which I had been reduced allowed me to reflect upon the positive fruits of adversity. Rather I had decided to seek the solution suggested to me by the flesh in its weakness. I therefore resolved to leave the monastery of Fly, less through the kindly authorization of my abbot than through the pressure of my relatives. My mother approved my initiative, thinking that I was taking

words, however, connote too much moral judgment. In the present circumstances Guibert is neither fully responsible for his soul states nor fully in control of them.

91. Guibert's image is literally that of being nibbled by his envious colleagues: "astruebant me ubique *rodendo,* pro scientiola superbire" (emphasis mine).

it with a pious intention, since the monastery I was planning to move to had a reputation for piety. She had a dream that warned her of the good and the bad things that were to happen to me.

She dreamed she was in the church of our abbey of Fly, which is called Saint-Germer. Going inside she found it completely deserted. As to the monks they were not only scattered and dressed in clothes entirely out of keeping with the rules of the faith; they had also been reduced to a cubit's stature, exactly like those creatures we commonly call dwarfs. But, because "where your treasure is, there will your heart be also" [Luke 12.34], and where your eye is, there your love lies, she turned her eyes toward me with a look of concern; and she noticed that my stature was no greater than anybody else's, nor were my clothes more dignified. She was saddened to see me and this once great church in such a state of abandon. But all of a sudden she saw a woman of unparalleled beauty and majesty walking up the middle of the church toward the altar. She was followed by what looked like a young maiden whose deferential appearance seemed entirely appropriate for whom she followed. As my mother seemed most curious to know who this woman was she was told that it was the Lady of Chartres. My mother understood immediately that this was the Blessed Mother of God, whose name and relics are worshipped at Chartres as objects of veneration for virtually the whole Latin world.[92] Drawing close to the altar, the Lady knelt to pray; and she who had been seen walking behind her, a noble lady of the court, did the same. Then the Lady arose, extended her hand as if in a gesture of intense indignation, and said: "I founded this church; why should I permit it to be forsaken?" Then, this standard-bearer of all piety turned her most serene eye upon me, and, pointing her dazzling white hand at me, she said: "As to this one, I brought him here and made him into a monk. In no way shall I permit him to be taken away." Her young lady-in-waiting then repeated the very same words after her. Hardly had the powerful Lady spoken, and faster than one could say it, all the desolation and ruin that could be seen beforehand was immediately repaired, and our ghastly shrunken sizes—not only mine but the other monks' as well—were returned to normal by virtue of the Lady's power and com-

---

92. The chief relic at Chartres was the tunic that the Virgin was alleged to have worn at the Nativity. It had been given to the church of Chartres by Charles the Bald, Charlemagne's grandson, around 876, and enclosed in a reliquary around the year 1000 (Benton, *Self and Society*, 85n.4).

mand. When my discerning mother had finished her detailed account of the dream, I greeted her beautiful story with great pangs of remorse and a great flow of tears. The meaning of the dream seemed so clear that I put an end to my notions of aimless travel and was never again attracted by the thought of changing monasteries.[93]

O Lady, mother of the heavenly realm, these experiences and similar ones made me anxious to return to you, rising above the horror of my sins and my innumerable defections from your love and your service. My heart keeps telling me that whatever the mass of my iniquities may be, the broad bosom of your enfolding clemency cannot be closed. I always remember, heavenly Lady, how as a little child I aspired to take the religious habit. One night I dreamed I was in a church dedicated to your name, and it seemed to me I was carried off to the roof of the basilica by two demons; then they fled, leaving me intact within the confines of the same church. I often remember these things as I consider how incorrigible I am; and even though I repeatedly commit the same sins, and even add worse sins to the worst ones, it is to you, most holy Mother, that I hurry back, if only to avoid the peril of despair, running a middle course between overconfidence and hopelessness.

Because my penchant for sin is the outcome not of obstinate arrogance but of the impulse of a weak nature, I never lose hope of amending my ways. The "righteous man falls seven times, and rises again."[94] If the number seven is normally taken to imply fullness,[95] then no matter how many ways one falls into sin if one has the intention of rising up again to live according to justice, and if, though fallen because of the flesh, one exhibits the pain of sincere repentance, one does not deprive oneself of

---

93. Like Monica, Augustine's mother (*Confessions* 1.13), Guibert's mother has a dream with what seems to the modern reader a clearly manipulative end. At a time that believed firmly in dreams as a direct sign from God, and in their power to predict, inhibit, or direct human actions, the manipulation of one conscience by another could seem an easy matter.

94. Prov. 24.16. Guibert's text is very close to that of the Vulgate: "septies enim cadet iustus et resurget."

95. Augustine comments on the text of Prov. 24.16 (to which Guibert is here alluding), and to the universality of the number seven, in *The City of God against the Pagans*, trans. David S. Wisen (Cambridge, Mass.: Harvard University Press, 1968), 11.31: "Accordingly let it suffice to observe that the first odd integer is three, that four is the first even integer, and that the sum of these is seven. For this reason seven is often used to indicate universality, as in 'A righteous man will fall seven times, and will rise again.' "

the right to be called just. Why, indeed, do we pray to God to "bring us out of our distresses" [Ps. 25.17], unless it be that the corruption of our nature condemns us, whether we choose so or not, to the servitude of sin. "I see," says the Apostle, "something leading me captive to the law of sin; for I do not do the good that I want to do but the evil that I do not want to do."[96] There is a depth of wickedness that brings contempt to the impious [Prov. 18.3] once they have plunged in; and yet from other depths there comes a supplication to God [Ps. 130.1], and petitioners cannot doubt that their voice will be heard. There is even a certain contempt born of despair due to an excess of sin, which can be a depth "where there is no foothold" [Ps. 69.2], in which misery itself cannot stand. And there is also a depth, the kind from which Jeremiah was delivered by a rope of knotted rags,[97] which yet has a bottom to it. Thus even though the soul may have slipped, owing to the enormity of its sins, it still possesses the restraining limit of reason to prevent it from falling into bottomless depths where it loses the knowledge of its total iniquity.

17

My flirtation with poetry. I am saved by Scripture

Meanwhile, I had fully immersed my soul in the study of verse-making. Consequently I left aside all the seriousness of sacred Scripture for this vain and ludicrous activity. Sustained by my folly I had reached a point where I was competing with Ovid and the pastoral poets, and striving to achieve an amorous charm in my way of arranging images and in well-crafted letters.[98] Forgetting the proper rigor of the monastic calling and

96. Guibert is conflating Rom. 7.19 and 23: "non enim quod volo bonum hoc facio, sed quod nolo malum hoc ago . . . video autem aliam legem in membris meis . . . captivantem me in lege peccati quae est in membris meis."

97. Jer. 38.11–13. Cast into a cistern of Malchiah, son of King Zedekiah, Jeremiah was rescued by ropes made of rags and worn-out clothes.

98. None of these adolescent writings having survived, so we are left wondering what Guibert might have meant by the "arranging of images" ("specierum distributionibus"). Benton (Self and Society, 87) suggests a versification exercise similar to that of the "blasons du corps féminin."

casting away its modesty, my mind became so enraptured by the seductions of this contagious indulgence that I valued one thing only: that what I was saying in courtly terms might be attributed to some poet. I failed to realize how much harm my industrious pursuit was doing to my intention of taking sacred orders. In point of fact, I was doubly chained for I was enmeshed not only by the sweet words I had taken from the poets but also by the lascivious ones I had poured forth myself. Moreover, by repeating these poetic expressions, I was sometimes prone to immodest stirrings of my flesh; and although my fickle spirit, chafing under any discipline, meditated on these matters, no sound could issue from my lips than what my thoughts could suggest.

My inner turmoil reached such a point that I began to use a few slightly obscene words and to compose little poems entirely bereft of any sense of weight and measure, indeed shorn of all decency.[99] When my tutor (whom I mentioned earlier) got wind of this, he took it very badly. While still in a state of exasperation and disgust, he fell asleep, and the following vision came to him: an old man with beautiful white hair — the same man, I dare say, who had led me to my tutor and predicted the love he would have for me[100] — appeared to him and spoke to him sternly: "I want you to render an account of these poems that were composed; the hand that wrote them is not that of the man who drew these letters." My tutor related this scene to me, and we both had the same interpretation of the dream. We were deeply embarrassed, yet we rejoiced at the hope we had in you, Lord, and at seeing your disapproval express itself in such a fatherly correction. The meaning of this vision gave us confidence that a healthy change from my frivolous ways was coming. Since we were being told that the hand that had written the letters was not that of the scribe who had copied them, clearly this meant that this hand would not persevere in these shameful activities. This had been my hand, but it was

---

99. In condemning (retrospectively) his earlier love for writing, and presumably reciting, poetry, Guibert is repeating a Platonic (and Augustinian) trope. Guibert's love of poetry makes him doubly captive: to the sweetness of words ("verborum dulcium") and to the tinglings such words elicit in his flesh ("carnis meae titillatione"). Similarly, Augustine realized that his love of epic and dramatic poetry is closely linked to love of death and love of physical sensation, whether pleasurable or painful, and conceals one from the truth of one's own soul which is to be estranged from God (*Confessions* 1.13.21; cf. 3.2.2–3).

100. In 1.4, Guibert has already described an earlier dream his tutor had, of an old man leading him by the hand into the tutor's room.

to be no longer; for it is written: "Turn over the impious and they shall be no more."[101] Indeed, when the hand that had been mine for a vicious purpose decided to pursue virtue instead, it lost every capacity to perform such an unworthy task.

You know, Lord, and I do confess, that at that time neither fear of you nor shame nor any respect for this holy vision caused me in any way to restrain my behavior. Clearly I was harboring irreverence within me so that I refused to tone down the scurrilous humor of frivolous writers. I forged these poems in secret, hardly daring to show them to anyone, except a few of my like-minded peers, while concealing the author's name. I would recite them to whoever I could, and I was happy if they were praised by my cohorts. It would have been unseemly to admit that they were my doing; and what produced no praise for the author allowed him to enjoy the fruit, or rather the shamefulness, of sin. But you, O Father, punished me when you were ready. When misfortune mounted against me over such works, you tightened my wandering soul with the belt of adversity and oppressed it with bodily infirmity. The sword "reached my very life" [Jer. 4.10] and my understanding was stricken with "sheer terror" [Isa. 28.19].

When the chastisement of sin had brought understanding to the hearer, then the folly of my useless study withered away. But since I found it difficult to do nothing, it was almost inevitable that I should reject vain fantasies, and, paying heed to spiritual things once again, I took up more appropriate exercises. Although I had lost time I began longing for things that had been taught me by several good scholars. I pored over the commentaries of Scripture; I dug more deeply into the writings of Gregory, in which the keys to the art of commentary are chiefly to be found; and finally, I closely examined, in keeping with the rules of the ancient authors, the words of the prophets or of the Gospels according to their allegorical, moral, and anagogical sense.[102] The per-

---

101. Prov. 12.7: "The wicked are overthrown and are no more, / but the house of the righteous will stand."

102. Scriptural texts were open to a fourfold level of interpretation: the literal, the allegorical, the moral, and the anagogical. The meaning of each level was summed up in a couplet cited around 1330 by Nicholas of Lyre: "Littera gesta docet, quid credas allegoria, / Moralis quid agas, quo tendas anagogia" ("The letter teaches the things that were done, the allegory what you should believe, / The moral what you should do, the anagogical where you are headed") (Henri de Lubac, L'Exégèse medievale [Paris: Seuil, 1968], 1.1.23).

son who encouraged me most in this enterprise was Anselm, abbot of Bec, who later became archbishop of Canterbury. He came from the transalpine area, from Aosta, in fact. His teachings were incomparable, and his life perfectly holy. While he was still prior of the aforesaid monastery, he wanted to make my acquaintance, even though I was still a child at the time and lacking the experience of years and intelligence. With great attention he set about teaching me how I was to conduct the inner self and how I was to use the laws of reason to govern my little body. Before becoming abbot, and afterward, he had free access to the monastery of Fly, where I lived, because of his piety and his erudition. He was so determined to make me benefit from his learning, and he pursued this end so persistently, that I might have seemed to be the only reason for his frequent visits.[103]

His teaching was to divide the mind three- or fourfold, to treat the operations of the entire inner mystery under the headings of appetite, will, reason, and intellect. He showed that the first two—appetite and will—which most people, including myself, consider to be one (broken down into sure divisions), are not in fact identical, even though one can readily assert that from the viewpoint of intellect or reason they are practically the same.[104] With his method he explicated several passages of the Gospels for me and explained with a consummate clarity what it is that distinguishes will from appetite. I noticed that he got these interpretations not from himself but from a few volumes he had close by, which nevertheless explained these matters far less clearly than he did. I,

103. Saint Anselm was born at Aosta ca. 1033 and died in 1109. He became prior of the abbey of Bec in 1063, was elected its abbot in 1078, and became Archbishop of Canterbury in 1093. Anselm's moral and intellectual impact on Guibert was obviously a powerful one. In the following passage Guibert summarizes Anselm's teaching that appetite and will were separate functions, although under the control of reason they might be considered as one and the same. Among Anselm's chief works are the *Monologion, the Proslogion, and the Cur Deus Homo.* Anselm described the theological venture as "fides quaerens intellectum." Some twenty-two years older than Guibert, Anselm was certainly one of the most prestigious theological thinkers in Christendom at the time Guibert is describing. The *Monologion* and the *Proslogion,* both considered highly original works, belong to the years 1077–78. See Richard W. Southern, *Saint Anselm and His Biographer* (Cambridge: Cambridge University Press), 50.

104. Benton's note here (*Self and Society,* 89n.9) is very informative: "Augustine described the faculties of the soul as memory, intelligence, and will. Anselm's novelty was to replace memory with reason and add appetite or desire; this allowed him to argue that the will was always free, since appetite was a separate function."

in turn, began to apply his reasonings to similar commentaries whenever I could and to examine all Scripture attentively to find anything agreeing, morally, with those interpretations.

One day, as I accompanied my abbot to a monastery in our province, I suggested to him—he being a very religious man—that he give a sermon at the opening of the chapter meeting. He made a countersuggestion, exhorting me, in fact ordering me, to take his place. It was the feast day of Mary Magdalene. Taking the text of my sermon from the Book of Wisdom, I restricted myself, for the purpose at hand, to the following words: "Wisdom triumphs over malice, it extends with strength from one end of the world to the other, and it arranges all things gently."[105] I elaborated upon this text as best I could, and I pleased my audience with the appropriateness of my words. The prior of this community, whose remarkable learning made him no less diligent in studying sacred writings, kindly insisted that I write him something that might be useful for a future sermon. But I knew that my abbot (in whose presence I had spoken) would look askance at my writing anything. I therefore approached him cautiously and begged him to give me permission to accept the prior's request as a favor toward a man he was fond of. I asked as if I were requesting on that friend's behalf and as if I were indifferent to the whole matter. He gave his assent, assuming I would write something short. When I finally extracted his permission, I began working on what I had in mind.

I therefore set about making a moral commentary on the opening text of Genesis, that is, on the *Hexameron*. I prefaced that commentary with a treatise of moderate length on how to construct a sermon.[106] Having finished this, I undertook an explanation on the moral level of the work of the six days, not very eloquent to be sure, but saying all that my mind wanted to say. When my abbot noticed that I was writing a commentary on the first chapter of sacred history, he looked less favorably on my undertaking.[107] In quite hostile terms, he ordered me to put a stop to my

105. Guibert is quoting the *Liber sapientiae* (Vulgate): "Sapientiae autem non vincit malitia / adtingit enim a fine usque ad finem fortiter / et disponit omnia suaviter." The feast of Saint Mary Magdalene falls on 22 July.

106. These two works of Guibert's can be found among his complete works (*PL* 156.19–338). The *Commentarii, seu moralia, in Genesin* is preceded by a short treatise entitled *Quo ordine sermo fieri debeat*.

107. Guibert was writing a commentary on a book of Scripture that, according to an ancient Jewish tradition mentioned by both Jerome and Origen, should not be read by anyone under thirty years of age (Benton, *Self and Society*, 91n.14).

writing. Seeing that my project amounted to sticking thorns into his eyes, I pursued my work secretly, taking care to avoid not only him but anyone who might relate my activity to him. I did not write either an outline or a first draft of these works on tablets but rather committed immediately to paper a definitive version of the text and the commentary. While the abbot was about, my work was carried out in utmost secrecy. After he resigned his post I took advantage of an interim vacancy to finish the work quickly. It was divided into ten books, according to the "four movements of the inner self," which I have previously mentioned. In each book I provided a moral interpretation, and I was so consistent to the very end that no change was needed in the order of the original text. I don't know whether my treatise was useful to anybody, but I am certain that it pleased many learned scholars; and it was unquestionably a most useful experience for me, insofar as it freed me from idleness, which is the source of all the vices.[108]

18
My mother's anxieties and visions

Since that time I have written a little book with chapter divisions on several Gospel passages as well as passages from the prophets, inserting into it excerpts from the Books of Numbers, Joshua, and Judges. I have put off writing a conclusion to this book.[109] When I have finished explicating the passages I'm working on right now I intend (if God gives me life) to continue explicating similar passages in the future. As I did in my study of Genesis I search for the tropological meaning in most of these texts and for the allegorical in a few of them. Moreover, if in Genesis I was particularly attentive to the moral meaning, it is not because lack of material prevented me from talking about the allegorical

108. Guibert's commentary actually disagrees with Anselm's teaching. For Guibert, reason is identical with intellect, and the soul, which he compares to the moon, is unstable.

109. Guibert's complete works include commentaries on minor prophets such as Hosea, Amos, and Jeremiah (*PL* 156.338–487). There are, however, no manuscripts attributed to him of commentaries on Numbers, Josiah, and Judges.

meaning on which I could have spent more time. It is because the moral meaning is in my opinion far more important than the allegorical. For if the faith that comes from God has remained the same, practically everybody's morals have been corrupted by vices of all kinds.[110] It is also because I had neither the time nor the will to embark on an excessively long work.

As much as my mother admired my scholarly successes, she was greatly worried by the excesses that occur on the slippery path of life. She constantly urged me to imitate her way of life. This woman, whom God had blessed with such great beauty, disregarded the compliments that were addressed to her, as if unaware that she was beautiful. She cherished her widowhood as if she had always borne the duties of the marriage bed with horror. Yet you know, Lord, what faithfulness, what love she showed for her spouse, even after he was dead. You know how persistently she struggled—with virtually daily Masses, prayers, tears, and much almsgiving—to redeem the soul of a husband whom she knew to be shackled by his sins. Thanks to the remarkable privilege granted by you she was allowed to experience frequent visions wherein she saw the most graphic images of the sufferings he bore in expiation of his sins. (There can be no doubt that visions of this sort come from you.) A spurious beauty only produces a false sense of security, the sight of suffering and torment is a wonderful incentive for prayer and almsgiving, and the dead (or rather the angels who watch over those who have died in the faith) require the remedies of the divine office: all of this is sufficient proof that such visions come from you because demons never busy themselves to promote anyone's salvation. So the signs my good mother saw rekindled the fire of her anxious soul, and the terrifying vision of her late husband's inner torments gave her the incentive she needed to seek intercession for him.

One summer night, for instance, on a Sunday after matins, she lay down on a very narrow bench to rest and soon fell asleep. She then had the physical sensation that her soul was leaving her body. She felt she was being led through a colonnade and then came out next to the opening of a well. When she approached it phantom human shapes seemed to leap

---

110. Guibert is not being puritanical here. It is very much in the Christian scriptural tradition to insist on the necessity of moral conversion, *conversio morum*, to be derived from a reading of Scripture. One can know Scripture with the mind and not let it affect one's way of living.

out from its depths. Their hair seemed to be eaten by worms, and they tried to take her by the hand to drag her down with them. Suddenly, from behind this terrified woman who was so lamentably upset by their attack, a voice shouted: "Touch her not!" [Ps. 105.15] They were paralyzed by this order and plunged back into the well. Now I forgot to say that as she was walking through the colonnade, she kept praying to God for one thing only, to be allowed to return to her body. Once delivered from the phantoms who dwelt in the well, she was standing near the edge when she suddenly saw my father standing next to her looking as he did when he was young. She stared at him and asked in a supplicating tone whether his name was Evrard (for such was his name in life). He answered no.

It should not surprise us that a spirit should refuse to answer to the name it had in its earthly life. A spirit can only answer another spirit in a manner befitting a spirit. To believe that souls know one another by their names is ridiculous, for if it were so we would be able to have only a limited knowledge of our own kin in the afterlife. It is obviously not necessary for spirits to have names, for their whole vision, as well as the knowledge of that vision, is internal. My father's spirit had therefore refused to be called by its name, but my mother continued to be persuaded it was he and asked him where he lived. In reply he pointed to a place not far from where they stood. She then asked him about his condition. In response he bared his arm and his side, and she was so horrified to see how both had been torn and flayed by repeated lacerations that she felt sick to her stomach. I might add that the phantom of a small child was present, filling the air with wails that greatly troubled my mother. Shaken by those wails she said to the spirit: "How can you put up with the wailings of this child, my lord?" "I have to put up with them," he answered, "whether I like it or not."

The child's cries and the lacerations on my father's arm and side had the following meaning. In his youth, when the maleficent influence of some people had prevented my father from having legitimate intercourse with my mother, some depraved counselors (his mind still being very immature) suggested to him most perversely that he should experiment to see if he was able to have intercourse with other women. Young as he was, he went along with them, and having had evil relations with some woman of loose morals, had a child by her who soon died without baptism. The laceration in his side signified that he had broken his marriage bond; as to the wails of that confounded voice it meant the damnation of

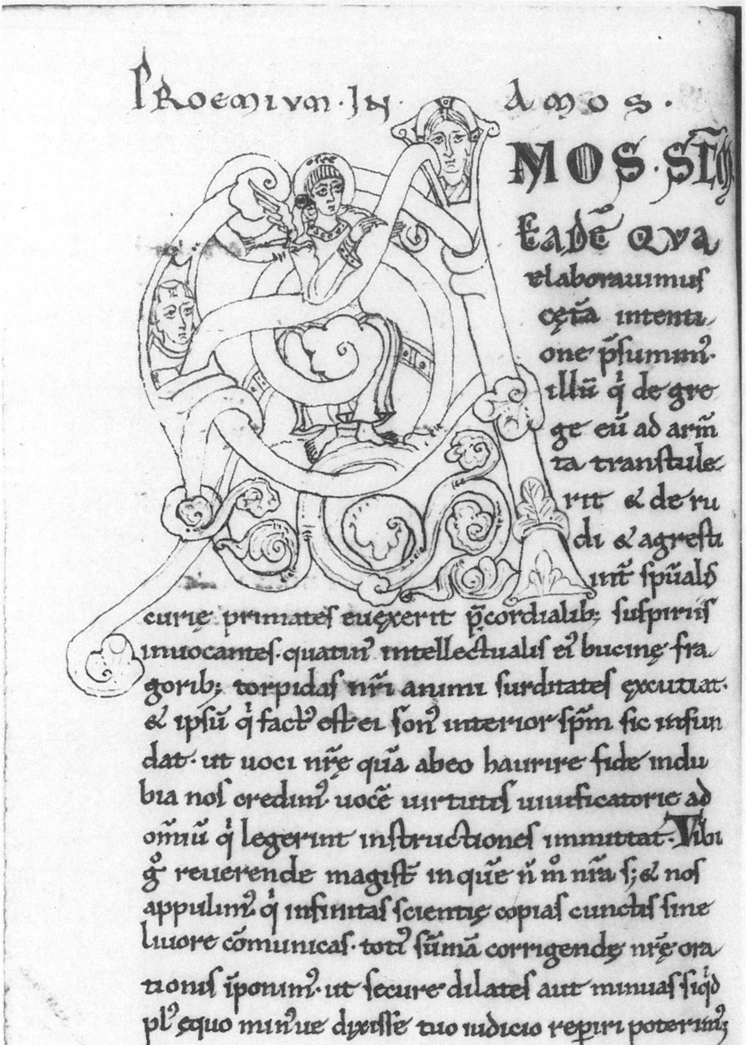
PROEMIUM IN AMOS.
AMOS SCI
EADEM QUA
e laboravimus
certa intenti
one presummi
illum qui de gre
ge eum ad armen
ta transtule
rit et de ru
di et agresti
inter spiritales
curie primates euexerit precordialibus suspiriis
inuocantes quatinus intellectualis ei bucine fra
goribus torpidas nostri animi surditates excutiat
et ipsum qui factus est ei sonus interior spiritum sic infun
dat ut uoci nostre quam ab eo haurire fide indu
bia nos credimus uocem uirtutis uiuificatorie ad
omnium qui legerint instructionem immittat. Tibi
ergo reuerende magister in quem non modo nostra sed et nos
appulimus qui infinitas scientie copias cunctis sine
liuore communicas totam summam corrigende nostre ora
tionis imponimus ut secure dilates aut minuas si quid
plus equo minusue dixisse tuo iudicio reperiri poterimus
INCIPIT TEXTUS.

Fig. 1. Prologue page of Guibert's commentary on the Book of Amos. Bibliothèque Nationale, lat. 2502, fol. 100 (back).

a child conceived in sin. Such, O God of inexhaustible holiness, was your retribution on the soul of this sinner of yours, whose soul was yet "alive through faith" [Rom. 1.17]. But let us return to the dream and see how it continued.

My mother asked her husband whether prayer, almsgiving, or sacrifice might bring him some relief. (Indeed, he was aware she was doing these things frequently for him). He answered yes and added, "But among you lives a certain Liutgarde." My mother understood that he mentioned this woman's name so that she might ask Liutgarde to remember him. This Liutgarde was truly "poor in spirit" [Matt. 5.3] and lived for God in simplicity, not according to the ways of the world.

As my mother was bringing her conversation with my father to an end, she looked at the well, over which there was a large tablet. On that tablet she saw a knight named Renaud, who was highly respected among his own kin and who that very day—a Sunday, as I have already said— had been treacherously killed by members of his clan at Beauvais after dinner. Renaud, then, was pictured on this board, bending his knees and stretching out his neck before a funeral pyre, and with his swollen cheeks he was blowing on the fire. My mother saw these things in the morning, and at noon on the very same day he died, plunging himself into a fire that his own sins had kindled. My mother also saw on the same board, helping Renaud, one of my brothers (who died long afterward), making horrendous oaths by the Lord's body and blood. It is easy enough to understand why, making oaths as he did and taking the holy name of God for a vain purpose, this man would have deserved his punishment and the place where he was being punished.[111]

In the same dream sequence, my mother also saw that old woman

111. According to Jacques Le Goff (*La Naissance du purgatoire* [Paris: Seuil, 1981], 249–50), this vision of the "poenales locos apud inferos" by Guibert's mother represents one of the key moments in the growing awareness of a place of purgation in the Church's teaching about the afterlife. Twelfth-century texts relating a trip to, or a sojourn in, Purgatory have several common characteristics: (1) Purgatory is described as a place, entered into by means of a well, or temple, from which black diabolical figures emerge; (2) it is a place of torment, where spirits who do not know one another's names are expiating the sins of their past lives with physical suffering; (3) the living can abbreviate or end the sufferings of their loved ones in Purgatory with prayer, almsgiving, offering of masses and other spiritual means, including the assumption of sufferings similar to those suffered by the departed soul; (4) there is a striking expression of solidarity between the living who pray and the dead who suffer; and the actions of the living have a direct effect upon the fate of the dead and its mutability.

who, as I said, lived with her at the beginning of her conversion to the religious life. That woman was to all appearances always intent on mortifying her body superficially; but it was said that she was less intent on avoiding the appetite for vainglory. My mother saw her being carried away by two very black demons, and her appearance was like that of a shadow. While that old woman was still alive and they were both living together, it happened one day, while they were talking about the destiny of souls and the circumstances in which they would die, that they made a mutual pledge: whichever of them died first would with God's permission appear to the survivor to let her know whether her condition was good or bad. They confirmed their resolve through prayer, sincerely asking God to allow the one who dies first to let the other know with some revealing vision whether her fate was to be happy.

Then, as this old woman was about to die, she had a vision: she saw herself deprived of her body, heading toward a temple with others like her, and as she went she seemed to be carrying a cross on her shoulders. But when she arrived at the temple with the others she found the doors locked and was forced to remain outside. Once she was dead she appeared to another person, in the midst of a great stench, and thanked her profusely: because thanks to this person's prayers she might be delivered from that stench and that suffering. Right before she died, by the way, she had seen standing at the foot of her bed a horrendously ugly demon, with large, repulsive eyes; but having invoked God's holy sacraments she ordered him away and told him to seek nothing from her. With this terrific counterattack she forced him out.

My mother, therefore, drew her conclusions from the coincidence of her visions with reality. Her instant premonition concerning the soldier who was soon to be killed and whose place of suffering she had seen being reserved in hell, made her interpret the cries of the infant (whose existence she had not been unaware of) as indicating beyond the slightest doubt that she should concentrate fully on bringing help to my father. Fighting fire with fire she decided to adopt a small orphan who was only a few months old with the intention of raising it.[112] But the Devil hates

---

112. By assuming a suffering similar in nature to the suffering of the soul in Purgatory the living can diminish the departed soul's suffering: such is one of the assumptions of what Le Goff calls "the purgatorial system" (*La Naissance du purgatoire*, 250). Guibert's mother adopts an orphan child in order to diminish the torture her husband is subjected to in Purgatory, having to listen to the constant wailings of the illegitimate child he sired with a prostitute during the early years of their marriage.

pious intentions as much as he does faithful deeds. This child would be perfectly quiet all day, whether playing or sleeping, but at night it proved so exasperating to my mother and to her servants with its fits of wailing and crying that no one was able to sleep in the same room with it. She told me that even paid nurses, who were continuously with him, kept shaking the child's rattle all night, his perversions being not his own but stemming from inner agitation. Even feminine ingenuity was powerless to drive out such an invader.

My dear mother suffered immensely. The child's incessant crying made any relief of those nightly hours impossible. Her brain was utterly exhausted by the child's frenzy, which was whipped up by a source outside itself, and by the presence of the all-perturbing Enemy. In spite of her sleepless nights, however, no one ever found her slothful when it came to attending nightly office. She knew that her pains helped diminish her husband's, which she had seen in her dream, so she graciously put up with her own. It seemed to her (which is the truth) that by her suffering she was making the sufferer's pains somewhat lighter. Never did she send the child away from her house, and never was she less solicitous about its well-being. On the contrary: whatever inconvenience the situation presented she decided to bear with an even temper, all the more so because she felt how ferociously the Devil was raging against her, trying to break her determination. The more she had been able to feel that he was the one stirring the child's rage, the more she was convinced that the horrid cries she had heard issuing from her husband's spirit had begun to diminish.

19

Ecclesiastical ambition. I am elected Abbot of Nogent

You revealed many other things to your handmaid, O Lord my God, as well as to the master you had personally designated for me, things that would only seem boastful of me if I wrote them. These were visions with a ray of hope in them, and even today, sweet Jesus, I expect them to come true, with the help of your most merciful Mother, under whose protection I was placed from my own mother's womb. Some things that were revealed to both of them when I was yet a child I am now marvelously experiencing as I grow older. Nevertheless, I began to be fired with ambitions all the more fervid because the love of knowledge you had instilled in me was already warm. Moreover I had been blessed with a physical appearance well-suited for worldly life, and I came from a privileged background. Both my own heart and some of my closest friends (who were being less helpful than they thought) began suggesting that it would be good for me to assert myself in the world by acquiring some prebend or other. I know, Lord, that your law forbids "going up by steps to your altar," for you have shown that this is how one can "expose" the shameful "nakedness" of any holy leader [Exod. 20.26] The fall of those who have used what I might call the "rubbish of external excellence"[113] to reach positions of spiritual power is all the more shameful if they have striven not for things that are at their level but for marvels beyond their reach. I had this sort of ambition, and it was nourished by my relatives. Their advice that I should go after high positions kept ringing in my ears. Many people flattered me like hypocrites, merely sounding me out so they could report what they learned to people who bore me no friendship. Either they thought they were pleasing me by pretending to honor me, or they said that what was to my advantage would also turn out to be theirs. So they were always hoping that my advancement would somehow benefit them as well.

Finally, spurred on and inspired by you alone, my Creator, I reached the point where my fear of you made me disdain asking favors of anyone. I decided to grant my attention and my consent to nobody who wanted to procure me favors, especially ecclesiastical benefits, which come from you alone. And you know, Lord, that in these matters especially I want nothing, nor have I ever wanted anything, except what I receive or have received from you. What I want, in this as in other things, is to be made by you, not by myself [Ps. 100.3]. Otherwise, Israel would be wrong to "rejoice in Him who made her."[114]

O my God, what adversities, what envies I was burdened with at that moment! Inside me my spirit was stirred by what was being suggested to

113. I have attempted to translate Guibert's alliteration, "exterioris excellentiae excrementa."

114. RSV. Guibert is here quoting Ps. 149.2 (Vulgate): "laetetur Israhel in eo qui fecit eum," in slightly altered form.

me from outside, as if that offered a way out of temptation. But even though this ambition was on fire within me I never allowed my tongue to give it expression. Of course I was troubled, but I did not speak. O Jesus, you remember how one fellow was making me some such offers, not prompted by me, and choked by my sinfulness I told him that whatever he was doing, he should do it quickly. You know, I repeat, how guilty I felt for having spoken this way. For however often I may have lapsed in other ways, I have always been reluctant to buy or, worse, sell doves in your temple. There is only one dove, to be sure, but for these people there is not one sales-counter but several.[115] Any division, in God or in the Church, is not of Christ, who suffers from it. "Let them be one as we are One" [John 17.22], he says. Again: "There is a variety of gifts, but the same Spirit, apportioning to each one individually as he wills" [1 Cor. 12.4, 11]. And again: "The throne of God (not the thrones) is for ever and ever" [Heb. 1.8], and "One of the sons of your body I will set on your throne" [Ps. 132.11]. What is united in God becomes divided because of human perversity.[116] Considering all these things and not unaware that "the head and the body are one" [Col. 1.18], I wanted to usurp nothing in the body, for whatever forces itself in from the outside can in no way be in harmony with the head, and no one can doubt that the head ignores something that is not supposed to be in the body. To those who say, "Did we not prophesy in your name, and cast out demons in your name?" [Matt. 7.22], I might answer that they are apostates, not co-members, of the body. And so they hear, "I never knew you" [Matt. 7.23], as if the Lord were telling them, "I do not feel them as part of me, because they do not live from me."

Therefore hope, however fragile, made my disgust more bearable, so I prayed to you, Lord, that if something should happen on my behalf, it should happen only at your bidding. I was ashamed to hear others say that my relatives were going after these church prebends for my sake, while others were being chosen only through divine action, not earthly intervention. By behaving in this manner, my relatives were in fact acting

115. This discussion of simony naturally reminds Guibert of Jesus's chasing the money-changers from the temple, Matt. 21.12–13: "And Jesus entered the temple of God and drove out all who sold and bought in the temple, and he overturned the tables of the money-changers and the seats of those who sold pigeons."

116. Guibert typically quotes extensively from Scripture in making his point about the sinfulness of simony.

in their own interest, not mine. They did not let me in on any of their negotiations. Clearly they didn't want to irritate me with these matters, being the sensitive boy I still was. At last, God would not allow me to be deluded any further, and therefore he inspired those who were acting in my behalf to move elsewhere, so that they might save their souls; and the monks of those abbeys who were counting on them to procure my election had to resort to different tactics.

O God, I thank you that my childish ambition of those days faded away entirely and that never again was I tempted to long for any other position of worldly honor. You whipped me at that time and afflicted me, O Father, O God, chastener of my ambition and my frivolousness. You forced me to reflect upon myself, forced me back into myself,[117] and kept my ever straying thoughts from wandering so that I might desire in my very marrow nothing but humility and sincerity of heart. For the very first time, Lord, I tried to experience that blessed solitude of mind, where one finds your presence. I began to draw closer to the Mother of the heavenly kingdom, Mary, Mother of God, my only refuge in all of my needs, and to offer her all of my inward fervor. I found the utmost delight in being humble. I found the thought of a more elevated rank or the mere shadow of a great name in the world utterly repulsive. Tasting of your inner sweetness I learned for the first time what unity of will means, what purity of will means, what an unflinching desire for perpetual poverty means. Dare I add, Lord, how transient this feeling of paradise was, how short my moment of repose, how brief and uncertain this sensation of sweetness?

This foretaste of paradise lasted barely a few months. Your Holy Spirit had led me into a land of righteousness, and had hardly made his abode for a while in my newly enlightened reason when suddenly it was as if you were saying: "When you willed it I did not. Now you no longer will it and it displeases you. Take it, whether you will it or not!" Consequently I came out victorious in an election conducted by a group of faraway monks whom I knew nothing about. What kind of election was this? Can I call myself outstanding, compared with all the other

---

117. "Et me ad cognitionem redegisti, ita ut me intra me constringeres." The theme of the forced "return to oneself" is typically Augustinian. Cf. *Confessions* 7.10, 16: "Et inde admonitus redire ad memet ipsum intraui in intima mea duce te. . . . intraui et uidi qualicumque oculo animae meae."

candidates in the running, when I was in your judgment the most wretched, even the most repulsive? The modest literary stature I had attained and the outward trappings of a scholar, so-called, had made my electors blind! Good God, what would they have said if they had seen me from the inside? What would they have felt if they had known how I would govern them and still do? You made this possible in a way that still escapes me. You know how unworthy I feel, you know how much I detest sitting above people who are better and more worthy than myself, completely reversing what is normal and proper. You, who "try men's minds and hearts" [Ps. 7.9] before they do, realize that I in no way wanted such a thing. On the other hand, I did not want to be spewed out or shamefully rejected, so I prayed to you from the bottom of my heart that I might be spared this charge, hoping I could avoid such a daunting burden, which I feared more than was justified. Being insecure, I was afraid to be heartbroken if I failed.

That my mother was greatly distressed by the prospect of my elevation to abbot was no secret to you, Lord, for what seemed an honor to others was to her a source of unbearable grief. She did not want this to happen to me, because she feared that I was dangerously inexperienced at this stage of my life. As a matter of fact, I was entirely ignorant about legal matters; having been entirely absorbed in literary studies I had taken no steps to learn law. Yet, like all those who knew me well, she had often filled my ears with talk about how it would not be long before I had some promotion or other.

Seeing things with her inner eye, Lord, she would talk to me about the good and the bad things that would happen to me if I were ever promoted. I am experiencing these things today, and they are no secret to anyone, least of all myself. She had many visions in which I and many others played a role. She would foresee events far ahead of time, and I realize that some of her predictions have come true. I also expect some of the remaining ones to come true, and I have deliberately decided not to add them to my narrative. God! how often she would warn me to keep lusts of all kinds away from my mind, predicting that certain misfortunes (which I have since experienced) were absolutely sure to come. She was always lamenting the immorality of youth, and she would keep my fantasies in check as they did tend to wander. To hear her talk about these matters you would have thought her a mellifluous bishop rather than the illiterate woman she was.

Now the monastery I had been chosen to govern is called Nogent.[118] It is located just inside the border of the diocese of Laon. A small stream called the Ailette, which sometimes overflows its banks, is the only boundary between this territory and that of Soissons. If God gives me the strength, I plan to discuss the monastery's antiquities in this work.

I have already related that I was raised at the monastery of Fly, under the patronage of God the Father and of Blessed Germer, the place's founder. It is only fitting, therefore, that I should recall some of the events I have heard of or witnessed there.

20
The Devil and the monk Suger

After the restoration of Saint-Germer de Fly following its sack by the Danes, a monk by the name of Suger, a man of good life, who held the office of prior, lay sick and dying. If I am not mistaken, he was the brother of the old woman who was in my mother's company at the start of her conversion to the religious life. As he lay in his bed, the Devil came up to him holding a book in his hand and said, "Take this and read it; Jupiter sends it to you." When he heard this loathsome name, the dying man was horrified. So the Devil added: "Do you love this house?" "I do," said the man. The Devil said: "You should know that it will lose all the rigor of its observance, and that after a short while it will fall into chaos." When the monk had confounded these words spoken by Satan with the appropriate responses, the Enemy withdrew, but after relating what he had seen, the monk went mad and had to be chained. Before dying, however, he came back to his senses, and he died after making a good confession.

Since we know that the Devil is "a liar and the father of lies" [John 8.44], we should believe that he spoke out of his usual envy. God forbid that this prophecy should ever come true! The church continued to thrive after this incident and is still doing so.

118. Guibert was elected abbot of Nogent (about eighty miles from Saint-Germer) in 1104 (Benton, *Self and Society*, 100n.15).

21

The story of a simoniac monk

In our own time I knew of a certain elderly monk, formerly a knight, who was considered a decent man. His abbot appointed him to live in a cell, which was part of the monastery church in the Vexin, since he was native to this region. There, with the consent of his prior, he proposed to restore the base of a public road that was damaged. He carried out his project with contributions from the faithful, but when it was finished he kept some of the moneys for himself. Then he was stricken with a fatal illness, but he refused to confess his hidden crime. He was brought back to the monastery to which he belonged, but even then he confessed neither to his abbot nor to his prior, though he was feeling the excruciating pains that were a sign of his impending death. He entrusted the money to a servant who ministered to the sick. That night, at some untimely hour, his pain reached such a point that he lost consciousness and lay on the ground as if dead. Summoned by the striking of the board,[119] we rushed to his side and recited psalms, prayers, and the appropriate rituals for those about to die. Then, in keeping with monastic custom, we left him lying on a hairshirt, since he seemed to be in his final agony and barely breathing. No one expected him to live; he was like someone already dead, and we expected the final ablutions to come soon.

As soon as we left he began to breathe again. He called the prior (for the abbot was away) and told him of the fraud he had committed as well as the name of the servant to whom he had entrusted the money. After he had spoken, he received the prior's absolution and soon thereafter began gasping again, and then he expired. The prior at that time was my master whom I have mentioned so often. Thus, the Lord's mercies are great, that we are not consumed [Lam. 3.22], for He saves whomever He wills "out of distress into a broad place" [Job 36.16].

After the monk had departed from this world, the question of the money fell entirely upon the servant, who had hidden the treasure in the straw of his infant daughter's cradle. One night, while the child was in

---

119. Benton (*Self and Society,* 103) translates "the beating of the wooden signal." The monks were summoned by such a signal to the bedside of a dying brother, where they recited prayers, laid the body on sackcloth and ashes, and performed final ablutions.

bed, demons looking like small dogs began to jump around her from every side, beating her here and there, sometimes biting her, and forcing her to cry out and weep. Both parents asked her why she was crying, and she answered that she was being eaten by dogs. Then her mother, who was my mother's servant at the time and occasionally her handmaid, ran to her mistress (that is, my mother) and told her about the evil treasure that had been concealed in the house and about the child who was in danger of being eaten by dogs. My mother said: "You should know that those are demons who are overjoyed about that damned money and bouncing up and down on it as if it were theirs." When he heard this, the husband, although reluctant and although "vexed by many vexations" (as I would put it), handed over what was being demanded through force, in secret or by entreaty, and no longer denied the invasion of devils he had endured.

We have heard it said that God "has mercy upon whomever he wills, and he hardens the heart of whomever he wills" [Rom. 9.18]. We might gather this from the following. O wonderful judgments of God! The man whose story I have just told spent his entire youth in exercises of horsemanship and in the sordid company of prostitutes, but the man whose story I am about to tell had been apathetic for a time, but nothing immoral had been reported about him. Clearly this vice of avarice is more detrimental to monks because it is less natural.[120] It is difficult to imagine a crime that the Devil uses more effectively to trap people than that of stealing.

22
Another case of monastic avarice

Another one of our monks, an ordained priest, whose only weakness was a passion for horsemanship, had received two sous from a certain noble lady. Soon after, being seized with dysentery, he stopped at Saint-Quen-

---

120. Guibert uses the pedantic Greek "philargyriae" to describe what he considers the most "pernicious" and "unnatural" vice in the life of a monk: "Est plane hoc philargyriae vitium intantum apud monachos perniciosum, utpote minus naturale."

Fig. 2. Eighteenth-century drawing of the abbey of Nogent-sous-Coucy, seen from the castle of Coucy. Reproduced with the permission of the Archives départementales de l'Aisne (Laon).

tin de Beauvais. When the abbey of Fly learned of this the monk was brought back to his own church by order of the abbot. Since he was eating a great deal and immediately evacuating what he had eaten, his abbot, who was about to go on a trip, came to speak with him, fearing that the monk might die during his absence. When the abbot arrived, however, the monk had sat himself down to satisfy the call of nature. He had placed himself on a pail, being unable to go outside. His abbot saw him sitting, and the terribly contorted lines on the monk's face incited terror. After they had stared at each other, the abbot was ashamed to be meeting with him in a place such as this, so the wretched fellow had neither the opportunity nor the will to confess his sin and be absolved. The abbot withdrew, and the monk made his way from the pail to the bed to rest, but he had hardly laid himself down when the Devil suffocated him. You could see his chin and his neck being violently crushed against his chest as if under some violent pressure. And so he died unconfessed and unanointed, having done nothing about that cursed money.[121] When his body was stripped naked for the final ablutions a small purse was found wrapped around his shoulder and hidden under his armpit. The monk who discovered it threw the purse to the ground in a rage, clapped his hands, and ran to the monks to regale them with this extraordinary tale. Certainly it was unheard of that any of their companions had ever died this way.[122]

They sent after the abbot, who was two miles beyond Beauvais and who had already sat down to dinner in one of his houses. The abbot had heard from a first messenger, who had reached him there, that the monk had died, but that messenger had neither known nor said anything about the sous. The second messenger, who was sent on behalf of his brothers, asked the abbot what should be done. Should a monk who had so shamefully severed himself from the communion of his fellow monks be buried with them? After consulting with men whose prudence he respected, the abbot ordered that the monk should be buried in a field without recitation of prayers or psalms, and that the money be placed on his chest. The monks did not, however, deprive their brother of their private prayer; in fact they prayed all the more intensely because they knew what need he had for their assistance. A sudden death such as this one made the others far more circumspect in matters of money. Let us now hear how they were punished for other reasons at other times.

23

Lightning strikes our monastery three times

At Fly just a few weeks later, on the vigil of Saints Gervais and Protais,[123] there was a little thunder and occasional lightning, and storm

121. Guibert describes the dying monk's condition of deprivation with an apt alliteration: "*Inconfessus* igitur et *inunctus,* et super maledicto illo suo peculio *intestatus*" (emphasis mine).

122. The monk who had accepted two sous from a noble lady died of suffocation by an incubus (1.22). The child in whose cradle the stolen money had been concealed was in danger of being eaten by devils disguised as dogs (1.21). Money stolen or concealed by a monk seems to attract devils quite as much as carrion meat attracts vultures.

123. 18 June.

clouds filled the air. In the morning we arose shortly after the summons, for the first hour had sounded. We assembled in the church with unusual haste and after a very short prayer, we chanted: "Deus in meum adjutorium intende!" (O God, come to my assistance).[124] We were about to continue when suddenly lightning flashed in the church followed by a resounding clap of thunder. As a result, the cock on the tower, as well as the cross and its staff, were either destroyed or burned, and the supporting beam was weakened. After burning and tearing out the wooden shingles nailed to the roof, the lightning bolt entered the church through the glass window in the western tower. It fractured, but did not burn, the image of the crucified Christ that stood below. The head was completely destroyed and its right side was pierced, while the right arms of both Christ and the cross were so burned and maimed that except for the thumb none of the remains of the whole arm could be found. (It is said that once the shepherd has been struck down the sheep are scattered abroad through blows and death.)[125] So on the right side of the church, over the broken crucifix, one could see a flame streaking down along the ridges of both arches, creating a two-armed black furrow. Then the flame entered the choir and struck two monks standing on either side of the arch, killing them on the spot. Then the bolt swept toward the left side of the church, stripping the paint off the walls, not everywhere but in spots; then like a stone being hurled, the bolt struck a monk who was standing there. No lesion was discovered on the monks in either accident, but in the second case, some dust, which had fallen from one of the arches, was found in the monk's upturned eyes. Another curious detail: the monks remained sitting after they were struck, but the rest of us, being frightened nearly to death by the shock of the bolt, were thrown on top of one another. Some of us lost all physical sensation from the waist down when we fell. Some of the monks were so badly hurt that we were afraid they might die so we anointed them on the spot. In some cases the flame even found its way under their cassocks, singeing all of

124. Ps. 70.1. The RSV translation reads: "Be pleased, O God, to deliver me, / O Lord make haste to help me." According to the Benedictine rule, each of the monastic offices must begin with this versicle: "In primis dicatur versi: Deus in adjutorium meum intende." See Benedict of Nursia, *The Rule of Saint Benedict,* ed. and trans. Abbot Justin McCann (London: Burns Oates, 1952), esp. chap. 18.

125. The allusion is to Matt. 26.31. On the Mount of Olives Jesus predicted to his disciples that they would all desert him: "I will strike the shepherd, and the sheep of the flock will be scattered."

their shameful pubic hair and burning the hair of their armpits (which some call the "goathair")[126] and making its way out of the extremities by piercing through socks and sandals. It is impossible to tell how equitable the judgment of God was in this case[127] or who was affected by it directly or indirectly, or to recount fully everything it struck, consumed, or broke. No one had ever seen anything like this happen in France in our generation.

I swear to God, during the hour that followed this event I saw the image of the Blessed Mother of God, which stood under the crucifix, with a face so troubled, so different from her usual serenity, that it seemed like someone else's face. I was unwilling to believe my eyes, but I heard others make the same remark. When we awoke from the stupor that this event had thrown us into we made our confession and began to meditate sadly on what we had suffered for our sins, which is more than ever can be told. Once God forced us to face up to ourselves and examine our consciences, we understood that our punishment had been a just one. Immediately we saw the Holy Mother's face regain her serenity. The grief and shame we felt for a while are truly beyond belief.

A few years later, when the memory of these events had almost been

---

126. Guibert's text reads: "pilos universos pudendae pubertatis adurens, et ascellarum, quas subhircos nominant." The term "subhirci," for "armpits," is from Isidore of Seville (according to Labande, *Guibert de Nogent*, 180n.3) and seems to have some reference to the underside of goats, *subhirci*. The only reference I have found in Isidore is to the word "hircus," which is discussed in chapter 12 of the *Etymologiae*, entitled "De Animalibus." Isidore describes the "hircus" as a "lascivious animal . . . always burning for coition, whose eyes gaze upon sexual pleasure in a crossgaze [cujus oculi ob libidinem in transversum], whence they derive their name. For 'hirqui,' are the angles of the eyes, according to Suetonius, and their nature is . . . extremely hot" (*PL* 82.426). The word *subhirci* may then be linked both to the fact that such hair is connected with our sexuality and to its location in the "angle" beneath the shoulder and the torso. Like Isidore, Guibert was essentially a Cratylist in his belief in the connection between the deep meaning of words and the essences of the things designated. Paraphrasing Isidore's belief in the power of words to designate essences, Howard Bloch writes: "[according to Isidore] the more we know about the sources of words, the faster we can penetrate the nature of things" (*Etymologies and Genealogies: A Literary Anthropology of the French Middle Ages* [Chicago: University of Chicago Press, 1983], 56).

127. Guibert's text reads: "Dici non potest, quam judicialiter in momento illo coelestis disciplina saevierit." Like most of his contemporaries, Guibert believes in a divine retribution that works immanently within history. Punishment for sin, which we inflict upon ourselves, is not reserved merely for "the afterlife."

erased from our minds, God gave us a similar warning, but this time no one was hurt. One night, a peacock had lain down to rest near the opening of a large fireplace within a certain room. His body was positioned in such a way that as he fell asleep he blocked the whole chimney. It was the feast of Saint James the Apostle, which happened to fall on a Sunday that year.[128] During the night, there was a tremendous clap of thunder, and the lightning streaked down the chimney, overturning everything in the room; but the peacock kept sleeping against the opening of the fireplace and did not budge. The noise didn't even rouse a young monk who was sleeping downstairs, but one servant was stricken with a kind of paralysis of the head and arms. According to the blessed Augustine, it is not in vain that God strikes mountains or inanimate objects. He does it to make us reflect that if he strikes in this manner things that don't sin, he prepares a discerning judgment for sinners. Augustine compares this with the nursemaid who strikes the earth with a stick to stop the baby's crying.[129]

While recounting the previous catastrophe I forgot to mention the character of the three monks who were killed. Two of them were novices who had hardly completed eight months of religious life. One of these appeared serious but in fact was not well-suited for the religious life; the other, who seemed frivolous, in fact had nothing reprehensible about him as far as we could tell. The night before they died,[130] they both behaved exactly the way their different temperaments would lead you to expect. On the morning of the tragedy, when the frivolous one heard the claps of thunder he began joking about them; but as soon as he entered the church he was struck by the very fire he had scorned. As to the third, whose name was Robert, he had been called "the dove" while he was still

128. The feast of Saint James the Apostle (25 July) fell on a Sunday in 1081, 1087, 1092, and 1098 (Labande, *Guibert de Nogent*, 183n.3).

129. In his *Enarratio in psalmum* 148,11, Augustine writes: "Why does the lightning bolt strike the mountain and not the thief? The mountain, which does not fear, is struck so that man, who fears, will change his ways. So when you are correcting someone, strike the ground with a stick, to instill some fear in the child" ("Et quare aliquando percutiunt montem fulmina, et non percutiunt latronem? . . . quia forte adhuc latronis conuersionem quaerit; et ideo percutitur mons qui non timet, ut mutetur homo qui timet" (*CCSL* 40.2173).

130. Guibert uses the expression "pridie quam pateretur," an expression taken from the canon of the mass, immediately before consecration (Labande, *Guibert de Nogent*, 185n.3).

in the world because he had a genuine simplicity about him.[131] He was a young man just on the verge of puberty. He was known for his perfect honesty, being so eager and helpful in the church offices and on behalf of his own brothers that he served everyone almost every day. He had, incidentally, begun to study grammar[132] and done very well. On the morning he was to meet his end, he awoke before me, as he usually did, and I found him sitting in the cloister. There, he made a sign to tell me that he was feeling violent pain in his knees and throughout his body. Immediately afterward he looked up and saw the commotion in the sky that was soon to rain death upon him. Before the catastrophe, then, the hearts of the first two were very fickle, but I think that God in his judgment was preparing a more severe judgment for them. In the case of the third his path to glory was paved with humility, and there can be no doubt that he had immediate access to the majesty of God. Soon afterward, in fact, someone had a vision in which he saw these three monks heading together toward Saint Peter's, in Rome. Two of them were in shadows, hardly visible, but the third was dressed in white, moving along swiftly and nimbly, with his customary keenness.

A few years later, a third chastisement was again reserved for those who had forgotten these incidents and had let themselves fall into a false sense of security. I had by this time already left the monastery. One morning, while a great storm was raging, the monks were walking in procession to the high altar in order to sing the litanies (they no longer dared to stand in the choir where the lightning had struck). Suddenly flame came dashing down from above and, according to the eyewitnesses, struck the altar, penetrating to its very base and filling the air around it with black, sulfurous smoke. One of the monks, a priest, was blinded on the spot. Two young boys were lying face down with their heads at the foot of the altar (one of them was a converted Jew but was deeply devout).[133] They were both lifted up over the altar and thrown some distance away with their feet toward the altar and their heads toward the wall of the apse — such was the force that turned them around without

131. Guibert is alluding to the text from Matt. 10.16: "Behold, I send you out as sheep in the midst of wolves; so be wise as serpents and innocent as doves."

132. The term "grammar," as it had been broadly used in classical and medieval schools since Quintilian's time, meant "recte loquendi scientia et poetarum enarratio" (*Institutio oratoria* 1.iv; cf. note 30 above).

133. Guibert's phrase, "alter ex Judaeo conuersus, *sed* praecordialiter fidelis," says a great deal about his suspicion toward Jews, even converted ones (emphasis mine).

their ever realizing what had happened. Finally, the bolt broke through the chest behind the altar, damaging parts of it; but even though most of the church's precious objects were kept there nothing was destroyed (and rightly so) but a chasuble that was considered rather precious. Let me explain this curious incident.

This chasuble had been expressly sought from the king of England, an absolutely faithless man and an enemy of the Church, whose surname was Rufus (he was red-haired). Since Rufus did not want to empty his own treasury he sent a monk, whom he assigned to this mission, to the abbot of a monastery called Battle Abbey, ordering the abbot to give the monk fifteen silver marks. When the abbot refused, the king violated the monastery by looting it and forcing the abbot to buy back what had just been looted for fifteen silver marks. God brought him to his end while he was hunting, with an arrow shot by his own minion. Thus, this chasuble was the subject of a sacrilegious negotiation, or gotten through sacrilegious means. Besides, it had been sewn together, acquired, bought, and manufactured by means no less fraudulent. It was clear that there was a curse on its very existence. It was not even worth half its price, which became clear after the lightning incident when it was taken apart for an expert evaluation. The way it was put together made it quite clear that the buyer had been cheated. It was only right that it should be destroyed by lightning while other ornaments were spared (although the merchant who sold it seems to have been spared a similar punishment).[134]

Before this event occurred another monk with an uneasy conscience had the following vision. He thought he saw the figure of the crucified Lord come down from the cross, with blood dripping from his hands, side, and feet. Walking through the middle of the choir he was heard to say, "If you do not confess your sins you will die." When the monk came to his senses he was disgusted with himself, but before confessing

134. William Rufus became king of England in 1087 (Benton, *Self and Society*, 109n.9). Battle Abbey was founded by William the Conqueror on the site of his battle with Harold at Hastings. Guibert's version of the "chasuble" incident is somewhat different from that written some time later by the author of the chronicle of Battle Abbey, who insists that God twice struck the abbey of Saint-Germer with lightning bolts because the chasuble had originally been stitched together with money procured sacrilegiously from the treasure of Battle Abbey by the abbot of Saint-Germer. The point of both versions is that the chasuble was justly destroyed because it had been procured by sacrilegious means. Guibert does not insist on the role played in its acquisition by the abbot of Saint-Germer (Labande, *Guibert de Nogent*, 188–91).

his sins he underwent the same danger as his fellow monks. Once he had made his confession, he revealed this great prophecy of a just judgment. In response to these dire forebodings fasting and almsgiving were instituted in perpetuity to commemorate the day when this event first occurred. Moreover a Mass was to be celebrated each day at the altar of the Virgin Mary, and the Mass of the Lord's Nativity was to be celebrated every Sunday at the altar of Saint-Michael. But it is time now to move on to other matters.

24

Strange happenings at Fly, Reims, and Caen

That same year, four months, in fact, after the first incident, a monk in priestly orders, who had been my mother's chaplain when she was in the world, fell seriously sick. He was apparently religious, but then, as later, he was in the grip of abominable vices that no surveillance by anyone could keep him from. Within a couple of days he unexpectedly found himself dying and began to cast wild glances all about him. Those who really knew him asked him what he was looking at. He replied: "I see a house full of barbarous men!" They understood that the creatures appearing to him were nothing other than demons hovering over him; so they urged him to make the sign of the cross and to invoke with confidence the Blessed Mother of God. "I would have faith and confidence in her," he said, "if these barons weren't hounding me so." It is amazing that he should have called them "barons," which, in its Greek sense, means "heavy."[135] And in fact how very heavy these creatures were, who could be removed neither through penance nor prayer. Finally they asked

---

135. For Guibert, as for Isidore of Seville, the Latin word "baro" is derived from the Greek *barus,* meaning "heavy." Labande (*Guibert de Nogent,* 192n.2) calls this etymology "fantaisiste," arguing that the word is in fact derived from the Frankish *baro,* meaning warrior. As is often the case, Isidore is far less "fanciful" and far more profound than he is given credit for. In *Etymologies* 9.4.31, he defines *barones* as synonymous with *mercenarii,* insofar as they are "fortes in laboribus." As a secondary meaning he provides the Greek *barus,* which is "heavy, that is to say, strong" ("Barus enim dicitur gravis, quod sit fortis" [*PL* 82.351]).

him what made him suffer the most. He answered that he felt as if an enormous, red-hot iron rod were burning his throat and his insides. Then, although it was a very peaceful night and not the slightest breath of wind could be heard, the windows of the house began to knock against the walls persistently as though crowds of people were coming and going. As the others in the house lay sleeping, the monk was being watched over by two of his brothers, who, being convinced that all these events meant nothing good, were very anxious. While he was uttering the words we have related he gave up the ghost. He was a man with many vices, and he died as he had lived.

In the cemetery of the same church a monk who had just died was being prepared for burial, and the gravedigger could not remember whether he had dug a grave in that same spot once before. He began to dig, and when he reached a certain depth, he found one of those slabs that are usually placed over a coffin. He removed it and found the coffin nearly empty, except for a hood (commonly called a capuchin) with a head inside. At the foot of the coffin he found sandals half stuffed with hay (this had been done at the time of burial so that the sandals would stay on the feet). But in between there was nothing. Some people went to see this and came back to tell us, and we were in awe at the incomprehensible judgment of God. What subtle and secret things we sometimes experience! In this miraculous recurrence the most noteworthy thing is that the head was left there, while the body had been taken the Lord knows where.

A similar event was reported to me by Archbishop Manasses, of blessed memory (he died very piously a few years ago), and certified by the monks of Saint-Rémi at Reims.[136] An archbishop of that town by the name of Artaud had been buried in former times at the feet of Saint-Rémi. Long afterward it became necessary to reconstruct the buildings nearby, so his grave was opened and absolutely nothing of his body was found in the coffin. The only item of clothing that remained was a chasuble, and it was clear that it had not decayed with his body, for it had remained absolutely intact. Surely if the archbishop's body had decayed in the grave, the rot would have affected the chasuble. We have seen in

136. This Archbishop Manasses of Reims, "qui ante hos annos fidelissime decessit," the second to bear that name, was archbishop of Reims from 1086 to 1106. His predecessor, Manasses I, is mentioned in *Monodiae* 1.11, as the one who used simony in order to gain control of the city.

our own time the confirmation of what Saint Gregory said about the judgments of God being renewed over the bodies of the guilty; for it is then clear they should not have been buried in sacred ground.[137]

There was a nun in the Abbey of Women at Caen, which was built by Mathilde, the queen of England and wife of William, the first count of Normandy, who had conquered the English and then become king.[138] This nun had fallen into some awful sins and could not be persuaded by any admonition to make her confession. She died in this state of obstinacy without saying anything that could.do her any good. One night, one of her sisters was sleeping in the cell where she had died. In her sleep she saw the fireplace of the house ablaze with a tremendous fire, and in the midst of the flames the dead nun was not only on fire, she was also being beaten with a hammer by two evil spirits on either side of her. While the nun lay watching the great torment that her unhappy sister was suffering a blow of the hammer blew shards right into her eye. The burning sensation caused by the burning spark woke her up. And she realized that what she had seen in her mind she had literally felt in her body. The lesion in her eye was there to confirm the truth of her vision.

25
Death of the monk Otmund

There was at Fly a monk named Otmund who, while he was still a cleric, had donated many things to the monastery before finally becoming one

137. The ancient Benedictine abbey of Saint-Rémi was the burial place of that great saint, who died in 533. Artaud was archbishop of Reims from 932 to 961. He may have been disinterred at the time of the building of the Romanesque abbey church, which was dedicated in 1049. Guibert is here repeating an idea expressed by Pope Gregory the Great (*Dialogues* 4.52), concerning the visible judgments of God "super noxiorum cadaveribus" who should not have been buried in sacred ground. It is significant that a century and a half after his death Artaud still struck Guibert as guilty, "noxius." It is equally significant that the chasuble, symbol of his priesthood, remained, while his body had rotted completely (Benton, *Self and Society,* 111–12)

138. Queen Matilda, wife of William the Conqueror, founded the Abbaye-aux-Dames, also called Abbey of the Trinity, in 1060, at the same time her husband was founding the Abbaye-aux-Hommes. Writing nearly a half century after William's con-

of its members. Having assumed the monastic state, he began to regret the good thing he had embarked upon and to deplore what he had done. But, God soon chastised him with a bodily infirmity that brought him to his senses; and he began to do things thereafter that were more in keeping with his well-being, and he conformed to the sacred rule through choice rather than compulsion. He was made custodian of the monastic church, and since he was more irritable than the average person, he was once excessively harsh in expelling from the church a poor man who was importuning him with a request for alms. This happened during the day. That night Otmund was making his way toward the church doors to open them and announce the hours of vigils when suddenly the Devil appeared before him in the guise of the poor man he had so rudely thrown out the day before and, raising a stick, rushed at the monk as if to strike him. He had already opened the doors of the screen that separates the clergy and the people and was proceeding to open the other doors through which the people enter when all of a sudden, the outer doors still being closed, a man jumped out from the middle of the nave through one of the doors in the screen as if to strike him. Otmund was terrified, because he recognized the man whom had ejected the day before; but then he came back to his wits, remembering that the other doors were still locked, and realized that this must be the Devil who was showing him with a sign what he had done to the other man.

One winter night, Otmund got up to satisfy the call of nature, and being too lazy to put on his usual dress, he wore nothing but a cowl. He was exposed just long enough to catch a deathly chill. Soon afterward, a great swelling in his limbs brought him to the brink of death, and he began to dread the very mention of death more than is usual. With continuous moans and groans he approached his final end. As he prepared to give up the ghost, he took communion, which by the grace of God he kept down (for he was vomiting everything else). These things were happening in the early hours of the night. Meanwhile, the sacristan, a saintly man, had gone to bed when suddenly he heard in the cemetery of the monks close by an innumerable horde of devils gathering together. His mind was perfectly free to perceive these things, but the movements

---

quest of England, Guibert identifies him as "Guillelmi ex Normannorum comite regis uxor, qui Anglos eosdem subegerat," that is, "that William who, from Count of Normandy [had become] king, he who had conquered the aforementioned English." Clearly King William I of England had not yet become a household name in monastic circles.

of his tongue and body were paralyzed as if by a spiritual force. The demons entered the church, went past the sacristan's bed, hurried between the choir and the altar toward the dormitory where the ailing monk was lying. While the sacristan, who realized everything that was going on, addressed a mental prayer to God, begging him to protect the dying monk—for he knew that death alone was the reason for such a gathering of demons—the demons reached the cell of the dying monk. The brothers surrounding him were beating on a board,[139] as is customary to call the others to assemble about him. No sooner were they gathered than their brother's soul was delivered. I have recorded this event not because I believe that the monk fell into the evil hand of these demons but to invite all of you to reflect with me that the Prince of this world once came to the Son of God, against whom he had no power [Matt. 4.1–11; cf. Luke 4.1–12]. And if he came against Him, how much more might we expect the Devil in his rage to use all of his quick wits against us, against whom he has all power!

In this same place, I once saw a woman so terribly angry with her little boy that among other slurs she hurled against this innocent child she even cursed the very waters of baptism in which he had been washed. Immediately the Devil took hold of her as she was ranting madly, saying and doing abominable things. She was led to the church and shown to the brothers. When prayers and exorcism had brought her back to her wits, she learned from the suffering she had undergone not to curse the Lord's sacraments.

It was there too that I saw one day a young girl possessed of the Devil brought before the relics of Germer the Confessor. She stayed there several days, after which she was brought to the altar by her parents.[140] While she stood there she turned her head toward the choir and seeing some young monks standing behind her she said: "My God, what handsome young men! But there is one of them who should in no way be living here!" When we heard this we were amazed, wondering who was the person these words were addressed to. Soon afterward one of them

139. Monks were summoned by the beating of a board, or a "wooden signal," to the bedside of a dying brother. See note 119 above.

140. There are frequent reports of miraculous cures effected in the early twelfth century by placing an afflicted person several days and nights in the presence of sacred relics. Compilations of *miracula* often cite perseverance in prayer as a key factor in obtaining an ultimate cure.

ran away from the monastery, and in the course of his flight death bore witness to the depravity of his life, for he had broken his religious vows.

26
The Devil initiates a lascivious monk

Since we have begun talking about demons, I think it useful to add a few things so that these examples might enable us to avoid both their pronouncements and the suggestions of those who speak with them. For demons admit no one to their evil doings except those whom they have first stripped of the honor of their baptism through some terrible sacrilege.

In a certain famous monastery a certain monk had been raised since early childhood and had attained some knowledge of letters. He was lodged by his abbot in a cell attached to the church.[141] While he was living there he fell sick, and this provided him with an unfortunate (for him) opportunity to converse with a Jew who knew something about medicine. They gradually became friends, and this made them bold enough to begin exchanging secrets. The monk, who was curious about black magic, felt that the Jew knew something about it and insisted on being initiated. The Jew agreed and promised to arrange a meeting between the monk and the Devil. The day and place of the meeting were agreed upon. On the appointed day, thanks to his mediator's intervention, the monk stood before the Devil and, at the Jew's instigation, asked to be initiated to the Devil's teaching. The Devil, abominable mentor that he is, replied that that was impossible unless the monk reneged his baptismal vows and offered him a sacrifice. The monk asked what the offering should be. "That which is most delectable in a man," the Devil said. "What is that?" asked the monk. "You will make me a libation of your sperm," the Devil replied. "When you have poured it out to me, you will taste it first, as it behooves the one offering the sacrifice." What

141. It was not uncommon to find small outlying cells of this type scattered about the main monastery buildings. They were usually inhabited by a small number off monks.

a crime! What a shameful act! And it was being demanded of a priest! This is what your enemy of old does, O Lord, to blaspheme and dishonor your priesthood and your sacred host! "Do not be silent" [Ps. 83.1], O God, and do not put off your vengeance! What can I say? How shall I speak? The wretched monk whom you had abandoned (O let it be for a time only!) did what was asked of him. He made the horrendous libation, and at the same time he abjured his faith. One example will suffice to show what kinds of arts he learned to master in this wretched bargain.

The monk had begun to have regular encounters with a nun from a well-known family. He shared his cell with another monk who ran the errands while our monk dilly-dallied at home. One day the monk and his female companion were sitting in the cell when the other monk returned from his errands. From a distance they could see him coming, but the woman saw no means of escaping, for she would have to cross the monk's path while attempting to leave. Seeing that the nun was shaking with fear, her lover, with his newly acquired powers of incantation, said, "Go straight toward him, and look neither right nor left. And don't be afraid!" The woman believed him and headed toward the door. Her lover stood at the entrance and, using incantations learned from the Devil, changed her into a giant dog. As she and the arriving monk drew close to each other the latter exclaimed: "Hey! where did this dog come from?" Meanwhile the nun slipped out the door in complete terror. Only the word "dog" let her know the nature of the disguise in which she had escaped. Finally the monk who had been out asked where such an exceptionally big dog could possibly have come from. "It belongs to one of our neighbors," the other monk said. "He's been around for a long time." His brother monk took this to be true, and said nothing.

Our monk lived a godless existence for a long time. Then one day, God permitting, he was stricken with a serious illness, and quite in spite of himself he confessed his wrongdoing. The case was referred to the judgment of wise men, particularly of Anselm, who was then abbot of Bec and later became archbishop of Canterbury. It was through Anselm's decision in particular that the monk, a filthy profaner of the divine mysteries, was banned from the celebration of them. But in spite of being under interdiction he could never rid himself of the idea that he would one day be a bishop. The devils, who are forever lying and did so in this case especially, had no doubt nourished this hope in him. The monk died a few years later: not only did he never become a bishop, he remained a defrocked priest forever.

Let me add another story with a similar beginning but a better ending. I knew a cleric from the town of Beauvais who made a living as a calligrapher. He had, in fact, come to Fly to work in that capacity. One day at the castle of Breteuil he was conversing with another cleric who knew something about black magic and heard him say something to this effect: "If you made it worth my while I could teach you a way to receive monetary gifts every day without any human intervention." "What do I have to do?" the cleric asked. The expert in black magic replied that all he had to do was offer sacrifice to the Devil, the citizen of hell. "With what victim?" asked the first. "With a cock," said the other. "But only on condition that the egg it was hatched from has been laid by the hen on a Thursday in March. You will roast the cock, and then, at nightfall, you will leave it on the spit and take it with you. We'll go to a nearby fish pond together. Whatever you see there, or hear, or feel, see to it you do not invoke God, or the Blessed Virgin or any of the saints." "It's a deal," said his companion.

But listen to this incredible ending! They came one night to the appointed place carrying with them the victim worthy of such a god. The sorcerer-cleric invoked the Devil by name while his wretched pupil held the cock. Suddenly the Devil appeared in a whirlwind and grabbed hold of the cock. Then, the cleric who had been led there called upon Saint Mary in his terror. When the Devil heard the name of this powerful Queen being uttered, he fled with the cock, but apparently he was unable to carry it away, since one of the fishermen found it the next day on a small island in the pond. O royal, sweet name of Mary, so dreaded in the regions of hell!

Our sorcerer-cleric, of course, grew angry against the other cleric and asked him why he had called upon so great a woman in such a circumstance. The cleric, however, was driven to penitence and went to call upon Lisiard of Beauvais, an archdeacon who was also my uncle. Lisiard was an immensely learned and wise man, renowned for his concern in matters like these. The cleric confessed his wrongdoing, and Lisiard ordered him to lead a life of penance, prayer, and fasting.

I have now said enough about the things I saw or heard in that monastery. Since I have written earlier about a certain position to which I was elected I should like, at the start of the second book, to speak of the nature of this abbey that I was, by the grace of God, transferred to. I should also like to mention how it was founded, and what antiquities can be found there.

BOOK TWO

The Abbey of Nogent

1

The origins of Nogent.
The legend of King Quilius

The place is called Nogent. Its use as a monastery is very recent, but its use for worship by worldly society is very old. Even if no written sources were available to sustain this conjecture, the uncustomary and, in my opinion, non-Christian arrangement of the tombs that have been discovered there would suffice to do so. Around and within the abbey church a large number of tombs has accumulated since ancient times; the countless number of bodies buried in such a crowded spot testifies to the great reputation that was enjoyed by a place that so many people flocked to. The tombs are not arranged the way ours usually are, but are grouped in a circle around one of them. Vases have been discovered in these tombs the likes of which are unknown in Christian times. I can therefore find no other explanation except to think either that these were pagan tombs or very ancient Christian tombs arranged according to pagan custom. In the abbey one can also see a few texts in verse to which I would ascribe no authority if I had not noticed that some facts exist even today bearing out what these texts say. Here is the history transmitted by these texts.[1]

It is said that a king once lived among the Angles before the assumption into heaven of the Incarnate Word. (They were not yet called Angles, which is a recent name derived from a segment of the Saxons who later seized their lands; since antiquity they had been called Britons.) As I have said: in this island of the ocean called Britannia there lived a king with a very rich background in poetry as well as philosophy. To this gift he brought a natural goodness that predisposed him to practice the works of mercy; and since his generosity in filling the hands of the poor was spurred not by any knowledge of God (whom he did not know) but by an overwhelming sense of humanity, it was only fitting that to his exercise of natural piety should be added the gift of clearer understanding.

He began asking himself the most subtle questions.[2] With so many representations of divinity before him, how could he hope one of these gods was the true one? What kind of harmony could possibly exist among them in their governance of heaven and earth when their marriages clearly were (while they lasted) nothing but a string of impurities and rivalries? Their administration of earthly lands revealed nothing but the cruelest hatred of one another: sons were set against fathers, fathers

1. Benton (*Self and Society*, 119–20) and Labande (*Guibert de Nogent*, 210–12), like earlier scholars, have remarked how methodical is Guibert's archeological reasoning, and how "modern" he is in evaluating both archeological evidence and written sources. What remained of the abbey of Nogent before 1914 was completely destroyed by the heavy fighting and bombing throughout the area. The only vestige of the abbey to be seen on a summer's day today is a solitary stone arch standing in an open field of sunflowers, with the ruins of the castle of Coucy (largely destroyed during World War I), in the background. All vestiges of the circle of tombs mentioned by Guibert have long since disappeared, as have the "texts in verse" (perhaps a verse chronicle?), which could be found in the abbey church in Guibert's time. The story of the Briton king Quilius that follows is taken from one of these lost verse texts.

2. Guibert's text is the only known literary source for the existence of King Quilius. The king's critical reflections upon the pagan gods before his adoption of the Christian religion is, however, a frequent theme in early medieval literature. Cf., in particular, King Edwin's deliberations with his chief men before adopting the Christian faith, and the declaration of his high priest Coifi, "that the religion which we have hitherto professed has, as far as I can learn, no virtue in it" (Bede, *The Ecclesiastical History of the English Nation*, trans. Vida D. Scudder [New York: E. P. Dutton, 1919; rpt., 1930], 2.13, 90).

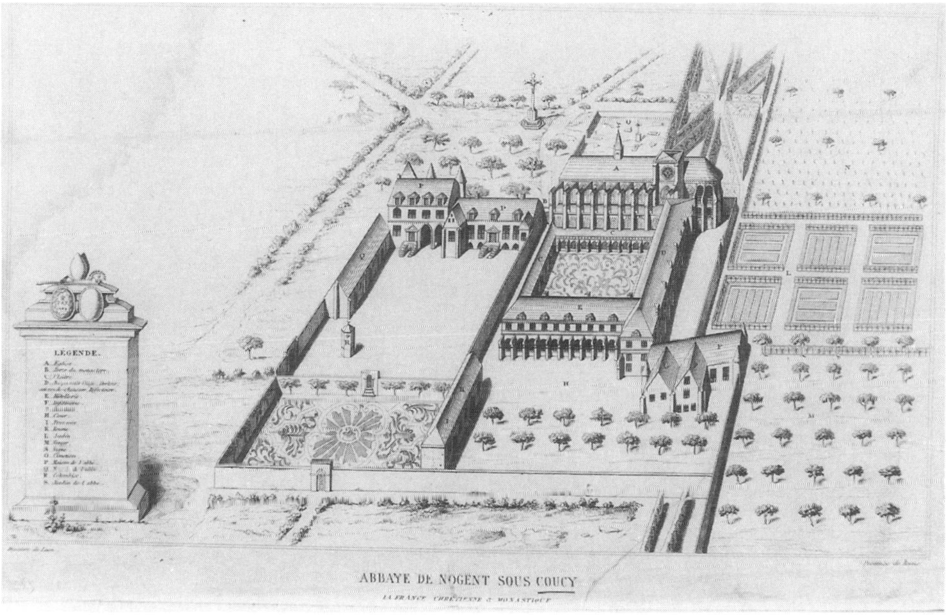

Fig. 3. Seventeenth-century drawing of the abbey of Nogent-sous-Coucy. Reproduced with the permission of the Archives départementales de l'Aisne (Laon).

against sons, all evicting, excluding, or killing one another. Since, thought the king, stories told about mortals could hardly be worse than stories told about the gods, he thought it sheer madness to believe that such beings have power to rule over earth, not to mention heaven. Who would turn over control of heavenly things to those who previously had been unable to wield their measly power over a few corners of land without behaving shamefully? The king kept pondering over these and similar matters. Finally he closed off his heart to images of what he now took to be vain gods, turning instead to the worship of one incomprehensible being: a being who, though without form, is worthy of worship and rules all things in perfect harmony. He came to understand "his invisible nature in the things that have been made" [Rom. 1.20]. While the king was in the midst of his fruitful meditations, however, a few lingering doubts remained in his mind. God, however, who shows the better way to those who seek the good, sent him a voice from heaven urging him to go to Jerusalem. There he would hear what he needed to know about God: how proceeding from God, the Son of God had lived among men for the sake of men, what he had endured and what he had come to reveal, and how he had left representatives after him to be models of the divine name. There he would also find witnesses to such great mysteries, namely the Mother of God and all the Apostles.

With this message of faith revealed to him this Briton king set aside his riches and his kingdom and resolved to set out quickly, to verify what he had just learned. He ordered a fleet prepared, left his country, crossed the nearby body of water, made his way through a number of fortified castles and towns, and finally reached the border of the province of Laon. At the village of Nogent, which I have mentioned before, he asked for hospitality. This village is situated at the foot of a castle called Coucy. They say the castle was built recently as a defense against attacks from the outside, by a very proud, rich local peasantry. The castle, then, is by no means ancient. In those days the place we are speaking of was surrounded by forests full of wild game. The river, which we have referred to earlier as the Ailette, could be described as more useful than its size might indicate. It is richer in fish than other more famous rivers, and unlike other rivers it is not contained within its banks but overflows, creating many pools of stagnant waters like fish ponds. Vineyards cover the slopes of the hills rising on either side of the river, and since the land on both sides is suitable for both Ceres and Bacchus, people praise its rich topsoil for yielding all kinds of abundant harvests. The charming meadows stretching far and wide on either side of the stream are an indication of its fertility.[3]

According to a credible ancient tradition, a very old temple once lay on this spot, dedicated not to the name and honor of any god then existing, but to the woman not yet born who would give birth to one both god and man. This temple, then, was dedicated to the mother of the god who was to be born. This idea did not seem absurd to any wise person, since those who worshipped the unknown god in Athens knew for certain that he would be born of a woman, just like the plethora of

---

3. Guibert seems to be describing the type of *locus amoenus* frequently to be found in medieval monastic literature (Labande, *Guibert de Nogent,* 216n.2). Even to this day, however, the area presents to the viewer's eye a rich, fertile, rolling landscape, where clumps of forest alternate with broad fields. The area where the abbey lay is now a broad, open field on the south side of the town of Coucy (about 20 km north of Soissons), with the ruins of its castle overlooking the town on a plateau. The Ailette, a stream about ten feet across, still flows in an east-west direction a mile south of the abbey site.

other gods whose mothers had a name.[4] If a sanctuary was already dedicated to the god who was to be born, his mother, like those of other gods, was surely deserving of a similar honor. It is not hard to believe that an honor granted in one place to the god to be born should be granted in another to the mother who was to bear him.

Our Briton king, then, happened to come this way. Charmed by such pleasant surroundings, he decided to rest here with his retinue after a difficult journey. He sent his animals out to graze for a week in the nearby pastures, after which time he set off and crossed immense distances on both land and sea until he reached the walls of Jerusalem. The Savior's passion, his resurrection from the dead, his ascension into heaven and, finally, the gift of the Spirit, were all recent occurrences. Thus the king found Jerusalem torn by dissension, some people being grief-stricken by these recent events, others delighted. He had no problem finding those he was seeking, since the great commotion surrounding these events gave him the clues he needed to find those who were proclaiming the new Law. They were no longer living in hiding, as they had been up to this time, nor did fear of reprisal from the Jews prevent them from being the Lord's witnesses. Just looking at them standing among the crowds he could see that their very presence lent authority to what they said. Need I add more? Peter was often visible among the crowds, together with the eleven others and an already large crowd of disciples behind him; and Mary, the mirror of our faith and of all our glory, bore witness by her very presence there to the incarnate God.

Immediately before making a sacrifice to God, the Briton king turned toward the disciples and the Virgin Mother and explained the reasons for his trip:

"Fathers and Lords, as you can see I have come from the remotest ends of the earth to hear you. Until now I have ruled over the Britons as scion of a legitimate line of succession going back to my ancestors. What they have mistakenly held sacred and venerable in the past, what I myself have honored until now, I now reject for the following reason. I have thought seriously about these beings who since ancient times have received the honorable name of gods. I have become convinced that they were far worse than any mortal ever was, and that after they had commit-

---

4. Guibert is here alluding to Saint Paul's speech to the Athenians in Acts 17.22–23: "I found also an altar with this inscription, 'To an unknown god.' What therefore you worship as unknown, this I proclaim to you."

ted the worst abominations nature took its revenge on them. With my rational judgment I have concluded that the human imagination alone has put these men in the heavens, where they have lived in pursuit of earthly things. In no way can they be said to have created heaven and earth and all that is in them, for clearly it is nothing else but the atmosphere's clemency and the earth's fertility that allowed them to thrive. All rationale for thinking them divine having disappeared, one thing is absolutely clear in my mind: they lack all divine authority. So one thing, and one thing only, is worthy to be believed: the power and providence of God, from whom alone all things come, and who governs all things that He embraces. Now that my mind has begun to focus on the thought of a single God, I find the idea of temples and of idols in them irrevocably repugnant. You might say my bowels have been purged of the dregs of idolatry, which the genuine purity of true religion has replaced. A divine voice has ordered me to come here. I have been promised a demonstration of the one true faith, through the grace of the Son of God's recent passion. I beg you, then, by that mother whom I see here present, by that light that was revealed to me, and by your own mission, to admit me to the mysteries of this second birth."

As Peter and his joyful co-disciples stood around Mary listening to this speech, they seemed like a reflection of heaven's court marveling at the magnificence of God and of his Son made man. Had God not just shown his glory right here at the earth's center?[5] The preachers of good tidings had not yet scattered in all directions, yet God was already proclaiming the news of his abundant grace to the remotest corners of the western world. The Briton king was therefore instructed in the teachings of the faith, after which he was washed in the waters of baptism and received the name Quilius. Then, through the instruction of these great masters, he was confirmed in his understanding of the sacrament he had just received. As he was about to take his leave and return to his homeland he begged them, with a heart full of faith, to give him some relics that were known to have touched the Savior's body. He requested, and devoutly received, some of the cords that (he learned) had tied the Lord

5. Medieval maps often portray Jerusalem at the center of the world, with Christian churches converging toward it. A text of Ezek. 5.5 (Vulgate) reads: "Haec dicit Dominus Deus: ista est Jerusalem, in medio gentium posui eam, et in circuitu eius terras." It was natural for medieval Europeans to think that the salvation of Christ had taken place at the world's center. To this day, of course, Jerusalem remains the sacred city for three of the world's major religions and a center of world attention.

to the whipping post; the whips used by an impious hand to flay the blessed body; the thorns that had crowned the Lord's sacred head; the wood of the cross on which he had hung; the gown that the Mother of God is said to have worn when she gave him birth; and finally, garments that had belonged to each of the Apostles.

Taking these relics with him in a small coffer, Quilius began the hard trip back home. Finally, after crossing many lands between, he reached the village where he had stopped to rest before. There he suddenly fell sick and took to his bed, where it was revealed to him that this would be the place of his death. It was also revealed to him that his remains would be buried under the same mound as the relics he had received from the apostles in Jerusalem. When he awoke from the dream telling him of his imminent death, the king began to concentrate on one thought, and one only: planning his final burial, with hope in the glory that he was soon to inherit. He died in this very place, paying back to his Maker in full the talents he had been entrusted with. The reliquary was buried next to him in the same spot. Long afterward it was dug up and given a precious covering of gold leaf, in the ancient style, by some faithful people whose names I don't know. It still looks the same today, continuing to bear witness to these ancient stories.[6]

This, then, is how Nogent is said to have started.

2
The first abbots of Nogent

As the Christian religion grew in strength, a small, beautiful church made its appearance in this place in the most ancient times, under the

6. There is, to our knowledge, no other source to this story than the verse texts that, according to Guibert, once adorned the abbey church: "Quae historia sic se habere secundum scripturae hujus seriem traditur." The story of the Briton king who sees the limitations of his pagan gods, travels all the way to Jerusalem to be baptized by Saint Peter (in the presence of the Virgin and the Apostles), returns to his homeland bearing relics of the sacred passion of Christ, only to be interred at Nogent, is a most telling illustration of the sacred nature of the site. To the medieval mind, the erection of an abbey, church, or cathedral on a site containing the relics of saints and martyrs

name of the Mother of God. Located at the foot of the stronghold of Coucy (already mentioned) and surrounded by ancient and very rich villas, it is frequented and venerated by a great number of people from the surrounding areas. When it was still small it was said to be illuminated often by the light of God and honored with frequent miracles. This did the place no harm, for many people thought that it suffered from insufficient exposure. The castle of Coucy had extended its domains in all directions under the leadership of most prosperous princes, barons endowed with wealth and generosity; so a group of devoted people inter-

Fig. 4. The only remaining ruin of the abbey of Nogent-sous-Coucy as it stands today. Damaged during the French Revolution, the abbey was almost entirely destroyed during World War I. This archway seems to have been the main entrance to the abbey church (see seventeenth-century drawing, center). Photo by Marianna M. Archambault.

was a proof of its miracle-bearing powers. Cf. Gregory of Tours's account of the dispute of the inhabitants of Poitiers and Tours over the possession of Saint Martin's body after his death at Candes in 397 (*The History of the Franks*, trans. O. M. Dalton [Oxford: Clarendon Press, 1970], 2.230).

ested in upholding the place's reputation for sanctity (which had spread like the sweetest of perfumes) suggested that the church be given to monks to assure the frequent recitation of the divine service. No one could possibly hope that an enterprise begun in this manner would ever grow, considering that the funds provided for its creation seemed sufficient to maintain no more than six monks. Furthermore, renovation of the church was begun by unskilled and uneducated persons who attempted some sort of construction or expansion. Since they had no leader or teacher with any skill for construction, what they did build was very flimsy when something more compact, useful, and suitable could have been made from these same materials.

The world enjoyed a greater abundance of things in those days than it does today. The monastery's treasury, which had already been endowed by the lords' generous donations, was increased with gifts from the barons of the castle to which were added donations from the outside. Upon the advice of the community's patrons and for the well-being of its brothers, it was decided that this little monastery would be directed by a great man named Henri, who was then abbot of Saint-Rémi and had for a long time directed the abbey of Hombliéres.[7] Henri was famous neither for his learning or his birth, but his remarkable skill as an administrator of worldly affairs made him equally attentive in caring for the internal running of the monastery. As overseer of three monasteries he could draw upon the abundance of the first two to supply the needs of the third, which was beginning to thrive. Among the many favors he generously bestowed on this church the greatest was the effort he deployed in obtaining its consecration. The dedication was performed by Hélinand, bishop of Laon,[8] a very rich man who was well informed about the foundation and the decoration of churches. Hélinand also showered privileges on the church, exempted it from most of its taxes, and lavishly endowed it with gifts.

Abbot Henri was handicapped by age and bad eyesight, so he withdrew to his two richer abbeys that, given his diminishing strength, were easier to administer. As for the third abbey, which could not be administered without constant attention, Henri decided to give it up. He called an assembly of the brothers in the monastery and tried to transfer his

7. Henri was abbot of Hombliéres before 1059. He was named abbot of Saint-Rémi at Reims about 1074. He died in 1095.

8. Hélinand was bishop of Laon from 1052 to 1098.

Fig. 5. Ruins of the castle of Coucy today, looking north from the field where the abbey of Nogent-sous-Coucy once stood. Photo by Marianna M. Archambault.

charge to a monk who happened to be his nephew; but he failed, and it was a young monk named Godfrey,[9] who came from the same area and had previously been a monk at Saint-Quentin, who was elected. Henri did not take this well, but once he saw that the electors were voting for a different person, being a shrewd old man he left the monastery that he had served with so much dignity and extraordinary generosity. Upon his departure he legally transferred his charge to the abbot-elect.

Once Godfrey was elected and the monastery placed under his stewardship he behaved very prudently. Since commoners and nobles alike had both the desire and the means to increase the endowments of monasteries, Nogent received a plethora of donations at that time, in lands and

9. Godfrey was the scion of a noble family near Soissons. He was Guibert's predecessor at Nogent, where he was elected abbot in 1085. He died at Amiens in 1115. The life of Saint Godfrey of Amiens is related by Nicolas de Saint-Crépin in the *Acta Sanctorum* (Benton, *Self and Society*, 126n.4).

in revenues. Godfrey knew how to adapt himself to people from the outside world, always being pleasant and hospitable with them, as he was with secular matters, to which he learned to devote considerable attention. To tell the truth, the people in those days, as I've mentioned them earlier in my book, were very liberal in establishing monasteries and in giving lands and money in abundance; they were happier doing things like this than their sons are today, who limit their generosity to fine words. At any rate, in the surrounding monasteries, religious zeal was not what it should have been, but Godfrey and his monks seemed spiritually very active. Thus the evident discipline of the monastery's leader, as well as the perfect response of those who were under his rule, provided an excellent opportunity for promoting his reputation, like the tiniest of candles in the midst of darkness.

Godfrey forbade simony and any toleration of it within his monastery. He banned all purchasing of offices and made merit the sole criterion for election to them, regarding the very mention of filthy lucre as abominable. However, he acquired a reputation for being more shrewd in matters of secular business than many of his fellow abbots, and so he became famous in the surrounding towns and cities. Soon the question was being raised of giving him richer abbeys, then of promoting him to bishop. At that time the bishopric of Amiens had been vacant for about two years, so Godfrey made himself the advocate of an archdeacon from that city who was putting himself forward for the office, with the support of some factions of clergy and people. It so happened that while playing the advocate for somebody else Godfrey himself was chosen, both because of his worldly shrewdness and of the monk's clothes he wore. It was Richard, onetime bishop of Albano and now legate of the Apostolic See in France (who had just finished assembling a council in the city of Troyes) who consecrated Godfrey bishop of the seat of Amiens.[10] So Godfrey was transferred from Nogent.

He had drawn high praise in that abbey and had been very happy there; so much so, in fact, that even bishops who were higher up in the hierarchy respected and even feared him. In a word he was honored everywhere as the very mirror of religious piety. Then suddenly came

---

10. Richard was deposed as bishop of Albano in 1079 by Pope Gregory VII, and in 1087 he became a schismatic and was excommunicated. He was relieved of his sentence in the same year, however, and sent to France as papal legate (Benton, *Self and Society*, 128n.7).

this promotion: whether he really wanted it or was reluctant to take it God only knows. My experience has taught me that a prize eagerly desired at the outset can turn out to be no blessing in the end. It is obvious in any case that although he was highly praised at the start of his episcopate and continued to be praised lavishly for some years, the fame that burst about the man like a fire not only started to fizzle out but to grow cold.[11] The first day of his reception, when he entered Amiens he stood up on an elevated platform to speak to the people and solemnly assured them that in the same way he would aim for the heights, being one who would not want the famous line of Horace to be applied to him in failure: "The mountains are in labor, they bring forth a ridiculous mouse."[12] Indeed, this is precisely the text that came to everyone's minds when subsequently they began observing the man in action. His reputation declined rapidly as the days went by, and his actions constantly fell short of his promises.

But enough said. Perhaps I'll have an opportunity to come back to this matter.

3

My installation as Abbot of Nogent

So Godfrey had left this abbey, which he had administered competently and properly. He could have been content with his condition and continued to live there in perfect happiness and freedom, obligated to no one, but it was my lot to be called there, after an election, as I have already said. Whether God disapproved of this election or merely tolerated it I

11. Guibert here shows a remarkable capacity for sustaining an image: "quidquid apud hominem gloriarum excandescere videbatur, non modo intepuit, sed refrixit." The implied image is that of a candle that seems to glow but slowly loses its flame and grows cold.

12. Horace, *Ars poetica* l.139: "Parturiunt montes, nascetur ridiculus mus." Godfrey's performance as bishop of Amiens turned out to confirm rather than contradict the Horatian line, delivering far less than he had promised, "seipsa deteriorem coepit indesinenter facere sponsionem."

don't know. This much I can say for sure, I was appointed to this position without soliciting it and without my knowing it, and without my family's exerting any influence.[13] In this respect all went well. I leave it to the reader of the remainder of my narrative to decide whether my being unknown to my electors and not knowing a single one of them was in itself a good and useful thing. When I arrived among them, in fact, a stranger to them as they were to me, it is not my impression that we felt any mutual hostility, yet some people felt this was the case. It has happened elsewhere, or might well happen, but nothing leads me to suspect it ever happened here. Now everyone knows that familiarity and acquaintance with someone commonly breeds boldness, and that boldness can easily break out into rashness. Clearly the less we know people the more respect we usually show them. When I entered this monastery, however, these monks by no means hid what they were thinking from me. They opened their hearts to me with confident confessions, and once their hearts were open we felt closer than I have ever felt with any other monks I have known.

O merciful Father, you know that I began this book not to be arrogant but to confess my iniquities. I would have confessed them even more explicitly if I were not afraid that by doing so my abhorrent actions might corrupt the minds of many of my readers. Yes I do confess my iniquities, but far more important, I confess your tender mercies, which reflect not my corruption but the grace that wells within you. If I happen to speak of any person I shall set forth that person's behavior and the ultimate consequences of his actions only to show the nature of your judgments.

You know, of course, that in these discourses, which are for you and dedicated to you, I do not use destructive or hateful speech with pleasure. For I am determined to write about my fortunes and misfortunes in the hope that they might perhaps benefit other people.

On the day of my installation, when the monks were preparing to greet me in procession, one of the monks, who knew his Scripture and was also curious, I suspect, about the future course of my life, opened the text of the Gospel, which had been placed for this purpose on the

13. Guibert, who harshly condemns the sin of simony and of monastic avarice, wishes to dispel the faintest suspicion that his appointment as abbot of Nogent might be due to family influence. Far from attempting to influence his election, his own mother, he tells us, was "vexed and displeased" at his promotion (1.19).

altar. He intended to take as an omen the first passage that caught his eye.[14] Now the book was handwritten, and arranged not in pages, but in columns. The monk fixed his eye on the middle of the third column, where he saw the following text: "Your eye is the lantern of your body."[15] To the deacon who was to carry the text of the Gospel during the procession he gave the following order: when the moment came for me to kiss the silver image that adorned the book's binding, the deacon would open the book for me to read (having kept his finger on the spot he had designated) and watch very closely on which part of the text my eye happened to fall. The deacon opened the book (which, according to custom, I had kissed on the binding), and as he watched to see which part of the text I would turn my attention to I fixed my eye not on the beginning of the page nor on the end, but on the very same verse as the monk who had started this whole business. He saw that my gesture, without my realizing it, had been in concordance with his whole intention. A few days later he came up to me to tell me what he had done and how his action had quite marvelously coincided with mine.

O God, you who "light the lamp" of whoever believes in you [Ps. 18.28], you know what light of good intention you have given me and what good will I bear toward others in spite of unfriendly gestures that have been made toward me. And though the filth and misery of my own heart may be due to my doing, you are not unaware that my spirit toils for the salvation of those whom you have entrusted to me. The more I consider the evil within me the more I am delighted by the good works of others when they occur. I know that I shall have freer access to the

14. Saint Augustine tolerates, but ultimately disapproves of, the practice of divination, which consisted of giving a prophetic value to the first passage of Scripture that one's eye fell on after opening the Book. He adds, however, that divination is better than consultation with demons (*Epistola* 55.20, in *PL* 33.222): "Hi vero qui de paginis evangelicis sortes legunt, etsi optandum est ut hoc potius faciant, quam ad daemonia consulenda concurrant; tamen etiam mihi displicet consuetudo, ad negotia saecularia, et ad vitae hujus vanitatem, propter aliam vitam loquentia oracula divina velle convertere." A capitulary of Charlemagne of 789 condemned this practice. Gratian declared that fortunetelling is prohibited to the faithful because of the danger of falling back into paganism (*Decretum* 26.2.1). Yet a century after Guibert, Saint Francis of Assisi still resorted to this practice before making any important decision (Labande, *Guibert de Nogent*, 236n.2).

15. Guibert is quoting the Vulgate version of Luke 11.34 verbatim: "Lucerna corporis tui est oculus tuus."

throne of your grace the more I have shown myself grateful for the deeds of men of goodwill.

Once I was received by the monks of Nogent and brought before the assembled chapter I delivered a sermon on a text from Isaiah—since it was the last Sunday before Christmas, when the prophet is read.[16] I said: The prophet Isaiah speaks as you have just heard: "A man will take hold of his brother living in his father's house and say to him: 'You have a cloak, be our ruler; we place this ruin under your hand.'" To which he will answer: "I am no physician and in my house there is neither bread nor a cloak. Do not make a prince of me. For Jerusalem is in ruins and Judah is crumbling."[17] The *man* in question is the one who conducts himself effeminately against the Devil. He *takes hold of his brother* when he comes to find someone who is born of God; the latter must *live in his father's house,* because anyone solicited for a pastoral office must not make himself appear ignorant of the mysteries of God's house. In fact, whoever is ignorant about the sacraments of the church is unworthy to be part of its administration because "a scribe who has been trained for the kingdom of God" [Matt. 13.52], faithful in observing its mysteries and wise in dispensing them, cannot be ranked as a "servant" [Matt. 24.45]. How can anyone administer a church if he does not know that church? Let him, then, be someone *from the house.* And what is the *cloak,* if not the fine dress of outward works? The owner of the cloak is begged to *become a ruler,* for it often happens that one is called to rule, who by his bearing, his words, and his actions shows himself to be one who chastises. The *ruin,* however, is perceived to be *under his hand,* because whatever he finds detrimental in his subjects becomes an object of concern for the ruler, who reasons as if he were saying: "At first glance you seem to be doing well, but see to it that you surpass others in virtue, knowing that it behooves you to hold up the *ruins* of others. Rendered more cautious by this meditation, the ruler says, '*I am no physician,* if this means being able to cure the ruins of recurrent illnesses. The *cloak* that you see is an external one, but *there is no one in the house,* because the

16. 18 December 1104 (Labande, *Guibert de Nogent,* 238n.2).

17. This is a verbatim quotation of the Vulgate version of Isa. 3.6–8: "Adprehendet enim vir fratrem suum domesticum patris sui / vestimentum tibi est princeps esto noster ruina autem haec sub manu tua / respondebit in die illa dicens / non sum medicus et in domo mea non est panis neque vestimentum / nolite constituere me principem populi / ruit enim Hierusalem et Iudas concidit." Note that Guibert does not choose this text at random, but that it is one of the readings for that Sunday before Christmas.

dress of the soul and that of the body are different.' Therefore the ruler declares *he is no physician,* because it is difficult, even with the needle of discernment, to pierce through to the cause and effect of every virtue and every vice. This condition might also be the result of his own short-comings, because *there might not be in the house that daily bread* that we ask God to "give us this day" [Luke 11.3], that is to say the comfort of divine refreshment that is poured into us spiritually, or as a confirmation within the inner person of that Christian charity without which there is never good rule. Rightly, then, does he *refuse to become a ruler,* for his strength, though bolstered from above, is unequal to the task before him. *Jerusalem falls into ruin,* which means that, when one has lost inner peace, the very confession of sin is blocked by utter despair, the worst of all ills, good reason for him to refuse the pastoral charge. For when the mind is disquieted by vices and shamefully overrun by them, it fails in its blindness to abhor them by confessing them. Unable to govern itself, it is only appropriate that some force outside the mind should prevent it (though it would be more appropriate for it to do so itself) from directing others."[18]

The points I have just made were developed in even greater detail in my sermon, and I underscored my main points with examples drawn from scripture.

4

My mother's death

I have long neglected to talk about my mother. Of all the blessings I received in this life she was the most special and the most unique. It is

18. This is a very characteristic example of a medieval homily based upon an exegetical development of a text of Scripture. The italicized passages are direct excerpts from the text of Isaiah, cited as an exordium. Trained as he was to interpret Scripture according to the literal, allegorical, moral, and anagogical levels, Guibert is indulging in typical exegetical practice. As newly elected abbot, Guibert's situation is clearly similar to that of the "brother" with the "cloak," who is asked to look after the "ruin." By subtly interweaving his interpretation of the text at all four levels, Guibert is stating that he, as abbot, cannot heal a house in ruin if the spiritual, inner state of the inhabitants of the house (including his own spiritual state as "prince") is not sound.

only fitting, then, that I tell briefly how her good life achieved an even better end. By her own admission she had managed to endure a considerable number of years with spirit unbroken; and while her frail body was tiring slowly the spirit of prayer had not in the least diminished in her. The weakness of her lungs kept her from sleeping, and a hundred times a night she would mournfully repeat the name of the Lord Jesus. Finally she took to her bed, overcome by her illness.

My brother and I were residing at Nogent at that time, two years (if I am not mistaken) before that return to Fly, which I have mentioned earlier.[19] This was a most inconsiderate thing for me to do, but thanks to God (who puts our misfortunes to good use) the story had a far better conclusion than might have been expected. God, in any case, spared my mother's feelings and did not allow her heart, which loved God so, to be pierced by the dagger of my dishonorable return to Fly.

When she was about to die, my master, who stood next to her in tears, said to her: "Behold, the sons of your master are far away,[20] and perhaps you will feel very sad if you die while they are gone. They will be even sadder." She stared right back at him and said, her eyes glaring: "Even if they were living in the neighboring monastery as they used to, God knows that I don't want them, or any other relatives, to see me die. There is only One whom I call out to with all my inner strength. May he alone assist me!" Those were her words, and that same night, at the very hour [of sunset] when the Angel Gabriel's Annunciation to the Virgin is sung and celebrated,[21] my mother went to meet her gracious Lady. I had always noticed the infinite love she had for her, and I am convinced she was gladly received.

A few years before her death a strong desire to take the sacred veil had started taking hold of her. I had convinced her not to do this, basing

19. Guibert is not referring here to the time he had been tempted to leave Fly for another monastery, only to be deterred by his mother's dream (1.16). Since he and his "brother" were, as he says, both residing at Nogent, the return to Fly from Nogent seems to be one of those embarrassing memories that he mistakenly thinks he has already recounted ("quod supra quidem meminimus"). This episode is alluded to once again in 3.7, where someone identifies Guibert as "ipse . . . qui . . . a vestris digressis monachis Flaviacum concessistis." As for the "brother" mentioned here, Guibert is clearly not referring to a member of his family, but to an unidentified brother monk.

20. A comparable expression is used of Rebekah in Gen. 24.51: "et sit uxor filii domini tui." Like Rebekah, who is to become the wife of Isaac, Abraham's son, Guibert's mother, in death, is to become the spouse of Christ, the Son of God.

21. At the hour of the last "Angelus Mariae," that is, around 9 P.M.

my argument on a text that says: "Let no bishop attempt to veil widows,"[22] adding that she could lead a perfectly chaste life without any
external robes. That wonderful man whom I have mentioned earlier,
Abbot Anselm of Bec, who later became Archbishop of Canterbury in
England, had denied her the same thing long before.[23] Nonetheless, the
more I talked the more she was determined not to let any argument deter
her from her purpose. She prevailed and took the veil in the presence of
the abbot of the local monastery, the reverend Jean, whom she had raised
as a child; and in the end she proved that the ultimate incentive for her
action had come from God himself.[24]

She said she had seen in a vision a very beautiful, imposing lady,
magnificently dressed, who presented my mother with a very precious
cloak. She seemed to be entrusting the cloak to my mother for safekeeping until the time came for her to give it back. We all agreed immediately
with what she was saying, especially as we were convinced that her pious
initiative had been encouraged with signs from heaven. For nearly three
years my mother kept her holy veil as conscientiously as she could; and
on the anniversary of the day when that most gracious Lady received the
happy Annunciation that would bring us salvation[25] she gave it back to
the Lady who had confided it to her keeping.

I commend my mother's soul to all the faithful who will read these
lines, as she never forgot any of the faithful in her frequent prayers.
What I have said of her I have said in God's presence, and as my heart
is my witness I have invented nothing.

I said earlier that I had gone back to stay at the abbey of Fly. Let us
pause there for a while before retracing our steps in the sands and returning to Laon.

22. Guibert may be alluding here to a decree of Bishop Yves of Chartres, based on
1 Cor. 7.8 and 39, where Saint Paul advises unmarried men and widows to "remain
single as I do" (Labande, *Guibert de Nogent*, 244n.2).

23. Guibert had a great respect for the teaching and the counsel of Anselm of
Bec, as in 1.17, where he calls Anselm "virum incomparabilem documentis et vita
sanctissimum," who taught him "qualiter interiorem meum hominem agerem."

24. Guibert's mother obviously was convinced that the Spirit spoke to her even
more clearly than Scripture.

25. On 25 March, the feast of the Annunciation. The exact year of Guibert's mother's death cannot be ascertained.

5

Some demonic doings at Saint-Germer de Fly

In that monastery of Fly there is a monk of Jewish origin. At the time when talk of a crusade to Jerusalem began to reverberate throughout the Latin world for the first time he was rescued from his superstition in the following manner.[26] At Rouen one day, some men who had taken the cross with the intention of leaving for the crusade began complaining among themselves. "Here we are," they said, "going off to attack God's enemies in the East, having to travel tremendous distances, when there are Jews right here before our very eyes. No race is more hostile to God than they are. Our project is insane!" Having said this they armed themselves, rounded up some Jews in a church—whether by force or by ruse I don't know—and led them out to put them to the sword regardless of age or sex. Those who agreed to submit to the Christian way of life could, however, escape the impending slaughter. It was during this massacre that a nobleman saw a little boy, took pity on him, whisked him away, and took him to his own mother.[27]

This lady was an aristocrat by birth, formerly the wife of the count of Eu (Eu is the castle that sits below the abbey of Saint-Michel by the sea,

---

26. This event, writes Guibert, occurred at a time when the crusade ("Hierosolymi-tani iter") was *first* being talked about in the Latin world, that is, before 1095. In 1108, Guibert wrote his famous account of the First Crusade, the *Gesta Dei per Francos, sive Historia Hierosolymitana* (*PL* 156.679–838).

27. Robert Chazan argues that while the First Crusade was "an expression of the new militance of Christendom against its external foes . . . it revealed also new potential for internal upheaval and disruption," but he adds that the persecution narrated by Guibert is "satisfactory evidence for but one specific persecution of Jews within the area of northern France" (*Medieval Jewry in Northern France* [Baltimore: The Johns Hopkins University Press, 1973], 24–26). While he is seemingly unaware of Guibert's text, Salo Baron writes: "Mundane and spiritual factors combined to make the Crusaders' march from France to the Holy Land in 1096–99 one of the most memorable events in world and Jewish history. Widespread failure of crops and mass starvation greatly swelled the ranks of desperadoes and adventurers to whom plunder and burning of Jewish, and occasionally also non-Jewish, communities appealed as much as the arduous expeditions to the Near East" (*A Social and Religious History of the Jews*, 2d ed. [New York: Columbia University Press, 1957], 4.94–95). Labande (*Guibert de Nogent*, 248n.1) seems to find Guibert's account unfounded, but Benton (*Self and Society*, 135n.1) finds it entirely credible.

in a place called Treport).[28] This marvelous woman took the child in and asked him in the most gracious terms whether he wouldn't like to be placed under Christian law. The child did not say no, thinking, in fact, he would otherwise be murdered just as he had seen his fellow Jews being murdered, and so the steps leading to baptism were speeded up. Then he was led to the font, and after the ritual prayers were recited, they reached the point where a candle is lit and liquid wax is dropped into the water. There was one drop in particular that traced in the water such a perfect sign of the cross that no human hand could ever have managed to trace anything of the kind with such a tiny piece of matter.[29] The countess herself related this incident to me, being a relative of mine and so close to me that she always called me her son. The incident was confirmed by a priest, and both of them swore several times in God's name that the story was true. Myself, I would not have paid much attention to this matter if I had not witnessed this child's extraordinary progress.

The name of the countess was Hélisende. Her son, who had rescued the child from the massacre and received him on the baptismal font, was called Guillaume and he gave the child this same name.[30] When the child was a little older he made the transition from the study of Hebrew, which he had learned first, to Latin, and was soon making great progress. Guillaume feared that the child's relatives would force him to readopt his old ways — they had attempted, unsuccessfully, to do so several times — and so he took him to the monastery of Fly. Once in the monastic life the child became so fond of the Christian way of living, showed such enthusiasm in absorbing everything dealing with divine learning, and accepted all the discipline that was required of him with such calmness that he ended up drawing considerable respect from people for mastering his former nature and for resisting all attempts to disrupt his new way of life.

The monk who had been designated to watch over him as a young child secretly made himself his teacher of grammar; being deeply religious he thought that a genuine knowledge of the Christian law was necessary for the child's budding mind. The monk took pains to teach

28. The abbey of Saint-Michel de Tréport in Normandy was founded with subsidies from the counts of Eu in 1053.

29. The "miraculous" cruciform shape of the wax in the water may have been due very simply to the officiant's tracing a sign of the cross over the water with molten wax.

30. William I, count of Eu, who was related to Duke William of Normandy.

the child, and his efforts bore fruit. The boy's naturally clever mind was so sharpened each day that in a place known for its great number of literary scholars no one had a greater reputation for brilliance or intelligence than he did. He was a deeply intuitive young man, never jealous or cantankerous, and always pleasant; and he had a special penchant for modesty. To increase the fervor of his already robust faith I sent him a little book of mine that I had written almost four years earlier against the count of Soissons, who was a Judaizer and a heretic.[31] Someone told me that he took such an intense interest in this book that he piously set about imitating it by writing a small book defending the faith through reason. The appearance of the cross at his baptism, then, was not a chance event but was divinely willed. It was a sign of the faith that would develop in this man of Jewish stock, a rare event in our time.

A simple, good-natured priest took monastic vows in this very same place [Fly] with his son, who was also a cleric. (The son imitated his father in every way, and because he was younger in years and not without learning, he became even more outstanding.) So long as he had lived as a priest in society the father had been generous to the poor, in keeping with his means. The Devil not only resented this man's goodness but was genuinely pained to witness his thorough contempt for the world. One night, when he was still a novice asleep with other novices he saw a throng of demons come up to him in a vision. They were carrying pouches slung around their haunches in the Scottish manner.[32] The demon who seemed to be their leader and spokesman stepped forward while the others hesitated, and said: "Give us some alms." Remembering that he was now a monk the novice replied: "I have nothing I can possibly give you, or anyone else." The "Scot" then said: "I have never seen a charitable priest," and with great fury he picked up a stone and threw

31. Guibert is alluding to his small treatise, *De incarnatione contra Judaeos*, written against John, count of Soissons, in the year 1111 (*PL* 156.489–527). In the opening chapter of this treatise (489–91), Guibert expresses shock that John, while a practicing Christian, is inclined to accept and even disseminate the rejection of the divine Incarnation of Christ preached by Jews. In 3.16 of the *Monodiae*, Guibert describes John of Soissons as one who is always out for his own advantage ("cujus tamen intentio sola sua utilitas fuit") (Labande, *Guibert de Nogent*, 422).

32. Guibert's text reads: "turba daemonum in morem Scotorum sitarcias suas . . . portantium." I have translated "sitarcias" as "pouches," Benton's words "scrip," or "sporran" being unfamiliar to the average reader. These pouches were used no doubt as purses and/or game bags. Benton notes (*Self and Society*, 137n.11) that "Guibert is the earliest author known to refer to the wearing of the sporran."

it with great force at the monk, striking him in the chest. He was in such pain that for forty days his anxiety drove him to the brink of death: it was as if the Scot had really hit him with a stone.

Long after this incident, when the monk had recovered, the Devil came to visit him again with intentions no less evil than the first time. One night, when all the other monks had withdrawn, the Devil tracked him down as he was sitting alone answering the call of nature. The Devil was disguised as a cowled monk and kept rubbing his feet against the floor of the stall, as monks usually do when they make some request at night. Our monk was so terrified that in his haste to leave the place he ran into the door, hitting his head against the top of the frame at the same time. So once again the Devil managed to hurt him, this time by bruising his forehead. Powerless to harm the monk's soul the Devil proved his own poverty of spirit by attacking his body.

There was another man, this one from a noble family of the Beauvais region, who also had great wealth in the Noyon area. He was already very old and physically exhausted; and he had a wife who was quite vigorous in bed, which in such circumstances is worse than the plague.[33] So he abandoned both married life and the world and became a monk [at Saint-Germer], where he spent his time weeping almost continuously and praying without ceasing, never tiring of hearing the word of God. To all of us he was most edifying to watch, and strict in observing the rule. Once he heard in the chapter assembly that no one should without good reason go into the infirmary in the place where he happened to be living. He took this prohibition seriously and kept it in mind.

One morning, while he lay in bed still half asleep with his eyes closed, two devils disguised in the habit of those religious commonly known as *deonandi* came up and sat on a little bench right next to the bed.[34] The old man woke up, looked toward the side of the bed, and was surprised to see such a familiar look on faces he did not know. One of those sitting

33. Guibert writes: "et effoeto jam corpore, quod talibus pestiferum est, uxorem habens vegetiorem officio thalamorum." It is refreshing to see a twelfth-century monk referring with humor to what will become one of the favorite themes of bourgeois farce in the fifteenth century.

34. Guibert's text reads: "duo daemones instar religiosorum illorum quos deonandos vulgo appellant." This seems to be the only instance, in Guibert 's work or anywhere else, of the use of the curious word *deonandi*, which may be a short, colloquial form of *deodonandi*. Guibert may be referring to some wandering monastic sect, possibly heretical (Benton, *Self and Society*, 138n.12; Labande, *Guibert de Nogent*, 256n.1).

there had his head uncovered; his beard was not sticking out but was tucked in. His hair was red. He must usually have walked in his bare feet, as do wandering monks of this type,[35] for he had dried mud between his toes as if he had recently been out walking. As to the second character he was so concealed behind the first that one could hardly see his face; he was covered with a long cloak and a black hood. The old monk, seeing these unknown people next to him, spoke to them in great irritation: "You are outsiders to this monastery and I don't know you. How did you have the gall to come here at this hour, in a place where even monks from this cloister don't dare come without good reason?" The first devil answered: "I had heard, Sir, that religious men live in this monastery and I had come to learn something about religion. Please don't take it badly." The old monk said: "This is not the place to learn anything about religion, or about the rule. If you want any instruction about those matters, go see somebody in the cloister. There you'll see the rule being vigorously practiced and you'll learn the rudiments of sanctity. Now you will please go, because what is prohibited to monks who live here is incomparably more prohibited to you."

When the first devil attempted to stay and repeat his speech, the old monk began screaming at them and forced them to leave the room. They went as far as the door but dallied on the threshold. Turning toward the old man the devil who was in charge of the conversation said: "Now you're trying to get rid of me. But if you allowed me to stay with you I could be very beneficial to you. I know one of your people who is guilty of theft. If he attempted to deny it I would go beat him up." The old monk laughed. "Now we can see from your speech what kind of danger you represent. You said you had come here to learn about religion, but in fact you're a fighter. You're such a liar that I don't have to listen to you or hold you back."

The old monk was still very irritated and wondered why people like this had been allowed in the house. He got up and walked over to the entrance of the house, where he found a few sick brothers who were staying there with him. He complained bitterly to them for allowing outsiders like this to come in. They were astounded, naturally, thinking

35. Guibert uses the word "circumcelliones," which he sems to have found in Saint Augustine's *Enarratio in psalmum* 132.3, meaning a monk who wanders from cell to cell, having no fixed place: "Nam circumcelliones dicti sunt, quia circum cellas uagantur: solent enim ire hac illac, nusquam labentes sedes; et facere quae nostis, et quae illi norunt, uelint, nolint" (*CCSL* 40.1928).

he was out of his mind, and they swore they had seen no one. The old man related his story—who these people were, how they had behaved, what they had said, at what time they had appeared—and it became clear to him as he confronted his testimony with everybody else's that he had been fooled by devils. Some devils are only interested in playing pranks; others are of a more cruel disposition and like to inflict physical pain. To illustrate this let us provide two examples, both pertinent to our present subject.

6

Other instances of demonic mischief.
Never to invoke the devil

At the castle of Chauny there was a servant belonging to the family of Wascelin, the lord of the castle, whose duty it was to stand watch over the castle at night.[36] One evening, as the light of day was waning very quickly, he found himself on the other side of the river and was very much afraid he would miss his dinner; so he called from the opposite bank for someone to come fetch him in a boat. When he realized that nobody had heard him he became furious and said: "Well, you devils, why don't you ferry me across?" Immediately a devil appeared and offered his services: "Climb in," he said, "I'll transport you." The poor man immediately climbed in. He was in for a hard time: the devil did not delay to carry him off to Italy, to the outskirts of a city called Sutri, and he was so "gentle" in laying him down that he broke his hipbone.[37]

Sutri is about a day's journey from Rome. The day before, Wascelin, the lord previously mentioned, had made a pilgrimage to the tombs of the apostles and had then left the city to spend a night at Sutri. Rising before dawn, as pilgrims usually do when they travel during the winter, he then left Sutri with his companions. When he reached the fields outside the city he heard a voice, not far from the main road, that sounded

36. Wascelin was lord of the castle of Chauny, on the right bank of the Aisne river.
37. Here as in other places, Guibert shows he can spice his narrative with wit and irony: "eum tanta benignitate deposuit, ut coxam ei frangeret."

like someone crying. He looked around and found his servant, who had recognized his master's voice, and whose voice his master had also identified. When they asked him what he was doing in this place he replied that he was still at Chauny the night before and that the Devil had transported him to this place. Wascelin could not get over this story. He brought his servant to the city nearby and gave some money to assure his recovery and his return home. The man's suffering had taught him a lesson: in any undertaking one should call on God, not on devils.

At Saint-Médard [in Soissons] there was another man who had duties similar to the previous one as nightwatchman of the abbey. Having once spent a part of the night over the tower gate near the fishpond, playing with rattles, singing, blowing on a horn (as watchmen do) he finally went down to the edge of the water to take a walk. As he stood there he saw what looked like three women appear to him, and he heard one of them saying: "Let's get into this man." Another said: "He is poor, he couldn't possibly keep us warm." The third said: "There's a clerk around here named Hugo who is fat and swarthy and who has everything. He would feed us well. Wouldn't it be good to attack him?" Then they disappeared. The man came to his senses and realized that the women represented three of the best known types of fevers; they had noticed his poverty with mock curiosity and they had despised it; and now they were setting their sights on someone whose meats and supplies seemed almost inexhaustible. Without waiting for the dawn the watchman went back to find his fellow monks. To the first ones he met he related what he had seen and heard. He asked them to send someone to inquire how Hugo was. They did this and he found Hugo suffering from a great fever.

From this we can deduce that such types of illnesses are administered by demons, with God's permission. We read in the Gospels, for example, that a certain woman was said to have been hunched over, bound by Satan, for seventeen years.[38] The same can be said about the man who suffered from epilepsy, that is to say the "falling sickness."[39] He was being thrown to he ground by an unclean spirit who caused him to foam at the mouth, gnash his teeth and grow very stiff; and it is written that

38. The text of Luke 13.11 mentions eighteen years: "et ecce mulier quae habebat spiritum infirmitatis annis decem et *octo*." This is one of many indications that Guibert frequently quotes Scripture from memory without checking his quotation.

39. Mark 9.28–29: "And when he had entered the house, the disciples asked him privately, 'Why could we not cast it out?' And he said to them 'This kind cannot be driven out by anything but prayer.'"

such a condition can be cured only through prayer and fasting [Mark 9.29]. Job, too, bore the attacks of devils, inwardly and outwardly, in his "bone and his flesh" as well as "what he had" [Job 2.4].

Who can interrupt a narrative once it is begun?[40] Well, let me write about the fourth case that comes back to my memory. There was a clerk from Reims who gave us a terrible example for our times. He was not very well read, but he was skilled in the art of painting. One day be began to feel nervous over having led such a frivolous life, and so he became a canon regular at Chalons, in the church of All Saints [Châlons-sur-Marne]. There he stayed a while; then, day by day, the fervor with which he had entered began to grow lukewarm while the flame of his old passions was revived. So he left the rule that he had submitted to and returned to Reims, where he got married. Several children had been born to him when, to chastise him, heaven sent him a serious illness. I should add that before he was stricken he had intended to go on the crusade to Jerusalem, which everyone was talking about at that time.[41]

He was ill for a long time. As his condition grew worse he came to his senses and urgently begged the abbot of Saint-Nicaise (whose name was Jean) to come to see him. In the abbot's presence he swore to renounce the world and asked his permission to wear the religious habit. The abbot was careful: his penitent's proven insincerity had made him suspicious. He dissuaded our man from his purpose and refused to give him the habit he was asking for; yet though the man was ill the abbot had him brought to his cloister. But since the man felt his illness was growing worse he went to see the abbot and lamented so much that he ended up forcing the abbot to give him the monastic habit against his better judgment. Having gotten what he wanted the man seemed contented, and for a very short while he seemed to behave more calmly. Then all of a sudden, as if moved by some sort of divine inspiration he called for the abbot and said: "I beg you, father, ask your monks to watch over me carefully; you should know that God's judgment upon me is imminent. That much is sure. You and your monks will have to bear much hardship because of me, but knowing it will be for a short time please bear up with it patiently."

Hearing this the abbot ordered him watched by fearless and vigilant

---

40. Guibert is gently mocking his own capacity to ramble on: "Conceptum sermonem tenere quis possit?"

41. The First Crusade, that of 1096–99.

guardians. Without warning, however, swarms of demons infinite in number appeared from everywhere and hurled themselves at the man. They began to pull at him, threw him to the floor, and dragged him around. In a violent rage they tried to tear off his sacred habit while he held on to his hood with his teeth and kept his arms together to avoid having his cassock torn off. He was particularly subject to these horrendous attacks during the night, being accompanied with frightful wailings. Sometimes, however, during the day the demons would withdraw, giving him some respite. Then one could try to ask him questions to ascertain what sort of frightful business was going on in the man.

He would talk at length about the souls of men he had known, or who were mentioned to him by those present, as if he had them under his very eyes. When a widow who was very much afraid that her husband's soul was in danger yet prayed very little for him heard about this, she came to consult the man. She asked whether she was allowed to pray for her husband and whether this man knew what had become of him. The man replied: "Why not? Pray for him with confidence. He was here a short while ago."

The man suffered afflictions of this kind for several days. Then he was overcome by a perfect sense of peace. Indeed while he had suffered he seemed at times to have peaceful intervals, but then he would see those hordes of devils coming out of the walls, out of the earth, from every side, and fly toward him as if to tear him to pieces. Finally, divine justice granted him clemency, and the evil spirits withdrew. The man called for the abbot and said: "My lord, God is repaying me for my sins. You know that soon after this examination it will be finished with me. Give me absolution for my sins as best you can, and please anoint me with holy oil to make the remission complete." The abbot responded swiftly and devoutly. The man was most grateful to receive absolution; and purged of every blemish for his sins when death came to greet him, he entered freely and joyfully into life.

BOOK THREE

The Uprising of the Laon Commune

1
Laon and its first bishops

I have already mentioned that I intended to talk about the people of Laon, or rather, to reenact their tragedies.[1] I should begin by saying that all their misfortunes, in my opinion, were due to the perversity of their bishops, which goes back a long time; but to tie things into my narrative I should start with Ascelin, who was also called Adalbéron.[2] Our re-

---

1. I have not translated the word play between "tracturi" and "acturi," which Guibert indulges in, quite typically, in this opening sentence: "De Laudunensibus, ut spopondimus, jam modo tracturi, imo Laudunensium tragoedias acturi." Guibert's "promise" ("ut spopondimus") to talk about events in Laon refers back to the end of 2.4: "antequam Laudunensi sabulo retrovaga vestigia conspergamus." Tragedies, in the classical sense, were not enacted on stage in France in Guibert's day, and this is one of many instances when our twelfth-century Renaissance humanist shows off his "classical" learning.

2. Since Guibert is convinced that the origin of all the ills of Laon resides in its bishops ("totius mali originem ex pontificum . . . perversitatibus emersisse"), he deems it necessary to go back at least a century in the history of the diocese, to Adalbéron's

search shows that he came from Lorraine, that he had a great wealth of goods and lands, which he attempted to transform into enormous donations for the See that he governed. He adorned his church with marvelous furnishings and increased the prosperity of the clergy and the bishopric considerably, but his generosity in giving was sullied by extraordinary wickedness. What could be worse or more ignominious than his betrayal of his lord the king, an innocent child to whom he had sworn fidelity, and his turning of the line of succession from Charlemagne toward another family?[3] Like Judas he committed this crime on the day of the Lord's Supper.[4] By overthrowing the ruler and his descendants, he was not looking to make a change that might have been useful at the time but was only concerned with fulfilling his own evil designs at the expense of innocent princes. But God deferred his punishment, so that the city and its bishop continued to enjoy material prosperity for a while.

2
Hélinand's episcopate

Then came Hélinand.[5] He was of obscure background, his family was poor, and he himself was not very well educated, and rather frail in his appearance.

---

administration. Hence the reader notices a genealogical tone in Guibert's history as he enumerates successive bishops and the string of "perversities" that led up to the uprisings of 1112.

3. Adalbéron was bishop of Laon from 977 to about 1030. He is buried in the church of Saint Vincent, at Laon, where his epitaph lists the many gifts with which he endowed his native church. Guibert seems to be referring to Adalbéron's contributions to the cathedral of Laon when he writes: "pretia ingentia ad sedem, cui praeerat, transtulisset." But the "extraordinarily evil" behavior with which Adalbéron "sullied" his generosity was, according to the contemporary monk Richer, his betrayal of Charles of Lorraine, his liege lord, in favor of Hugh Capet (Labande, *Guibert de Nogent*, 268n.1; Benton, *Self and Society*, 145n.2).

4. Richer, the monk of Saint-Rémi of Reims, and whose history of France covers the years 888-954, places Adalbéron's betrayal of Charles of Lorraine on the night of Palm Sunday 991. Another contemporary chronicler, Adhémar of Chabannes, seems to agree with Guibert that Adalbéron's crime, like Judas's, took place on a Maundy Thursday, "ebdomada majori ante Pascha, in qua est coena Domini" (Labande, *Guibert de Nogent*, 268n.3).

5. Guibert omits the names of two bishops, Gébuin and Liétry, who administered the diocese of Laon between Adalbéron and Hélinand. The latter was bishop between 1052 and 1098.

Through his acquaintance with Gautier the Elder, count of Pontoise, Hélinand (who was from this area) had entered into the good graces of Edward, king of England. (Edward's wife had established some sort of bond with the count, the details of which I am unaware of.)[6] So Hélinand became Edward's chaplain, and being well acquainted with French manners, Edward often sent him on missions to Henry, king of France.[7] Henry was very greedy and had the habit of selling bishoprics; so Hélinand showered him with lavish gifts while suggesting that if one of the bishops from the French royal domain were to die he, Hélinand, would be ready to wear the episcopal robes. England was very rich at the time. As chaplain to the king and queen Hélinand had amassed mountains of money, which allowed him to distribute largesses of the kind I've just mentioned. So his message came through very clearly to Henry. Hélinand had his way and received the bishopric of Laon. Even without the help of family background or great learning he knew how to put himself forward. He put his hopes in his wealth, which compensated for many things and which he distributed very carefully, and in his taste for luxurious living.

He set about building and decorating churches. Though he seemed to be doing much for God, it was abundantly clear that he was looking only for applause and for giving himself visibility through good deeds. He tried with similar tactics to obtain the archbishopric of Reims. He succeeded within two years, having spent considerable sums of money on King Philip,[8] a particularly corruptible man when it came to the things of God; but then the pope let him know that whoever has a wife cannot take another.[9] One

6. Guibert's text reads, "Gualteri comitis senioris Pontisarensis." Benton's translation, "Gautier, the old count of Pontoise," suggests that Gautier was advanced in age when Hélinand "entered into the good graces" of Edward the Confessor. In fact, Gautier was Edward the Confessor's nephew, being the son of his sister Goda. Guibert's term "senior" seems more accurately translated as "elder."

7. Henry I, son of Robert II the Pious, was king of France from 1031 to 1060.

8. Philippe I, the son of King Henry I, was king of France from 1060 to 1108. He repudiated his wife, Berthe de Hollande, and remarried with Bertrade de Montfort, in 1092. His remarriage drew upon his head an excommunication by Pope Urban II in 1095. See Georges Duby, *The Knight, the Lady, and the Priest,* trans. Barbara Bray (New York: Pantheon Books, 1983), 3–21.

9. Since the days of the early church, a bishop was considered married to his diocese as to a wife, *unicus cum unica,* and could not be transferred to another diocese. Hélinand's claim to the archbishopric of Reims, which fell vacant in 1067, was disputed by Pope Alexander II, who asserted in 1070 that "a bishop is married to his see and cannot be translated without papal permission" (Benton, *Self and Society,* 147n.3). Twenty-five years later, Pope Urban II would assert to King Philippe that "whoever has a wife cannot take another." Is Guibert aware of the ironic resemblance between

day, in response to someone who asked him why he behaved this way Hélinand said that if he could become pope he would not pass up the opportunity.

Whatever ambition or other human weakness he may have had, Hélinand should unquestionably be given credit for having magnificently defended the church's liberty and for having greatly enriched his own episcopal See as well as the other dependent churches of his diocese. It was right, in short, that he should have such wealth since he used it for the adornment of the houses of the Lord.

3

Bishop Enguerrand's complicity with Enguerrand de Boves

Enguerrand was Hélinand's successor.[10] Though he surpassed his predecessor in noble background and in education, he was terrible in defending the rights of the church placed under his protection. In the past the king would use royal force to confiscate revenues from Hélinand's See, forcing the bishop to resort to gifts and entreaties to get them back. The return was then confirmed by royal charter and Hélinand's seal. But Enguerrand began his disastrous accession to the seat of Laon by giving

---

Hélinand's attempted episcopal "adultery" in 1070, and King Philippe's adultery with Bertrade? Though he wrote the *Monodiae* around the year 1115, fully twenty years after Pope Urban II's excommunication of the French king, Guibert never alludes to that event in his autobiography. He does, however, refer to it explicitly in the *Gesta Dei* (written around 1108), and he clearly admires the decisiveness and incorruptibility shown by Pope Urban II on that occasion: "[the Pope] tanta auctoritate excommunicavit ut intercessiones spectabilium personarum, et multiplicium munerum illationes contempserit."

10. Enguerrand of Coucy, who became bishop of Laon in 1098 or 1099, died in 1104. He was first cousin to Enguerrand de Boves, whom Guibert will discuss shortly. With bishop Enguerrand we enter into the labyrinthine lineage of the lords of Coucy, who for nearly three centuries (1116–1397) will be among the most powerful of the French feudal barons. No fewer than eight of the lords of Coucy took part in the Crusades. Four of them perished.

everything back to the king; and for three successive bishops now, the church has been deprived of this income, a situation that could last forever.[11] It seems, therefore, that the bishop has made all of his successors accomplices in his simony: once they become bishops they live in such fear of the king that they do not dare claim what Enguerrand shamefully abandoned in order to become bishop.

Because Enguerrand had not the slightest idea what the love of God was, he made a mockery of any kind of moderation or piety. In public he made any conversation degenerate into chit-chat or scurrilous talk, worse than any jester or entertainer would. During his term of office there began to appear real risks that the city, the churches, and the entire province might deteriorate completely, with results that were far from pleasant for him.

A man with the same given name, Enguerrand de Boves, was a close relative: a very generous man, who loved to spend lavishly.[12] He showed great respect and munificence toward churches once he had assured himself that they were observing the rule. But he also had a great love for women, and whenever women surrounded him, whether legitimate or mercenary, he did only what their caprice dictated. Enguerrand de Boves had made some very unfortunate matrimonial choices, so he began looking around for other women. He secretly fancied the wife of a relative of his, the Count of Namur, seduced her in secret but married her in public. This marriage was condemned by repeated anathemas and was severely chastised by the councils.[13] The couple might easily have been pressured to renounce its scandal-

11. King Louis VI restored these rights to the bishopric of Laon in 1121. Guibert is clearly writing before that year.

12. Enguerrand I de Boves became lord of Coucy in 1086. Through his first marriage with Ade de Marle, by whom he had two sons, Thomas and Robert, he was also lord of Marle. He later abducted the wife of the count of Namur, Sibylle de Porcien, and subsequently married her. To expiate this foul deed, he left on the First Crusade, where he performed heroically. In the *Gesta Dei per Francos* 8.6, Guibert describes him as "a man who stood out by his physical appearance and his eloquence, would that he had done so by his piety!" ("vir sicut forma et eloquentia, utinam sic religione! conspicuus.") (*PL* 156.813).

13. No specific church council had condemned this marriage, but adulterous marriages in general had been condemned by many councils. The early twelfth century is very explicitly a period when the church "attempted to complete the integration of Christian marriage within the universal edicts of the earthly city," steering a course between allowing the marriage of clerics (Nicolaism) and radically rejecting marriage as evil. See Georges Duby, *Love and Marriage in the Middle Ages*, trans. Jane Dannett (Chicago: University of Chicago Press, 1994), 15–16.

ous behavior if the bishop (whom I've mentioned already) had not been softened by his kinship with the husband and by the woman's deft flatteries. Bishop Enguerrand's weak response encouraged these adulterous embraces and gave secret absolution to something that had been generally proscribed and publicly excommunicated. Oh shame! Surely this couple, whom he falsely gave assurance of absolution, never dared to presume themselves absolved.

It is written that "from the serpent's root will come forth an adder"[14] That is, evils once encouraged lead to something worse. Who can say how many murders were committed in the county of Porcien by the enraged baron whose wife had been taken from him? For this Countess of Namur was the daughter of Roger, Count of Porcien, his youngest child, to be precise. Dispossessing the sons and daughters whom he had had from a woman far nobler, Roger had married his last daughter, whose mother was a woman of lower rank, to a man from Lorraine named Count Godfrey of Namur.[15] The daughter's dowry was the county of Namur, her mother having insisted that her stepchildren be excluded from the inheritance.

While her husband, Count Godfrey, was off at war against some enemies of his, he had ordered his wife to remain at the castle of Tournes, in Porcien.[16] Her husband had been fulfilling his marriage debt far less than she would have liked. Whether or not this figured into her behavior, one thing is sure: she would never have gotten involved in such a monstrous public scandal had she not descended there, one step at a time, through clandestine acts of wickedness, especially considering that when she first came to her husband she was already pregnant from intercourse with another man. Everyone is in such agreement about her past debaucheries that I am ashamed to tell about them or even to remember them.

Godfrey was a very handsome young man, but Enguerrand, whom she took as a lover, was very old. War soon broke out between these two barons and raged with such intensity that any of Enguerrand's men who happened to fall into the hands of the Lorrainer was either hanged on a gibbet or had his eyes put out or his feet cut off. The results are still

14. Guibert is quoting Isa. 14.29: "de radice enim colubri egreditur regulus," with a slight alteration.

15. Roger de Porcien's daughter Sibylle, whom Guibert never mentions by name, had married Godfrey, the future count of Namur, around 1088.

16. This is no doubt Thour, about fifteen miles east of Laon.

plainly visible today to anyone visiting the county of Porcien. I was told by a man who witnessed that butchery that in a single day about twelve men were captured and hanged. Some of the leading figures of Porcien were either intermediaries or instigators of this adulterous affair, and their names lived in infamy while they were alive and after they died. When Vulcan's fires fail to satisfy Venus she proceeds to Mars: the heat of lust, that is, boils over into cruelty. Who can recount the lootings and the burnings that were committed everywhere, not to mention the other misfortunes that this kind of calamity gives rise to? Anyone attempting to recount these events is struck speechless.

So the lord bishop Enguerrand in his madness gave his absolution to that diabolical union.[17] Many other things might be reported about his ways that were better left unreported. His most notable characteristic is that no awareness of sin toward God ever made him remorseful. Toward the end he fell sick, which did not restrain him in any of his pleasures. A sudden stroke brought him to the dark threshold of death and robbed him of his ability to speak coherently. Those who were administering to him forced confession, anointing, and communion upon him without his consciously requesting them. As he lay awaiting death with paralyzed tongue and eyes staring blankly, the other Enguerrand showed up, being bound to the bishop by his wicked absolution. While the last rites were being administered the clerics had prevented Enguerrand de Boves from entering the room, treating him as though he were excommunicated. But the latter cried out in tears: "My lord bishop, it's me, Enguerrand, your kinsman." And the bishop, who had been unable to ask for confession, or anointment, or communion, threw his arm around his vassal's neck and pulled him forward as to kiss him. Everyone present was shocked to see this happen, and from then on nothing but delirious utterances came from the bishop's lips until he breathed his last. The very woman for whose love he had acted so shamefully, the Countess of Namur, herself told this story openly many times, thus proving that the evil that he had committed in life now lay over him like a tombstone of wickedness. Take notice, therefore, that "the heavens will reveal his iniquity, and the earth

17. Guibert is suggesting for the second time in this chapter that the scandal might not have been so protracted had bishop Enguerrand of Laon not been "softened" by his blood ties with Enguerrand de Boves and by the charms of Sibylle, countess of Namur: "Facili utique instanti flagitium abjurassent, nisi praefatum et mariti consanguinitas et foeminae adulantis dolositas mollivissent."

will rise up against him,"[18] and they shall be found displeasing to those whom they had attempted to please by disgraceful means.

4

Enguerrand's succession. I defend Gaudry's nomination at a papal inquiry

After Enguerrand's death his church was vacant for two years, until we finally convened to elect a bishop.[19] Among those present was that same Enguerrand de Boves, who had previously intervened to dissuade the king when he had tried to disqualify Bishop Enguerrand's election on grounds of the latter's immoral ways. Clearly, he was using all his energy and eloquence to ensure the election of a bishop who would be obligated to him (the king and the clergy gave him their full confidence as a bishop-maker) and who would not dare contest his marital situation.[20] To the city's ruin, and to the detriment of the

18. Guibert is here quoting Job 20.27.

19. The see of Laon was vacant from 1104 to 1106. This passage provides a good idea of the composition of an episcopal electoral body. In an election involving the *clerus* and the *populus*, one finds highly influential members of the *populus* like Enguerrand de Boves. As to the *clerus*, it involved members of the regular and the secular clergy.

20. Guibert's text reads: "Inter quos affuit ipse idem Ingelrannus, qui et superiorem episcopum [the late bishop Enguerrand], cum eum rex pro suis levitatibus a pontificiis abjurasset, sua apud eundem regem interpellatione crearat. Ad hoc nitebatur plane animus et sermo ejus [Enguerrand de Boves] ut, qui eligeretur episcopus, sibi esset obnoxius, cui potissimum in efficiendo episcopo rex faveret et clerus, et ideo minus adversari auderit conjugio ejus." Benton's translation, "The king and the clergy most strongly favored one candidate, who as a consequence of the favor would be less likely to dare to oppose the king's [*sic*] union" (*Self and Society*, 151), cannot be justified. Since Guibert has spent a good part of the preceding chapter discussing Enguerrand de Boves's adulterous union with Sibylle de Porcien, which bishop Enguerrand had accepted, the main clause, "Ad hoc nitebatur . . . ut, qui eligeretur episcopus, sibi esset obnoxius, . . . et ideo minus adversari auderit conjugio ejus," can only refer to Enguerrand de Boves's striving to elect a bishop who will not interfere with his own marriage. Guibert never explicitly mentions King Philippe's adulterous union with Bertrade de Montfort in the *Monodiae*, but he does so in the *Gesta Dei*.

whole province, they elected a certain Gaudry, who was chancellor to the king of England,[21] and who, it was reported, possessed gold and silver in abundance.

Before this election, two archdeacons of the church of Laon, Gautier and Ebal, had been raised to the episcopal seat by competing groups of electors. But a judgment of the Apostolic See disqualified them both. Gautier had always behaved more like a soldier than a churchman, while Ebal was more than an average womanizer. Once these two were eliminated, a third candidate, another shining light of the church,[22] came to the court with the intention of slipping into the episcopal See, and while seeming to plead on behalf of someone else he drew attention to himself as a candidate for the bishopric. Why beat around the bush? He promised the king an abundance of gifts, and bloated with his own expectations he embraced the hope and the promise of wealth. But wealth eluded him. He returned home, expecting his installation by the king's legates on the following Sunday. God, however, sets traps for people like this and casts down those who raise themselves up. This arrogant man was stricken with a fatal illness; and on the day he saw himself receiving the cathedraticum[23] from the clergy and the people it was only his dead corpse that was placed in the church. I am told his body had hardly been brought in when it burst open, and a stinking liquid flowed out of it into the middle of the choir. But let us come back to what we were discussing before I digressed.

21. Gaudry became chancellor to King Henry I Beauclerc in 1102. According to a text in Ordericus Vitalis's *Ecclesiastical History of England and Normandy,* Gaudry received the diocese of Laon as a reward for his capture of the king's enemy, Robert Curthose, duke of Normandy, at the battle of Tinchebray, in September 1106 (ed. G. Forrester [London: Henry G. Bohn; rpt., New York: AMS Press, 1968], 3.380). "Public opinion," comments Forester, "revolted at seeing a mere clerk attached to the court, who was not even a subdeacon, raised to the episcopal and ducal see of Laon" (380n.3). The uprising of the Laon commune was already present in this unprecedented nomination.

22. Guibert curiously abstains from naming this mysterious candidate to the bishopric of Laon, whom he characterizes, no doubt ironically, as "ecclesiae candor" ("the shining light of his church"). He clearly dislikes this venal beacon of virtue, and describes the fate of his corpse in the terms reserved for the traitor Judas in Acts 1.18: "crepuit medius/ et diffusa sunt omnia viscera eius."

23. The "cathedraticum" mentioned here was the annual tithe paid the bishop by the churches of his diocese as a sign of their subjection (Labande, *Guibert de Nogent,* 283n.6).

Gaudry, whom I've already mentioned, was elected by clerics who were completely misled by the hope of getting rich. At the instigation of Enguerrand de Boves and of others who added to his criminal dishonesty, the king of England was asked, at Rouen, quite against all the canons,[24] to allow Gaudry to leave his court. Gaudry could hardly be more assured of being elected; but having no ecclesiastical title and having received no holy orders except those of a cleric, he used his influence to be ordained a subdeacon immediately and to receive a canon's stall in the church of Rouen, though until this time he had been nothing more than a soldier.

When everyone had approved Gaudry's nomination, the only dissent came from Master Anselm,[25] whose knowledge of the liberal arts made him a beacon for all of France and, indeed, the whole Latin world. Anselm had learned from irrefutable sources what sort of man Gaudry was, whereas we, perhaps in spite of ourselves, continued to favor an unknown entity. Some of us, to be sure, didn't like Gaudry, but we wrongly feared others who outranked us, so we followed the lead of the powerful.[26]

Gaudry arrived at Laon, where he was received with the emptiest sort of pomp. Soon afterward he requested that we accompany him to Rome, persuading Abbot Adalbéron of Saint-Vincent (a very cultured man who came originally from Soissons), the Abbot of Ribemont (also a very cultured man), and me (the youngest of the group in both age and learning) to go with him, all expenses paid.[27] So we left; but by the time we reached Langres we learned that Pope Pascal had left Rome shortly

24. It was contrary to canon law, "contra canones," to seek a candidate for ecclesiastical office among courtiers (Benton, Self and Society, 154n.12).

25. Master Anselm [Ansellus], who died in 1117, was a student of Saint Anselm of Bec and one of the leading figures of the school of Laon. Among his pupils were Guillaume de Champeaux, Gilbert de la Porrée, and especially Abelard, who came to study under him at Laon around 1113. In the Historia Calamitatum, Abelard contemptuously calls him a "fire [that] filled his house with smoke but did not light it up; he was a tree in full leaf which could be seen from afar, but on closer and more careful inspection proved to be barren." Anselm of Laon was in fact a greater scholar than Abelard allows for; but he was a traditionalist who relied on authority and who must have been intimidated by Abelard's dialectical prowess. With his brother Raoul and other members of the Laon school, Anselm produced the Glossa Ordinaria on the Bible (Benton, Self and Society, 152n.6).

26. Passages like this one reveal the essentially timorous but sincere nature of Guibert's character: "aliorum male timidi, qui nobis praeerant, potentias sectabamur."

27. Adalbéron, abbot of Saint-Vincent (of Laon), Mainard, abbot of Ribemont, and Guibert, abbot of Nogent were considered three powerful figures in Gaudry's attempt to convince Pope Pascal II to approve his designation to the bishopric of Laon.

before and was now close to the borders of that diocese.[28] We stayed in Langres for eight days. When the lord pope reached Dijon, the clergy of Laon, a great number of which the bishop-elect had brought with him,[29] went out to greet him; and once the pope was settled in Dijon they spoke to him in favor of their man. With many there to inform him, the pope was soon well acquainted with all the facts of the case, and he promised to do everything he could to satisfy their request. Their contention was that the election was within the law so long as exceptions were made for certain provisions that Anselm had brought to the pope's attention. But members of the curia, especially his close advisers, were delighted to discover how rich Gaudry was and supported his cause, singing his praises. It is customary for people to become compliant when the word "gold" is mentioned.

The day after the pope's reception into the city of Langres he opened a discussion on the subject of our election. In his presence I read the written report on the election, which was immoderate in its praise of Gaudry's life and character. The pope then asked those abbots among us who were present, as well as a few priests from the church of Laon who had accompanied the bishop-elect, to stay; and he began questioning us about the report that had just been read. The assembly was filled with high-ranking people: Italian and French bishops, cardinals, and other very learned men.

The pope began by asking us why we had elected someone we did not previously know. Since none of the priests was answering—some of them hardly knew the rudiments of grammar—he turned toward the abbots. I was sitting between the other two abbots, both of whom kept silent but began urging me to speak. Being so young I felt shy, and I feared I would be thought rash for daring to speak in such a place and about a matter such as this.[30] In fact I was so shy I hardly dared open my mouth.

28. Pascal II, originally a monk of the abbey of Cluny, succeeded Urban II in 1099. The chief purpose of his trip to France during the winter months of 1107 was to gain the approval of King Philippe I of France against the German emperor Henry V, in the Investiture Controversy. He arrived at Langres on 24 February 1107 (Benton, *Self and Society*, 153n.7)

29. Besides Adalbéron, Mainard, and Guibert, Gaudry had brought with him "plurimam turbam" of clerics from Laon, whose names we shall unfortunately never know.

30. Guibert describes himself as "meae timidus juventutis." He was, in fact, about fifty-two, but the youngest, no doubt, of the three abbots who had accompanied Gaudry. Related in indirect discourse, the ensuing dialogue is one of the most endearing moments of Guibert's account of himself. In spite of a personal shyness to which he has

The discussion was being conducted not in our native French tongue but in Latin.[31] Finally I spoke up, giving full expression to what was on the tip of my tongue and in my mind. I gave fitting answers to the pope's questions, speaking in carefully weighed and well-phrased sentences not veering too far from the truth. I said that, indeed, we had not known Gaudry from personal experience before his election but that we had been favorably impressed by the good things that had been said in his behalf.

The pope tried to put off this argument by citing the testimony of the gospel: "He who saw it has borne witness."[32] Then, setting that point aside he objected (not in the plainest of terms) that we had elected someone from the royal court. Upon which I thought it pointless to keep arguing back and forth, and I conceded that I had no response to this argument. The pope was very pleased with this statement.

The pope's level of education was not equal to his high office.[33] Though he had seemed quite pleased by my words I felt that my evasive circumlocutions had not really answered his first question. So I changed the drift of my argument and began talking about the pressing needs of the church of Laon adding, to be brief, that no one there was qualified for the rank of bishop. The pope then asked what orders Gaudry had received. I answered that he was a subdeacon. Then he asked in what

---

already referred several times, Guibert is able to overcome his inhibitions, to speak like a mature man in the pope's presence. Passages of third-person narrative like this one perhaps reveal more about Guibert's personality than many passages of first-person discourse wherein he speaks about the "I."

31. Guibert addressed the pope "non materno sermone, sed literis." Pope Pascal II being Italian, Guibert spoke to him in Latin. The silence of the other clerics from Laon is due presumably to their ignorance of Latin ("quidam elementa vix norant"). The silence of the other two abbots, Adalbéron and Mainard, is more mysterious, especially in view of the fact that Guibert described both as *literati*.

32. John 19.35: "et qui vidit testimonium perhibuit / et verum est eius testimonium." The Pope is implying that Guibert's testimony, not being that of an eyewitness, is unreliable.

33. "Erat enim minus quam suo competeret officio literatus." *Literatus* is a term used by Guibert to measure the intellectual stature of several of his contemporaries. Abbot Adalbéron of Saint-Vincent has just been described a few pages earlier as "virum . . . bene literatum," and the abbot of Ribemont as "non sine literis." It seems all the more mysterious that these two chose to remain silent in the pope's presence. Guibert no doubt gives the appropriate clue when he suggests, at the end of the papal audience, that he and Adalbéron came to the papal investigation already bearing some of Gaudry's bribes.

church Gaudry had served. Here I hesitated, not wishing to lie; but prodded by my colleagues I answered "in the church of Rouen"; but to be truthful I added, "only recently." Finally the pope asked whether Gaudry was a legitimate child, having clearly heard that he was a bastard.[34] On this matter I proved firmer than on the others, having no doubt about the matter. The pope asked: "Have you any proof?" To which I answered: "On other matters I will be silent, but on this one I can confidently assure you that he is legitimate on both sides of the family."[35] My lord the pope then withdrew his objections, seeing them well refuted, as he had his earlier ones. The reason the pope had raised this series of objections was not to bar Gaudry from being elected but to see if Master Anselm, who was present and had secretly made all these charges against Gaudry, would make them to his face.

Now Master Anselm had by this time gotten a better idea of what the members of the papal curia—I won't say the pope himself—wanted and was finding it hard to pry the club out of Hercules's hands. Seeing these members of the curia arguing with each other Anselm, as a good schoolman, refrained from contradicting either my lord the pope or—if I may say so in jest—even me. The whole discussion came to an abrupt halt, and the bishop-elect was ushered into our midst to have the powers of bishop conferred on him by the pope. When the assembly had been dissolved and the pope was gone, a group of cardinals came up to me and, very excited, they said: "We were very pleased by what you said." My lord God, you know very well that they were complimenting me less because I had been eloquent than because they hoped very much they

34. Though an exceptionally qualified subdeacon might qualify for the office of bishop, illegitimate birth was a bar to entering orders. The proscription was intended principally to discourage concubinage among clerics by barring their "illegitimate," therefore unrecognized, offspring from holy orders. See "Bâtard," in *Dictionnaire de droit canonique* (Paris: Letouzey & Ané, 1937), 2.254: "C'est en s'efforçant de faire disparatre l'habitude du mariage chez les clercs ou plutôt de leur concubinage—puisque leur mariage est considéré comme nul—que l'Eglise fut amenée à frapper les clercs en premier lieu et par contre-coup tous les enfants naturels. N'était-ce pas le plus sûr moyen d'avoir une action efficace sur la conduite des parents que de les atteindre dans leurs affections les plus chères? L'aversion de l'Eglise pour les relations charnelles hors mariage devait conduire à refuser à tous les bâtards l'accès aux ordres sacrés."

35. Guibert answers, literally, that Gaudry is "neque . . . nothus, neque spurius." In his *Etymologiae* 9.5.23, Isidore of Seville defines *nothus* as one having a noble father and a non-noble mother (for example, a concubine), and *spurius* as one born of a noble mother and a non-noble father.

would receive some of that Rouen money that Gaudry had come loaded with. In fact, Abbot Adalbéron of Saint-Vincent and I were both carrying on us some twenty pounds of that money, which may have fulfilled some of their expectations. That's why they were so enthusiastic in supporting Gaudry and his backers.[36]

The cardinals withdrew. Then Peter, a Cluniac monk and one of the pope's chamberlains (the one who had made the acquaintance of Gaudry at Rouen when we were asking the English king to release him), came up to me secretly and said: "Now that my lord the pope has received your testimony in favor of the person you want and has lent you a generous ear, you must suggest to your bishop-elect that he is to obey my lord the pope's orders in all matters and defer to him in such a manner as to make him willing to listen to you in the future, whether for Gaudry or for anybody else." Talk about coating the lip of a poisoned cup with honey! For what could be better than obeying the pope's orders, and what could be worse than having to pay other people for a favor that is God-given? Myself, I found the whole idea of being an intermediary in such a negotiation abhorrent.[37]

When Gaudry was consecrated bishop in the church of Saint Rufus at Avignon,[38] the Gospel text proved to be a bad omen. It read: "A sword will pierce through your own soul."[39] At Langres, however, it had

36. Gaudry admits, quite ingenuously, that both he and Abbot Adalbéron arrived at the papal interview each carrying twenty pounds given them by Gaudry, in anticipation of bribes that may (*forsitan*) have been distributed after the interview to expectant cardinals. Guibert's disarming admission strengthens the credibility of this entire narrative, but it is hardly consistent with Guibert's condemnation of "philargyria" as the most pernicious of monastic vices (1.21).

37. Guibert's text reads: "Ecce mel illitum per ora virosi poculi." Unlike Labande (*Guibert de Nogent*, 292n.3), who sees here an allusion to *Metamorphoses* 8.670, I fail to detect any Ovidian flavor to this passage. I see nothing in common between Guibert's conversation with Peter the Cluniac monk and the simple, rustic meal set out by the aged couple Philemon and Baucis for Jupiter and Mercury, with "cups hollowed out, coated with scented wax." Cf. Ovid, *Metamorphoses*, trans. Frank Justus Miller (Cambridge, Mass.: Harvard University Press, 1977).

38. According to Benton (*Self and Society*, 156n.1), the place of Gaudry's consecration is problematic. While the Labande Latin text reads "Avinione" here, the Dachéry text (*PL* 156.914) reads "apud Sanctum Ruffum de Anione." Dachéry adds a note (*PL* 156.1166), clarifying that what is meant here is the monastery of canons regular of Saint-Ruf at Avignon ("Avenione monasterium canonicorum regularum"). Why Gaudry was consecrated bishop at Avignon, so far from Langres, remains a mystery.

39. Luke 2.35: "et tuam ipsius animam pertransiet gladius."

been different. Once he had received papal approval he had gone up in procession to the altar of Mamertus the martyr while the clergy was singing "Te Deum laudamus," and opened the text of the Gospel to find some prophetic omen. The first verse he had fallen on he had applied to himself, namely: "Woman, behold your son,"[40] and he was soon proudly repeating it everywhere he went.

In his speech, as well as his behavior, Gaudry proved remarkably unstable and shallow. He loved talking about military matters, dogs, and hawks, as he had learned to do while in England. One day he was on his way to dedicating a church, and I was riding with him with another cleric, a pleasant young man. All of a sudden the bishop caught sight of a peasant holding a lance; and while he was still wearing the mitre he had worn for the consecration he snatched the lance from the peasant's hands, gave his horse the spurs and went charging at some imaginary target. The cleric and I both cried out (he in French and I in Latin verse): "The mitre and the lance do not sit well together."[41]

Within a short time he had squandered the fortune in English money, cups, and vessels, which he had made by dishonest means. Master Anselm (already well-known to the reader), who once traveled to England with Gaudry, has assured me that when they arrived in English territory they were battered with complaints from every side, some Englishmen clamoring for the return of their precious vessels, some for the return of their money. Anselm immediately understood that the wealth that Gaudry was so grandly showing off had been stolen, not honestly earned.

5

The murder of Gérard de Quierzy

About three years after his consecration Gaudry gave his contemporaries an unmistakable sign of his true character. There was a noble of Laon

40. John 19.26: "mulier ecce filius tuus."
41. "Non bene conveniunt, nec in una sede morantur/ Cidaris et lancea." Guibert is modifying to his purpose Ovid's comment about Jupiter, who is about to turn himself into a bull for the purpose of seduction: "non bene conveniunt nec in una sede morantur maiestas et amor" (*Met.* 2.846).

named Gérard, a very energetic man, who was warden[42] of the young women's monastery in that town. Though he was short and looked rather scrawny, Gérard was quick-witted, a fast-talker, and so strong at handling arms that he was feared and respected by just about everybody throughout the provinces of Laon, Soissons, and Noyon. Though he had a reputation for integrity far and wide on occasion he could be bitingly sarcastic toward those around him, though never toward well-intentioned people. It so happened that he began secretly maligning, then openly attacking the countess whom I have mentioned earlier.[43] In doing so he was acting very stupidly since doing so meant he was also attacking Enguerrand, the countess's lover, who had previously used his enormous fortune to help Gérard. Moreover Gérard had been on too intimate terms with the countess before his marriage. They had been lovers for a long time before Gérard had succeeded in breaking the chains of his passion by taking a wife. Both women then began to hurl insults at each other. They were both fully acquainted with each other's previous debaucheries and could therefore be quite lurid when they spoke of each other. The countess would fly into a rage, like a woman scorned, when she spoke of the other's husband, or of his wife, knowing that this other woman was also spewing insults at her. More venomous than any serpent, the countess's determination to ruin Gérard by any means grew with every day that went by.

Because God places a stumbling block in the way of those who sin intentionally, the occasion arose for Gérard to meet with destruction. A dispute arose between Gérard and Bishop Gaudry, and Gérard made some unfortunate remarks about the bishop and his associates. The bishop did not say anything, but he did not take these remarks well; and along with his companions and most of the nobles of the city he plotted Gérard's undoing. They all took an oath to come to one another's aid to achieve this end, being joined by a few very rich women who also participated in the plot.

Now Gaudry, driven by the worst possible motive, left the whole business in the hands of the conspirators and headed for the tombs of the

42. As *castellanus,* or *avoué,* of the Benedictine monastery of Saint-Jean de Laon, Gérard de Quierzy played the role of warden, or counselor, in the secular affairs of the nuns who were housed there. Gérard had served with distinction during the First Crusade (Benton, *Self and Society,* 157n.1).

43. Sibylle de Porcien, wife of Enguerrand, count of Amiens, and later mistress to Enguerrand de Boves before marrying him, was first mentioned in 3.2.

Apostles. For you know very well, Lord, that he was not at all interested in making a pilgrimage to the Apostles' tombs but in letting his absence make it seem that his hands were clean. So Gaudry left for Rome around the feast of Saint Martin[44] and stayed until he had learned that the man he hated had been murdered. (Good people did not find Gérard hateful, but bad people did.)

Here is how the deed was done. On Friday in the week of the Epiphany,[45] Gérard rose from his bed by the faint light of dawn and made his way to the cathedral of the Blessed Mary. One of the nobles belonging to the conspiracy came up to tell him of a dream he had had that very night which had left him quite terrified. He said he felt as if two bears had wanted to tear his liver (or his lungs, I'm not sure which) right out of his body. But alas! How sad it is to say that Gérard had not received the sacrament. In fact he had been banned from communion, for the following reason. A monk residing at Barisis Saint-Amand had invited to his monastery two young boys who spoke only German, with the intention of teaching them French. Now Barisis, along with the domains attached to it, was under Gérard's protection.[46] When he saw that these boys had fine manners and deduced that they were of anything but poor background, Gérard kidnapped them and held them for ransom. Along with the sum of money they had agreed upon, the boys' mother sent Gérard a long fur tunic made of ermine and commonly called a *reno*. Gérard was wearing that tunic, with a purple mantle over it, that morning when, with a few companions, he went to the church on horseback.

Gérard went into the church and paused before the image of the crucified Lord, while his companions wandered about looking at various altars to the saints. The conspirators' agents, who had been watching, went to the bishop's quarters to announce to Gaudry's inner circle that Gérard of Quierzy (as they called him, since he was lord of that castle) had come to the church to pray. Rorigon, the bishop's brother, and one of his companions snatched up their swords, hid them under their cloaks, and going by way of the ambulatory surrounding the choir of the basilica, they reached the spot where Gérard was praying. He was leaning against

44. Around 11 November 1110, according to Labande (*Guibert de Nogent*, 298n.3), who assumes that Gaudry was crowned in March 1107 and that Guibert means three years after Gaudry's ordination. Undertaking a pilgrimage under false pretenses was not uncommon, even for a medieval bishop.

45. 13 January 1111.

46. Gérard was *castellanus*, or guardian, of both Barisis and Saint-Jean of Laon.

a column, called a pillar, at a few columns' distance from the pulpit, toward the middle of the church. At that early hour when the morning was still dark and there were few people to be seen in the vast church, the conspirators approached Gérard from behind as he prayed. The straps of his cloak were thrown back, and he held his palms together over his chest.[47] One of the conspirators seized Gérard's cloak from behind and wrapped it around him so tightly that he could not move his hands. The bishop's steward held him tight in this position and said to him: "We've got you!" Ferocious as usual, Gérard turned his eye toward him (for he had only one eye)[48] and shouted: "Get out of here, you dirty bastard!" The steward then shouted to Rorigon: "Strike!" Rorigon took aim with his sword from Gérard's left side and struck him between the nose and the brow. Gérard was badly wounded. All he said was: "Take me where you want to." The two men then stabbed him several times and pressed down on him hard. In desperation Gérard cried out with all his strength: "Holy Mary, help!" With these words he was thrown into his final agony.

Two archdeacons of the church, Gautier and Guy, were in this conspiracy together with the bishop. Guy was also the church's treasurer and had a little house located on the side of the church. Two servants presently came out of the house and joined in the carnage. For the conspirators' sacrilegious oath had clearly stated that if the bishop's courtiers deemed it necessary, reinforcements would be despatched from that very house. The servants, inflicting further wounds on Gérard, slashed his neck and his legs. Gérard's pain was now at its zenith as he lay moaning in the middle of the basilica. The few members of the clergy who were in the choir, and a few very old women who wandered about praying and murmuring, were paralyzed with horror. No one dared voice the slightest protest.

When the deed was done, these two carefully picked soldiers went back to the episcopal palace accompanied by the city's leading nobles (who were now proving how treacherous they were), and were presently joined by a few archdeacons. Then the royal provost, a very clever man by the name of Yves, assembled the king's men and those of Saint-John's abbey, of which Gérard, the murdered man, had been warden. With

---

47. Guibert states four times that Gérard was in prayer ("orabat . . . orantem . . . Orabat . . . inter orandum"). In doing so he intensifies the dramatic pathos of the scene.
48. Gérard had lost an eye at the siege of Jerusalem in 1099.

them he attacked, plundered, and set fire to the conspirators' houses and expelled them from the city.[49] The archdeacons and the nobles followed Gérard's assassins wherever they went as a sign of their loyalty to the absent bishop Gaudry.

6

The reconsecration of the cathedral. I preach reconciliation. Gaudry returns

In the meantime Gaudry remained in Rome, as if he were continuing to enjoy the pope's presence; but he kept his ear attuned to see if some favorable news might not reach him from France. At last he learned that his prayers had been answered. It did not escape the pope's attention that a great crime had been committed in a great church; but Gaudry had a talk with him and, using gifts as a means of flattery, managed to dispel any suspicion that he had been involved in this murder in any way. So Gaudry returned from Rome more pleased than ever.

A church that a criminal hand had so flagrantly violated needed to be reconciled;[50] so Hubert, bishop of Senlis, who had been suspended from his functions on grounds of simony some time before, was brought in to perform the ceremony.[51] The dean of the church, Master Anselm, and the canons all urged me to use this gathering of people and clergy to

49. The *prévôt* was the king's officer in Laon, which was both a royal and an episcopal city. The scene highlights the state of tension and latent war between the king and the bishop. The king's men may have been noble vassals or serfs. The "men of Saint John's abbey" were no doubt serfs of the abbey.

50. A church in which a murder had been committed was "violated," and in need of purification and reconsecration according to a specific Roman rite: "Ecclesia . . . quam adeo violatam constat opere." (Labande, *Guibert de Nogent*, 306n.1).

51. Hubert was bishop of Senlis from 1099 to 1115. He had temporarily lost his office in 1103 on charges of simony. Guibert seems to have an ax to grind here in making it seem as if Hubert were still suspended when in fact he had already been reinstated at the Council of Troyes in 1104 (Benton, *Self and Society*, 161n.1).

deliver a sermon to the people about the calamity that had just occurred.[52] Here is the general tenor of what I said:

"Save me, O God," I intoned, "for the waters have come up to my
neck. I sink in deep mire and there is no foothold."[53] Even though you
have suffered all kinds of evils until now, the sword has *now come up to
your neck* [your very soul]. You are now *sunk in deep mire,* which means
that your sins have brought you to the limits of despair and ruin. And
there is no foothold there, because those whom you might have had re-
course to in your peril, the church authorities and the nobles, have seen
their honor and their strength crumble into ruin. If your bodies have
been crushed on occasion by the hostilities raging among you, yet your
souls were free; because the church, which had maintained its purpose,
which is to save you, rejoiced to see itself flourishing so and without
stain. Now the *waters* and the sword have *crept into the soul,* as tribulation
and discord have infiltrated and polluted what was holy. Now what dignity do you think this temple still holds for you, who are ignorant of
spiritual things, if it can no longer provide a physical sanctuary for those
who pray? Behold, God has hurled upon us the wrath of his indignation — indignation, and wrath, and tribulation — by the hand of his avenging angels. The *wrath of his indignation, the wrath born of his indignation.*
Indignation, as you know, is less than wrath. Did not God show righteous
indignation over your sins, when outside the city you constantly suffered
pillage, fire, and murder? Did he not show his wrath when wars from the
outside reached the inside of the city, when citizens began to be stirred
by mutual hatred, when after mutual provocations lords hurled themselves against burghers and burghers against lords, men from the abbey
against bishops' men, and vice versa, in unjustified hostility?[54] And when
neither *indignation* nor *wrath* convinced you to mend your ways, then God

52. It is a sign of the Abbot of Nogent's high standing in the area of Laon that, in
Gaudry's absence, Guibert should preside at this ceremony.

53. Ps. 69.2–3 (RSV). Guibert is quoting the Vulgate version (Ps. 68.2–3) with one
slight modification: "Salvum me fac Deus quoniam intraverunt aquae usque ad animam
meam/ infixus sum in limum profundi et non est substantia."

54. In this excellent commentary on a scriptural text, Guibert shows a remarkable
capacity for dramatic eloquence, punctuated with rhetorical questions, symmetrical an-
titheses, and neologisms (for example, *abbatiani / episcopani*): "civilia inter nos agitari
coeperunt odia, cum domini in burgenses, burgenses in dominos mutuis irritationibus
moverentur, cum abbatiani in episcopanos, episcopani in abbatianos indebito hoste de-
furerent?"

sent *tribulation* to your stubborn minds. For it was not just any church that was sullied with Christian blood, nor was it refugees from skirmishes that had begun elsewhere taking refuge in a church to be undone there; no, it was the most perverse intention, criminally carried out, which murdered a man praying before the image of Christ Jesus hanging on the cross.[55] It was not, I repeat, just any church, it was the most prosperous of the churches in Gaul, a church whose fame extends well beyond the boundaries of the Latin world. And who was the victim? Was it not a man whose illustrious birth should have commanded anyone's respect, whose frail body harbored a great heart, whose brilliant feats as a warrior were famous throughout France?[56] Now, therefore, the name of this place will forever be synonymous with crime and dishonor. If the horror of such a wretched deed does not trouble you deep in your hearts, if this violation of sanctity stirs no compunction in you, then you can be sure that God will surely "make a path for his anger" [Ps. 78.50]; he will let his resentment, which has been concealed until now, explode and destroy you openly. Is it possible you can imagine that God will spare your herds — your bodies, that is — from extinction when, because of your incorrigible ways, he did not even spare your souls from death? Since God's revenge comes step by step toward us like a funeral march, be sure that if you do not mend your ways swiftly under his scourge you will fall into the worst possible situation through the civil wars that have arisen among you."[57]

Pursuing my sermon, following a request from the clergy and with the assent of the people, I stated that the bishop who would reconcile the church should also be the one to excommunicate the murderers of the noble Gérard, the crime's instigators and accomplices, and any who

55. Guibert insists once again on the doubly sacrilegious nature of a murder committed in a church, and against a man in prayer before the crucified Christ: "ante Christi Jesu in cruce pendentis imaginem virum trucidavit orantem." As a churchman, Guibert is less intent on pointing his finger at the guilty ones than on dramatizing the violation of the church's essential purity.

56. Because of Gérard de Quierzy's tragic death in the position of *miles orans*, Guibert seems quite willing to forget that, just a few pages earlier, he described Gérard as a scandal-monger, extorter, and adulterer.

57. Guibert has most effectively used a classic ploy of ecclesiastical rhetoric in times of disaster: he presents the murder of Gérard as a sign of God's vengeance, and of greater wrath to come if his hearers do not mend their ways. Can one wonder that Guibert viewed the uprising of the Laon commune the following year as a fulfillment of his prophecy?

might have assisted them or granted them asylum. The excommunication was approved by a unanimous voice, after which the church was solemnly reconciled. The news of the excommunication did not delay in reaching the ears of the archdeacons and the nobles who had left the urban community for exile. The sermon I had preached and the excommunication that had been pronounced focused the hatred of all the exiles upon me. Gautier the archdeacon, in particular, loathed me more than anyone else. It was like hearing a tremendous clap of thunder that, thank God, is not followed by lightning. In secret he was against me, but openly he showed respect.[58]

Now back to my story. Bishop Gaudry came back from Rome armed with papal bulls and other texts. After Gérard's murder, the king, realizing full well that Bishop Gaudry was completely involved in the crime — an involvement he had attempted to disguise by his absence — had ordered the bishop's palace completely emptied of its supply of grain, wine, and lard.[59] While still in Rome Gaudry had, of course, been informed of this spoliation and of its motives. He therefore sent a letter to the king, who had taken measures to deprive him of his seat and his possessions. Letters were also addressed to his fellow bishops, to the abbots of his diocese, and to a few others.

I have already said that a bridge over the Ailette river sits on the boundary separating the dioceses of Laon and Soissons. It was here that the archdeacons and the nobles whom we had just excommunicated came out to greet Gaudry when he reached his own territory. Gaudry greeted them with so many tender kisses and embraces that he did not even see fit to visit the church of Blessed Mary, the very first church within the limits of his diocese, which by God's will we serve. Instead he spent a long time in the vicinity of the church talking to these people, whom he considered his only trustworthy friends. Then he continued his journey until he came to Coucy, where he spent the night in their company.

I was shocked by Gaudry's behavior and refrained completely from either greeting or meeting with him. Three days later, if I'm not mistaken, after he had succeeded (on the surface, in any case) in appeasing

58. Archdeacon Gautier, one remembers, was one of the instigators of the conspiracy to kill Gérard de Quierzy. Before Gaudry's election they had both been elected bishop by factions, but the Apostolic See had invalidated the election. Guibert had earlier said of Gautier that "non clericum, sed militarem se semper exhibuerat."

59. Invoking *ius spolii*, King Louis VI was already treating Gaudry as guilty of murder, and Gaudry's possessions as if he were already deposed.

the hatred that kept churning within him, he ordered me to come to him. Recent events, of course, had led his entourage to bring all sorts of accusations against me. When I showed up at his house and saw it full of murderers and excommunicated people I became enraged. He showed me a papal document and pressed me not to work to have him deposed. I promised to help him as much as I could, but only you, O God, know how insincere and hypocritical I was in speaking this way.[60] I could see how evil the man was by the way he chatted with people who had just been excommunicated from a church they had soiled in every possible way. There was Enguerrand—the same old Enguerrand of Coucy—sitting next to him; and that same old countess [Sibylle] who, the day before Gérard's murder, had sharpened the sword of his two assassins with her own tongue; and now they were showering Gaudry with compliments.

The king had given orders that Gaudry be kept away from Laon, but Gaudry, whose arrogance knew no bounds, kept threatening to enter the city with the military assistance of others. What had hardly been possible to the Caesars and the Augustuses he boasted he would accomplish by the force of arms. So he assembled a troop of knights on horseback and spent extraordinary amounts of money (crookedly amassed), but all this amounted to nothing. Having done nothing more, finally, than make a laughing stock of himself with so many auxiliaries, he negotiated peace, through intermediaries and by means of a huge bribe, for himself and his accomplices in Gérard's murder (the nobles of Laon, that is, and the two archdeacons) with Louis, the son of King Philip.[61]

Then Gaudry entered the city. Later on he held an assembly at Saint-Nicolas-aux-Bois,[62] and while he was celebrating Mass there he announced that he would excommunicate those who, after Gérard's murder, had damaged the conspirators' possessions and forced them to leave the city. When I heard him say this, I whispered to one of my fellow

60. Guibert's deeply emotional nature and his hatred of duplicity are evident again in this confrontation with Gaudry: "aestuavi . . . fallaciter, tu scis, Deus, et non ex corde spopondi." Like Augustine, his model, Guibert calls God, who sees all things, to witness his deepest feelings when he is forced to repress them publicly.

61. Louis VI, son of Philippe I, had been associated with his father's rule since 1100. He was sole ruler of the French kingdom from 1108 to 1137.

62. A Benedictine abbey about eight miles from Laon. Guibert calls the assembly a "conventiculum," which, in the language of Augustine and Cyprian, would have connoted an illegal assembly held by heretics (Labande, *Guibert de Nogent*, 314n.1).

abbots sitting next to me: "Did you ever hear of anything so preposterous? Instead of excommunicating the people who polluted his church with their wicked crime, here he is avenging himself against people who rightly wanted to punish the murderers!" When Gaudry saw me whispering, being the type of person afraid of anyone with a clear conscience, he suspected I was talking about him. "What are you saying, my lord abbot?" he asked. Then Gautier the archdeacon intervened, even before he had permission to speak, and said: "Go on, my lord, with what you were saying. The lord abbot was talking about something else."[63]

Gaudry then excommunicated those who had attacked the accomplices of the sacrilegious murderers, an act that was passionately denounced by the clergy and the people. For a long time, the city and the whole diocese resented the bishop for delaying the excommunication of Gérard's murderers. At last, sensing that he was an object of suspicion and loathing to everyone, Gaudry excommunicated the perpetrators of the deed along with their accomplices. Moreover, he had promised big monetary rewards to the king's counselors who had taken his defense, and that of the murderers' accomplices before the king, so now that he was beginning to go back on his promises you can well imagine the insults he heard in public. None of Gaudry's supporters dared enter the royal court so long as Gaudry did not ransom them with gold and money from the threat of violent death that was held above them. On the other hand Gaudry could not be accused by the church since it was known that he had been excused by the Apostolic See.

7

Chaos at Laon. The origins of the commune

A short time later Gaudry left for England to extract money from the king, his former master and old friend. While he was away Gautier the archdeacon and Guy, with the nobles of the city, devised the following plan. Laon had for a long time fallen into such chaos that no one,

---

63. Guibert's impression of Gautier was right: though Gautier was secretly against him, openly he showed respect ("Clam in me in promptu reverentia").

whether God or master, was held in any reverence. Without restraint, public authority was entangled in acts of pillaging and murder.[64] To begin with the worst instance, whenever the king came to Laon he was the first to be taxed shamefully, in spite of the respect due his royal rank. If his horses happened to be led to the drinking trough, morning or night, his servants would be beaten and the horses stolen.[65] Members of the clergy themselves were so exposed to humiliations that neither their persons nor their goods were spared. As the text says: "As with the people, so with the priest."[66] And what about the common folk? There wasn't a peasant coming into the city, unless he enjoyed the surest protection, who wasn't put into jail and put up for ransom or dragged into court on any pretext.

Let me give one example, which, if it had occurred among barbarians or Scythians, people who have no laws, it would have been considered the highest form of profanation. Every Saturday country people from various parts would come there to buy and sell. The citizens of Laon would carry around for sale in the marketplace vegetables, wheat, or other produce in bowls, platters, or other containers. They would offer these to the peasants, who were anxious to buy them; and once a price had been fixed and the purchaser had agreed to buy, the seller would say: "Come over to my house and I'll show you the full supply of this product I'm selling you; once you've seen it you can take it with you. So the peasant would follow and, once he had placed himself in front of the bin, the "honest" seller would lift and hold the lid and say: "Bend your head and shoulders over into the bin to be sure that this product is the

64. Labande (*Guibert de Nogent*, 317n.2) sees a similarity in this passage between Guibert's description of conditions at Laon and Cicero's description of events in Rome toward the end of the Republic. Guibert writes: "Urbi illi tanta ab antiquo adversitas inoleverat, ut neque Deus neque dominus quispiam inibi timeretur, sed ad posse et libitum cujusque rapinis et caedibus res publica misceretur." Cf. Cicero, *De lege agraria*, 2.91, 221: "Homines non inerant in urbe, qui malis contionibus, turbulentis senatus consultis iniquis imperiis rempublicam miscerent."

65. Laon being a royal city, it is difficult to imagine King Louis VI, who had not hesitated to dispossess the powerful Gaudry, remaining passive in the face of insults like these. Guibert is either exaggerating something he has heard, or, as Benton suggests (*Self and Society*, 166n.1), giving a "distorted reporting of something he has heard."

66. Isa. 24.2 (RSV). Guibert is giving an abbreviated version of the Vulgate: "et erit sicut populus sic sacerdos / et sicut servus sic dominus eius."

same as the one I showed you in the market." The buyer would then hoist himself up and lean over the edge of the bin on his stomach, with his head and arms dangling inside. Then the good vendor would come from behind, lift the unsuspecting peasant by the feet, dump him into the chest and keep him in this safe prison until he had paid a ransom.

These and similar things were happening in the city. The city leaders and their retainers were openly committing thefts, even armed robberies. No one was safe going out at night for he was sure to be robbed, captured, or killed.

Seeing these conditions, the clergy, the archdeacons, and the nobles were looking for a way to extort money from the people, so they sent them messengers and made the following proposition: in exchange for a good offer the people could obtain authorization to create a commune.[67] Now "commune" is a new and evil name for an arrangement by which all persons are subject to a yearly head tax that they owe their lords as a result of their servitude. If they have committed a crime they will be subject to a legal fine but all other forms of taxation that used to be inflicted on serfs are abolished. The people of Laon seized this opportunity to ransom themselves and contributed vast amounts of money to fill the gaping holes in these moneygrubbers' pockets. The moneygrubbers in turn were delighted to see so much money raining upon them so they confirmed under oath that they would respect the pact that had just been agreed upon.[68]

67. Guibert uses "communio" here. In subsequent passages he uses variants like "communia" and "communitas."

68. The entire section on the Laon commune has been quoted and commented at length by historians since Augustin Thierry's *Lettres sur l'histoire de France* (Paris: Garnier, 1828), 250–93. Writing in 1827 as a liberal "Republican" historian in a period of Bourbon Restoration, Thierry saw in the Laon uprising a distant predecessor of the French Revolution. Using Guibert as his almost exclusive source, Thierry establishes a more causal link than does Guibert between the inept and corrupt rule of successive Laon bishops and the creation of the commune. Thierry describes the Laon prelates as "elevated through favor" and "without merit," "displaying their power and their lavishness," and "imposing increasingly arbitrary taxes which were subsequently shared between the dignitaries of the cathedral church and the nobles" (250–51; cf. Ceri Crossley, *French Historians and Romanticism* [New York: Routledge, 1993], 62). It is difficult to sort out Guibert's thinking about the commune, which he initially calls "novum ac pessimum nomen," as if he were opposed to this show of popular strength as a potential threat. He then gives a very restricted definition of "communio" as the people's way of limiting arbitrary payments and servile dues to the clergy, the archdea-

Once this promise of mutual assistance had been signed between clergy, city leaders, and people, Bishop Gaudry returned from England with a large amount of money. He was angry with the instigators of this new movement and stayed away from the city for some time. Then he began to quarrel with his accomplice, Gautier the archdeacon, over questions pertaining to honor and glory. The archdeacon said some very unbecoming things about his bishop in connection with Gérard's murder. As for the bishop, I'm not sure what he was saying to others about this matter, but I do know what he told me one day when he was complaining about the archdeacon. "My lord Abbot," he said, "if Gautier ever brings accusations against me in some council or other, don't just shrug it off. Isn't this the same Gautier who was praising you publicly, while secretly sowing discord when you took leave of your monks to retire to Fly?[69] Isn't he the man who took up your cause in your presence, while in secret he was stirring me up against you?" With words like these Gaudry was luring me into making an enemy of this dangerous man.[70] He knew, of course, that he shared with Gautier the heavy charges that had been brought against him, and he was fearful and suspicious of universal condemnation.

Though Gaudry declared himself implacably hostile toward those who had sworn an oath to the commune and to the principal instigators, large offers of gold and silver quickly silenced his high-sounding rhetoric. He swore to maintain the rights of the commune of Laon, following the same

---

cons, and the nobles, whom Guibert seems to dismiss as greedy and insatiable ("maximos tot avarorum hiatibus obstruendis"). Guibert then goes on to describe the commune in essentially positive terms as a peace-making association: "Facta . . . inter clerum, proceres et populum mutui adjutorii conjuratione." As abbot of a prosperous, self-sufficient monastery at Nogent, some twenty miles from the scene of these events, Guibert should not have felt threatened by the Laon commune. Ultimately, his condemnation of the commune, like his condemnation of Gérard de Quierzy's murder, rests on his instinctive dislike for real or potential violence, and on his abhorrence for any violation of church property.

69. Guibert seems to want to conceal the fact that he once took leave of his community at Nogent to return to his earlier community at Saint-Germer de Fly. He has once before hinted at this incident (2.4), but the circumstances of his leaving were never clear.

70. Guibert is here showing how Gaudry is attempting to distance himself from Gautier the archdeacon, to prove that he was not involved in the plot to assassinate Gérard de Quierzy.

terms as they had been written down and sworn to in the city of Noyon and the town of Saint-Quentin.[71] A large bribe from the people also convinced the king to confirm this written text with an oath.[72] But, my God! after so many gifts from the people, after so many oaths sworn, who can count the judicial maneuvers that followed to overturn what they had sworn to respect? Indeed, once the yoke of oppressive taxation had been lifted from the serfs an attempt was made to return them to their former condition. The truth of the matter is that the bishop and the nobles nursed an implacable hatred against the burghers; and once Gaudry realized that he would not succeed in crushing this French show of liberty as had happened in Normandy or in England, he forgot his promises and gave in to his insatiable greed. Whenever one of the people was brought to court, he was judged not according to the law of God but according to his ability "to pay up" (if I may coin a phrase) and was robbed of everything he had.[73]

Accepting bribes usually subverts all forms of justice. So the money coiners, once they realized that they could always ransom their crooked operations with money, corrupted it with so much base metal that many people were reduced to the direst poverty. They made their coins of the cheapest bronze that, through dishonest practices, could immediately appear brighter than silver;[74] and, unfortunately, since the people were unsuspecting when they bought goods, whether cheap or expensive, they received nothing but the basest dross in exchange. Bishop Gaudry was rewarded for allowing this practice to continue, and so many people

71. Guibert does not necessarily mean that the wording of the text sworn to by Gaudry was identical to those sworn to by the communes of Noyon and Saint-Quentin, but simply that events in Noyon and Saint-Quentin constituted significant precedents.

72. Louis VI is said to have accepted many bribes. Since, however, the word *largitio* in medieval Latin can mean a charter of donation, Guibert is perhaps punning when he writes: "Compulsus et rex est largitione plebeia idipsum jurejurando firmare," meaning "The king was also constrained, by a popular charter of donation" (cf. Benton, *Self and Society*, 169n.6).

73. Guibert here begins describing the events, particularly the breach of a written agreement between the bishop and the nobles, which led to the uprising of the Laon burghers.

74. Benton (*Self and Society*, 169n.7) suggests that these dishonest practices ("pravis artibus") may have consisted both of cheapening the billon alloy with which the coins were made, and producing a "deceptively enriched silver surface" on the coin by heating it in an open flame, leaving a "silver-rich layer which will not flake off if the metal is then hammered."

became increasingly ruined not only within the diocese of Laon but far beyond its boundaries. When the bishop realized that he was power-less—and deservedly so—to sustain or improve the value of his own currency, which he had wickedly debased, he decreed that the small coins of Amiens (which were also much debased) would be current in the city for a while. He could in no way enforce this currency, however, so he decided to coin his own money and stamped it with a pastoral cross as his personal sign. Privately, of course, this was greeted with such laugh-ter and scorn that the bishop's currency was valued even less than the cheapest coinage. With the issuing of each of these new coins came an edict that attempted to prevent people from laughing at their dreadful designs. This gave Gaudry many opportunities to accuse people of carp-ing at his ordinances, and hence of exacting the heaviest of fines when-ever possible.

A monk by the name of Thierry, who in everyone's opinion was the worst sort of fellow, began bringing in great quantities of silver from his native town of Tournai and from Flanders. He converted all of this metal into the basest money of Laon and scattered it all over the surrounding province. By appealing to the greed of the rich with his hateful gifts he sowed lies, perjury, and misery while depriving his city of truth, justice, and prosperity. Never was the province more hurt by warfare, pillage, or fire. To think that the very walls of Rome had once held the old money of Laon in high favor! But "even a long-concealed impiety cannot be hidden forever and ends up piercing through the most artfully disguised modesty; for as light shines through glass, so does it radiate in the face."[75] What Gaudry had secretly managed to do to Gérard [de Quierzy], while pretending to have done nothing, he did some time later to another Gérard, giving this time clear proof of his cruelty.

This Gérard was some sort of manorial director, or bailiff, of the peasants who belonged to him. The bishop loathed him more than any-one else because he was rather favorably inclined toward the worst man I have ever known, Thomas of Marle, presumed to be the son of Enguer-rand de Boves (whom I've already mentioned). The bishop had him arrested, threw him into a dungeon in his episcopal palace and ordered

75. Guibert is perhaps quoting his own verses here. He also quotes these lines with a slight alteration in *Moralia in Genesin* (*PL* 156.73): "Arte superductum violat quando-que pudorem/ impietas contecta diu, nec passa [= clara] recondi. / Ut lux clara vitrum, sic penetrat faciem" (cf. Labande, *Guibert de Nogent*, 326n.2).

an African[76] in his service to put out his eyes. In behaving this way Gaudry was risking public reprimand, for he was reopening an old wound that he had inflicted against an earlier Gérard. Neither the people nor the clergy were unaware of a certain canon of the council of Toledo (if I am not mistaken) forbidding any bishop, priest, or cleric from killing, condemning to death, or mutilating anyone.[77] The news of this deed angered the king. I'm not sure it reached as far as the Holy See, but I do know that the pope suspended Gaudry from his office, and I suspect he did it for this very reason. Gaudry then piled offense upon offense by consecrating a church while under suspension. So he left for Rome, where he once again mollified my lord the pope with gifts, then was sent back to us with his privileges restored. God could see that masters and subjects alike were participating in a common iniquity of both deed and intention. Able to restrain his judgment no longer, God allowed pent up evils to break out into an open fury, which was motivated by human pride and crushed by divine vengeance, but only after it had sown tremendous devastation.

Gaudry had sworn to uphold the commune and had used bribes to coerce the king to do the same. Now, toward the end of Lent, during the holy days of the Lord's passion, the bishop had decided to destroy the commune with the help of the nobles and of a few clerics. To this pious duty he called the king, and on the eve of Good Friday,[78] which is the day of the Lord's Supper, he instructed the king and his whole entourage to break their oath after he had put his own foot in the trap. As I have said earlier it was on that very same day that his predecessor, Bishop Ascelinus, had betrayed his king.[79]

On the very day, then, when he should have been fulfilling the most glorious of episcopal functions—the consecration of the holy oil and the

76. This Aethiops, later called *maurus*, was probably a baptized slave in Gaudry's service.

77. The eleventh Council of Toledo (Canon 6) reads: "It is not permitted to those who are charged with the Lord's sacraments to inflict a death sentence ["judicium sanguinis"]. Nor should they presume, urged on by their own private deliberation, to condemn anyone to death by their own judgment, or to allow the mutilation of any member of any person to be carried out, whether by themselves, or by someone else" (text in Labande, *Guibert de Nogent,* 328n.3; my translation).

78. 18 April 1112. Guibert is being heavily ironic in calling the destruction of the commune a "pium officium," when the true pious duty of a king on Maundy Thursday was to wash the feet of the poor.

79. Cf. 3.1.

absolution of the faithful from their sins—Gaudry was not even seen
entering the church. He was scheming with the king's courtiers so that
after the commune was destroyed, the king would restore the city's laws
to their former state. But the burghers, fearing they too might be top-
pled, promised the king and his men four hundred pounds (or even more,
I'm not sure). As for Gaudry he asked the city leaders to accompany
him to speak with the king, and they in turn offered seven hundred
pounds. King Louis, Philippe's son, was a remarkable man[80] who seemed
well-suited only for royal majesty. A vigorous warrior, intolerant toward
inaction when conducting his affairs, fearless under fire, he was an excellent man, equal to his office in every way but one: he gave too much
attention and confidence to wicked, greedy people. This was his own
fault, and it led to his undoing and to the ruin of many, as this episode
and others make clear.

As I was saying, the king's appetite was whetted by alluring promises;
and in disregard of God's will he decided to break all his solemn oaths,
as well as the bishop's and those of the city leaders, in complete disre-
spect for the sanctity of those holy days. On the night of Maundy Thursday the king, conscious of the great rancor he had stirred up in the
people, was afraid to sleep anywhere but the bishop's palace, even though
he had lodgings prepared elsewhere. Very early the next morning the
king left, and the bishop assured the nobles that they need not worry
about paying the large sum they had agreed upon with the king, but that
he, Gaudry, would pay any debt they might have incurred. He added:
"If I don't deliver on my promise, you can throw me into the royal prison
and hold me for ransom."

The pacts that had created the commune had been broken. The burghers were filled with such rage and stupor that all the artisans aban-

---

80. Louis VI, whom Guibert qualifies as "persona conspicuus, ut soli majestati re-
giae videretur idoneus, armis strenuus, etc." is better known to history as Louis the
Fat. Guibert's younger contemporary, Ordericus Vitalis, called him "fluent of speech,
pale, . . . tall in stature and corpulent" ("ore facundus, statura procerus, pallidus et
corpulentus"). Given to severe attacks of diarrhea, Louis VI died after one such attack
1 August 1137. The contemporary writer Henry of Huntingdon wrote of the event:
"Need I speak of Philip of France, and Lewis, his son, both of whom reigned in my
time; whose God was their belly, and, indeed, a fatal enemy it was; for such was their
gluttony, that they became so fat as not to be able to support themselves. Philip died
long ago of plethora; Lewis has now shared the same fate" (quoted in *Ecclesiastical
History*, trans. Forester, 4.181–82.

doned their shops; the tanners and the cobblers closed their stalls; no food or drink was to be had from the inn- and tavern-keepers, who were afraid that the lords would rob them of everything. The bishop and the nobles were, in fact, already calculating what everybody else owed. Whatever any citizen was known to have contributed to the creation of the commune, that same sum would be exacted from him for the commune's destruction.

These events took place on the Parasceve, which means "the Preparation." On Holy Saturday, when they should have been preparing their souls to receive the body and blood of the Lord, they were in fact preparing for a murder here, a perjury there. Need I say more? During these days prelates and nobles alike were focused on the one and only end of fleecing their inferiors of everything they owned. But these inferiors finally grew so angry that they were goaded into an animal fury. Binding themselves by mutual oaths they conspired to kill, indeed to massacre the bishop and his accomplices. It is reported that forty took the oath.[81] A conspiracy as large as this could not be kept entirely secret, and when Master Anselm got wind of it on the eve of Holy Saturday he sent word to the bishop, who was about to retire, not to appear at matins. If he did he should expect to be murdered. But Gaudry, puffed up with his usual arrogance, answered: "Nonsense, am I going to die at the hands of people like this?" However, in spite of his verbal contempt for them he did not dare rise for matins or go into the cathedral.

The next day, as he was preparing to follow his clergy in procession, he ordered his retinue and all the soldiers to place themselves behind him with their swords under their cloaks. During the procession a small commotion began to stir, as often happens with crowds, and one of the burghers emerged from the crypt thinking the assassination plot they had sworn to was already in effect. He began shouting over and over again in a loud voice: "Commune! Commune!" by way of a signal. Since it was a feast day his voice was easily drowned out, but the incident made the other party suspicious. After the bishop had celebrated Mass, he brought a considerable crowd of peasants in from his episcopal domains to guard the church towers and ordered them to defend the episcopal palace. It was clear, however, that these peasants were no less hostile to the bishop than the other people: they too realized that the masses of

---

81. Like the assassination of Gérard de Quierzy, the commune of Laon is the result of a "conjuratio" bound together by a "sacramentum."

coins Gaudry had promised the king would be taken from their own pockets.

On the Monday after Easter it is customary for the clergy to hold a "station" at Saint-Vincent.[82] Since the conspirators realized that the bishop had headed them off the previous day, they decided that Monday [22 April] was the day to execute their plan, and they would have done so if they had not learned that all the nobles would be accompanying the bishop. In an outlying district of the city they did find one of these nobles, a harmless man who had recently married one of my cousins, a very shy young girl, but they refrained from attacking them for fear of alerting the others. When the Tuesday after Easter came Gaudry was feeling more secure so he dismissed the peasants to whom he had committed his own defense in the towers and at the episcopal palace, making them live at their own expense.

On Wednesday I went to see Gaudry, because he had pillaged my grain reserves and stolen a few hams, commonly called "bacons."[83] I pleaded with him to put an end to the storm that was shaking the city. He answered: "What do you think they are going to accomplish with these riots? If my African servant, Jean, grabbed the most powerful of them and dragged him by the nose, not one of them would dare grumble. Haven't I forced them to renounce this commune of theirs (as they were still calling it yesterday) as long as I'm alive?" I attempted to answer, but seeing this Gaudry so incredibly arrogant I said no more. In any case, before I had left the city, we quarreled sharply with each other because of his antagonistic behavior. Many people tried to warn him of his imminent peril, but he would not as much as listen to anyone.

8

The commune erupts. Riot, fire, and murder

The following day, Thursday [25 April] that is, as Gaudry and Gautier the archdeacon were collecting money from people after the noon offices,

82. The "station,"or procession to the abbey of Saint-Vincent (in the manner of papal processions to various Roman churches at Eastertime) was held 22 April 1112.

83. "Quarto die," or 24 April 1112. This statement, which seems to imply that the abbey of Nogent had some sort of granary, or smoke-house, in Laon, helps one understand why Guibert, from a twenty-mile distance, seems personally involved in the events of the episcopal city.

a clamor arose throughout the city with people shouting "Commune!" At the same time a great crowd of burghers, bearing swords, double axes, bows, lances, and pikes, stormed the episcopal palace. They had come down the nave of the cathedral of Notre-Dame, going through the same door that Gérard's assassins had used for their entrance and their exit. Now when they learned of the start of this riot some of the nobles, who had sworn to come to the bishop's aid in case of attack, rallied to his side from every direction. As they were gathering, the castellan Guimar,[84] a very handsome elderly nobleman of irreproachable behavior, became the riot's first victim. After running through the church armed with nothing more than a shield and a pike, he had hardly set foot in the courtyard of the episcopal palace when he was struck behind the neck by an ax wielded by Raimbert, a man who had been his close friend. Soon afterward Rainier (whom I have mentioned already, the man who had married my cousin)[85] was struck from behind by a lance as he was running up the stairs of the bishop's chapel trying to enter the palace. Struck down on the spot, the entire lower half of his body was consumed in the ensuing fire from the bishop's palace. Adon the *Vidame,* who was keen in tongue and even keener in spirit,[86] tried to gain access to the bishop's residence and realized that there was little he could do fighting by himself. Yet he encountered the full force of the attacking crowd and resisted so well with his spear and sword that he struck down three of his attackers within seconds. Then he climbed onto the dining table in the great hall, where he was wounded in the knees as well as other parts of his body. At last he fell to his knees, continuing to strike his attackers; he kept striking at his attackers, now this way, now that, until someone

84. Guimar the "castellan," like *Vidame* Adon (mentioned below) were lay officers whose charge was to defend the bishop's worldly possesions and domains.

85. Guibert has just referred to his cousin Rainier in the previous chapter (3.7) as one of the nobles who had accompanied the bishop the previous Monday and had not been attacked, "a harmless man who had recently married one of my cousins." Rainier will be the first victim of the Laon uprising.

86. Guibert plays skilfully on words here: "Ado vicedomus, minis acer, animo nimis acrior." A *Vidame* (from the Lat. *vicedomus*) was an ecclesiastical officer responsible for protecting and administering ecclesiastical property. Benton (*Self and Society,* 174) assumes Guibert's "minis" to mean "minimis" and mistranslates "sharp in small matters and even keener in great ones." "Minis acer . . . animo nimis acrior" in fact means, literally, "sharp in his threats and even sharper in his spirit." Guibert is consciously punning anagrammatically on the words "minis"/"nimis."

finally pierced his exhausted body with a javelin. A little while later this body was burned to ashes by the fire that burned in the house.

Now the insolent crowd, which had been screaming before the walls of the palace, attacked the bishop. Gaudry, along with those who had come to his aid, kept the enemy at bay by throwing stones and shooting arrows. In this as in other moments Gaudry showed the fierceness in battle that had always been his hallmark; but because he had unjustly and wrongly taken up that other [spiritual] sword, he perished by the sword.[87] Unable to repel the fierce attacks of the people he took the clothes of one of his servants and fled to the cellar of the church where he hid himself in a small barrel. After one of his faithful followers had fastened on the cover, he thought he was safe. Meanwhile men from the mob were running in every direction calling out not for the "bishop" but for the "gallows bird." They laid hands on one of his pages, but as he was loyal to the bishop they could get nothing from him. Then they seized another page who showed them with a betraying nod of the head in which direction the bishop might be found. So they entered the warehouse, searched everywhere, and finally found him in the following manner.

There was a despicable wretch named Theudegaud, a serf of the abbey of Saint-Vincent. For a long time he had been a servant and a provost in the service of Enguerrand de Coucy, who had him collect tolls at the bridge of Sort, as it is called.[88] Theudegaud used to watch for the moment when there were few travelers, then he would strip them of everything they had; then he would toss them, weighted down with a stone, into the river so that they wouldn't bring action against him. How often he did this God only knows; to list his robberies and his petty thefts would serve no purpose. Let me put it this way: the incurable wickedness of his heart was plainly visible in his hideous face. Once he had fallen out of favor with Enguerrand he had dedicated himself heart and soul to the commune of Laon. This man, then, who had spared neither monk nor cleric nor pilgrim nor member of either sex, finally decided he would be the one to kill the bishop. As the leader and instigator of this wicked attack on the bishop he was now looking for this man, whom he hated more than anyone else.

---

87. An allusion to Matt. 26.52: "Omnes . . . qui acceperint gladium gladio peribunt." Cf. Luke 22.38.

88. A bridge on the Oise river, about ten miles north of Laon, linking Sort to Crécy.

As the others were searching for Gaudry among the containers, Theudegaud halted in front of the barrel in which the bishop was hiding, smashed in the cover and twice asked: "Who is in there?" Shaken by the blows Gaudry was hardly able to move his frozen lips to answer: "A prisoner." Now the bishop had the habit of calling Theudegaud by the derisive name of Isengrin, on account of his wolfish profile — that is the name some people give to wolves.[89] So this scoundrel called out to the bishop: "Might it not be my lord Isengrin hiding in there?" Now Gaudry who, sinner though he was, was nevertheless the Lord's anointed,[90] was pulled out of the barrel by the hair, repeatedly beaten, then dragged outside into a narrow street of the cloister, before the house of Godfrey the chaplain. There he began a most pathetic plea for his life, swearing that he would never again be their bishop, that he would give them immense sums of money, and that he would leave the country. The crowd jeered at him, their hearts being closed to all feeling. Finally a man named Bernard de Bruyères raised his ax over the head of this holy (though admittedly sinful) man and dashed his brains out. As they tried to hold him up, Gaudry fell between their hands; and then another blow, this one delivered sideways across the nose and under the eye sockets, finished him off. He died on the spot. Then they broke his legs and kept inflicting repeated blows on his corpse. Then Theudegaud saw the ring on the ex-bishop's finger; and as he was having a hard time trying to pull it off, he cut off the dead man's finger with his sword and seized the ring. The bishop's body was then stripped of its garments and thrown naked into a street corner, in front of his chaplain's house. My God! who can repeat the insults that were hurled at him by those who walked by, or how much mud, how many stones, how much dirt his body was pelted with?[91]

89. This allusion to Isengrin, the wolf of the *Roman de Renard,* antedates the earliest known texts of the tale. Presumably the tale was already well known by the year 1112, at least in its oral folk versions.

90. Cf. 1 Kings 24.11 (Vulgate): "Non extendam manum meam in dominum meum, quia christus Domini est." As in the case of Gérard de Quierzy's assassination, Guibert is conscious of a kind of tragic grandeur in Gaudry, whose many crimes and sins seem to be absolved by his assassination, and the dignity of whose office of bishop ("christus Domini") must ever be distinguished from the person holding the office.

91. The violence of Gaudry's murder, attesting to the hatred and contempt in which he was held, especially since the assassination of Gérard de Quierzy, is confirmed by Abbot Suger in his *Life of Louis VI:* "[The assassins] most cruelly killed bishop Gaudry, a venerable defender of the church, not hesitating to lay hands on the Lord's anointed, left him exposed naked to the beasts and the birds in the public place, and cut off the

Before continuing with my narrative I should point out that something Gaudry had done recently had very much contributed to his undoing. Some two days before his death, if I am not mistaken, some eminent members of his clergy who were in assembly with him in the nave of the cathedral had asked him why he had spoken ill of them to the king during one of the king's recent visits to Laon. Had he not told the king that his clergy was not worthy of respect since most of them were the descendants of serfs who lived in the royal domains? Gaudry's response to this accusation had been to deny it. "May the holy communion," he said, "which I have just received at this altar"—he then extended his right hand in that direction—"turn to my ruin; and may the sword of the Holy Spirit pierce my soul if I even whispered such things about you to the king!" When they heard this, some of the clergy had been amazed and had reasserted under oath that they had heard him speak these words in the king's presence. Clearly the inconstancy of his mind and tongue had led to his ruin.

9

Victims of the commune. Some women escape

The enraged mob was now heading toward the house of Raoul, the bishop's steward, who had been one of Gérard de Quierzy's closest friends. Here was a man small in stature but heroic in spirit. Wearing his coat of mail and his helmet and armed with light weapons he was determined to resist, but seeing the size of the crowd and fearing that he would die in the fire he dropped his armor and threw himself defenseless at their mercy with his arms spread out in the shape of a cross. But the mob,

---

finger that held the bishop's ring" (Labande, *Guibert de Nogent*, 344n.1; my translation). Augustin Thierry saw in the Laon uprising three "distinct periods" characteristic of all revolutions: (1) the subjects make peaceful demands for freedom, and the "possessors of power" make concessions with an apparent good grace; (2) those in power renege on their concessions and destroy the new institutions they had vowed to maintain; (3) popular passion takes over, goaded by resentment, desire for revenge, and terror in the face of the future (Thierry, *Lettres*, 267–68).

giving no thought to God, threw him to the ground and butchered him without mercy.[92]

Before Gérard's murder in the church, Raoul had the following vision. He thought he was in the cathedral of Notre-Dame, where perverse-looking men had come together and were preparing strange games and new spectacles for the assembled spectators. In the meantime other men were coming out of the house of Guy the treasurer, located next to the church. In their hands they were holding bowls containing a drink so nauseating that anyone smelling it found it unbearable; and they passed it around to the assembled spectators. The meaning of this vision is clearer than the light of day: it is immediately obvious what a horrid and wicked demonic game was being played there, and what a great stench of crime poured out of this house to spill over in every direction. The raging mob first set fire to that house, and from there the fire spread to the church and, finally, to the episcopal palace.

Raoul had another premonition of his coming fate. In a vision he saw his squire report to him and say: "My lord, your horse is unusually broad in its front part and unusually narrow in the back. I have never seen anything quite like it." Until this time Raoul had been an extremely wealthy and highly respected man, but all his prosperity was gradually reduced to the "narrowness" of his miserable death—the horse being a symbol of the world's glory.[93]

It was chiefly through one man's sin, then, that the marvelous church of Laon was brought to miserable ruin. From the house of the treasurer, who had bought his way to an archdeaconate, the fire was seen spreading to the church. Now in preparation for the solemnities of Easter the church had been magnificently decorated with draperies and tapestries, but when the fire broke out it is believed that a few of the draperies were stolen rather than destroyed by the flames. As for the tapestries, since a few men could not manage to unhitch them from the pulleys, they perished. The gold panels of the altar and the saints' reliquaries (as well as the baldaquin covering them, called *repa*) were rescued; but I think ev-

---

92. As bishop's steward and one of Gérard de Quierzy's closest friends, Raoul was quite open to the crowd's suspicion of having been directly involved in Gérard's assassination. Hence, perhaps, the mercilessness of his butchering at the crowd's hands.

93. The allusion may be to Ps. 33.17: "The war horse is a vain hope for victory, / and by its great might it cannot save." The sense of Guibert's image, as of the Psalmist's, in its context, is that a king cannot be saved by his great army, and the war horse is a vain hope for victory, if might is not combined with truth.

erything else perished in the fire. One of the most prominent members of the clergy sought refuge under these reliquaries and did not dare come out for fear of meeting the roaming mobs. As he heard the fire crackling about him he ran toward the bishop's chair, smashed the chevet window right above it, and managed to escape. An image of the crucified Lord, magnificently gilded and decorated with precious stones, and a sapphire vase placed under the feet of the image, melted and fell to the ground and were recovered though heavily damaged. While the church and the palace were burning, an extraordinary thing happened, one of those mysterious designs of God: a firebrand, or a piece of burning coal, flew through the air to the nun's monastery and set fire to the church of Saint John. As for the church of Notre-Dame, called La Profonde, and the church of Saint Peter, they were reduced to ashes.[94]

I am not ashamed to relate how the wives of the nobles behaved in such circumstances.[95] *Vidame* Adon's wife, seeing that her husband had sided with the bishop's party when the uprising began, knew that this meant instant death. She therefore began asking her husband's forgiveness for any offenses she might have committed against him. As they were embracing for the last time, lamenting tearfully and kissing, she said to him: "How can you abandon me to the swords of the townspeople?" Seizing his wife by the right hand and holding his lance, he ordered his steward to carry his shield behind him. But the steward, who happened to be one of the original conspirators, not only refused to carry the shield, he also hurled violent insults at *Vidame* Adon and attacked him from behind. He now refused to acknowledge the master whose serf he had been, and whom he had waited upon at meals even a short while before. Adon made his way through the mob while shielding his wife, and finally managed to hide her in the house of one of the bishop's porters;[96] but his wife, seeing the mob attacking and the fires spreading

94. Both the Benedictine abbey church of Notre-Dame la Profonde and the church of Saint-Pierre au Marché were founded in the sixth century. They were behind the Laon cathedral to the east (Benton, *Self and Society,* 179n.3).

95. Guibert seems to overcome a certain sense of embarrassment ("referre non piget") in telling of the behavior of several of the nobles' wives. Was it exceptional for a monk to chronicle the behavior of the "procerum conjuges" so admiringly, and in such detail? The women, in any case, come alive in these pages, and are vividly described.

96. In the previous chapter Guibert has already described how *Vidame* Adon was killed by a javelin while defending himself against heavy odds on the dining table of the bishop's residence. Guibert's account of Adon's final, pathetic separation from his wife

from building to building turned and fled wherever her feet carried her. As she fled she ran into some of the townswomen who stopped her, beat her with their fists and stripped her of the rich clothes she was wearing. Disguising herself as a nun she barely managed to find her way to Saint-Vincent's abbey.

When my cousin's husband [Rainier] left her, she disregarded all her household possessions, kept only her long cape and, with the agility of a man, she climbed over the wall surrounding her orchard and jumped down. Then she sought refuge in the hovel of some poor woman, but a few moments later she realized that the fire was drawing nearer. She rushed toward the door, which the old woman had locked from the outside, broke the latch with a stone and went to ask a nun, one of her relatives, for a habit and a veil to cover herself with. She thought she was safe with the nuns, but when she saw the fire raging there too she turned and headed for another house even farther away. Finally, the next day, she showed up at her parents' house—they had been looking for her—and when she learned that her husband had died, the pain she had felt at being afraid to die turned into an even more painful rage.

The wife and the daughters of the castellan Guimar and many other women sought refuge in humble places.

Gautier the archdeacon was in the bishop's company when he saw the palace being besieged. Realizing that he had always been one to fan the flames of dissension, he jumped out the palace window into the bishop's orchard, and, with his head covered, he made his way from the outer walls toward the vineyards; and from there, using small sideroads, he managed to take refuge at the castle of Montaigu.[97] When the burghers were unable to find him anywhere, they mocked him saying that fear had made Gautier take refuge in the sewers.

Ermengarde, the wife of Roger, lord of Montaigu, was in the city that day, for her husband had become the warden of the abbey replacing Gérard de Quierzy. I believe she took a nun's habit at the same time as the wife of Raoul the seneschal, and they both made their way toward

---

after a desperate attempt to protect her is presumably a flashback to events that occurred minutes or hours earlier. Guibert justifies this apparent discrepancy at the start of the paragraph by announcing that he is now "turning without shame" to the behavior of the nobles' wives during these same events.

97. The castle of Montaigu lies about ten miles southeast of Laon.

Saint-Vincent by way of the valley of Bibrax.[98] Someone else tried to save one of Raoul's sons, who was about six years old, under his cloak, but he fell upon a brigand who lifted the cape to see what he was carrying and summarily cut the boy's throat while he was in his arms.

That day and night the vineyards situated between the two spurs [Bibrax] of the mountain of Laon served as an escape route for clergy and women. Men did not hesitate to wear women's clothes, nor women men's.[99] So fast, too, was the advance of the fires that had started on the other side and were coming around in the direction of Saint-Vincent that the monks thought they would lose everything in the conflagration. Those who had taken refuge there were in such fear that it was as if they had swords suspended over their heads. Guy the archdeacon and treasurer, who had missed all the excitement, was a lucky Guy indeed![100] Before Easter he had left on a pilgrimage to Notre-Dame de Versigny. The murderers were particularly sorry to see him absent.

Once the bishop and the chief nobles of the city had been slain, the assailants headed for the homes of the remaining ones with the intention of besieging them. Throughout the night they attacked the house of Guillaume, son of Haduin, who had not conspired with his co-citizens in the death of Gérard. On the contrary, on the morning he was about to be killed, Guillaume had accompanied him to the church to pray. The assailants set fire to the house and demolished one of its walls with picks, axes, and spears; but those who were inside resisted fiercely. Finally they were forced to surrender. By some admirable divine dispensation, however, they shackled Guillaume's feet but did not otherwise harm him, though he was the most hated of all the noblemen. They treated his son in the same way.

98. According to medieval tradition, Laon was the site of the Bibrax mentioned in Caesar's *Gallic Wars*, so named because of the twin spurs ("bina brachia") of the mountain of Laon (Benton, *Self and Society*, 180n.5).

99. An allusion to Deut. 22.5: "A woman shall not wear anything that pertains to a man, nor shall a man put on a woman's garment: for whoever does these things is an abomination to the Lord your God." The law is clearly directed against transvestism for immoral purposes, such as the heathens frequently practiced. Guibert clearly insists on the exceptional nature of the circumstances that made men dress like women, and women like men: "Vir plane muliebrem non verebatur habitum, nec mulier virilem."

100. "Lucky Guy" no doubt exceeds the intention of the original, "Felix Guido," but Guibert would perhaps have found the pun to his liking.

In Guillaume's house there was a young boy, also named Guillaume, who was the bishop's chamberlain. During the defense of the house this Guillaume showed that he deserved the highest praise. Once the house was taken a group of burghers who attacked it surrounded the boy to ask him whether the bishop had been killed or not. He answered that he didn't know. Those who had killed the bishop were, in fact, a different group from those who had attacked the house. The burghers looked about for the bishop's body until they found it. Then they asked the boy whether he could tell by some distinguishing mark whether the corpse was Gaudry's. (His face and features had, in fact, been beaten so severely that he was disfigured beyond recognition.) The young Guillaume then said, "I remember that when he was still alive he often talked about military matters, which he liked too much for his own good. He told me that once in a mock battle on horseback he charged sportingly at another knight and was struck with a lance and wounded in the part of the neck called "the windpipe." The burghers examined Gaudry's corpse and found the scar.[101]

Adalbéron, the abbot of Saint-Vincent, heard about Gaudry's assassination and wanted to go to him, but he was told unequivocally that if he became entangled with an enraged mob he would soon meet a similar death.

Those who witnessed these events swear that this day and the following were as one continuous day: no darkness ever came as a prelude to nightfall. I objected that this was probably due to the light from the fires, but they swore (and this was true) that the fires had been put out during the day. Incidentally, the fire in the women's monastery was so devastating that some of the bodies of the saints were consumed.

10

Gaudry and other victims are buried

The next morning hardly anyone walked past Bishop Gaudry's corpse without throwing something at it or cursing it. No one even thought of

101. Many are the medieval literary accounts of a corpse so badly disfigured that it

burying him, so Master Anselm, who on the previous day had stayed in hiding while the rioting was at its peak, went to seek out the main actors in this tragedy, begging them to allow this man's burial, if only because he had held the rank and prestige of a bishop.[102] They reluctantly consented. Master Anselm then ordered the body to be covered with a sheet and carried to the Saint-Vincent's abbey,[103] because it had been lying naked on the ground, like a dead dog, from the time of vespers on Thursday to mid-morning of the next day. One cannot imagine the threats and insults hurled at those charged with carrying the body or count the curses with which the dead man himself was pelted. Once laid out in the church he received at his burial none of the offices to which any Christian is entitled, let alone a bishop. A grave was only half dug to receive his body, which was packed so tightly in a small box that his chest and belly nearly exploded. He had such bad undertakers to lay him out that the eyewitnesses have concluded that the body received the worst possible treatment. That day—what am I saying?—for many days following, the monks celebrated no office in their church. They feared for the safety of the refugees to the monastery, and they feared for their own lives as well.

It is painful to relate this, but soon afterward Guimar the castellan was brought in by his wife and daughters, a very noble family, who fastened his body to a cart and pulled it themselves. Rainier, in turn, was transported in similarly miserable circumstances by a young peasant of his and a young female relative. The lower part of his body had been picked up somewhere and placed on the axle of a cart between the two wheels; the part above the thighs was still sizzling.[104] About these two men "there was found something pleasing," as it says in the Book of Kings,[105] for anyone with his heart in the right place could only be sad-

---

can be recognized only by a secret mark. Judging by the brutality of Gaudry's murder, it is difficult to agree with Benton (*Self and Society*, 181n.9) that Guibert might have embellished his tale for literary effect. In his account of Gaudry's murder, which corroborates Guibert's gruesome details, Suger states that the body was thrown "bestiis nudum et avibus in platea."

102. Once again Guibert insists on Gaudry's dignity as "christus Domini."

103. The traditional burial place of the bishops of Laon.

104. Guibert is forgetting that he had stated earlier that Rainier had been burned in his lower half, "ab inguine inferius."

105. 1 Kings 14.13: "And all Israel shall mourn for him and bury him: for he only of Jeroboam shall come to the grave, because in him there is found something pleasing

dened by their deaths. They had done nothing wrong except to associate with Gérard's murderers, which explains why they were buried with far more compassion than their bishop. As to the mortal remains of *Vidame* Adon, a few fragments—very few—were found several days after the rioting and conflagration. These were kept in a very small cloth until the day when Raoul, the archbishop of Reims, came to Laon to reconsecrate the church.[106] When the archbishop came to Saint-Vincent's, he began by celebrating a solemn mass in honor of Bishop Gaudry and his accomplices, though they had been dead for many days. I should add that the body of Raoul the seneschal had also been brought in on the same day as the bodies of Guimar and Rainier. Raoul's body was borne in by his aged mother, along with the body of Raoul's small son; and both were given a summary burial, with the son placed over his father's chest.

After the archbishop, a wise and venerable man, had some of the bodies transferred to a more convenient burial place, he celebrated the divine liturgy for all the dead in the presence of grieving relatives and close friends. During the Mass he delivered a sermon flaying these wretched communes in which, against all law and custom, serfs violently overthrow the law of their lords. " 'Serfs,' said the Apostle, 'be submitted to your lords and fearful in all things.'[107] And so that serfs might not invoke the harshness or the greed of their masters as an excuse for revolt, they should also hear this: 'And not only to good and moderate masters but even to harsh ones.' In the accepted canons [the archbishop continued], those who advise serfs to disobey their masters even to enter the religious life or to run away, let alone resist, are damned with anathema. This interdiction is confirmed by the fact that no one can be admitted as a cleric, or receive religious orders, or enter the monastic life, unless he is first considered freed from servitude; even when admitted he

---

to the Lord, the God of Israel, in the house of Jeroboam." The reference is to Abiyya, the only member of Jeroboam's house in whom there can be found "some good thing."

106. Raoul le Verd was archbishop of Reims from 1108 to 1124. According to Labande (*Guibert de Nogent,* 359n.5), the reconsecration of the church of Laon took place on 6 September 1114. The "multi a mortibus eorum . . . dies" that Guibert refers to since the death of Gaudry and his accomplices would in fact mean nearly two and a half years.

107. Raoul is quoting not "the Apostle" (Saint Paul), but 1 Peter 2.18: "Servants, be submissive to your masters with all respect, not only to the kind and gentle but also to the overbearing."

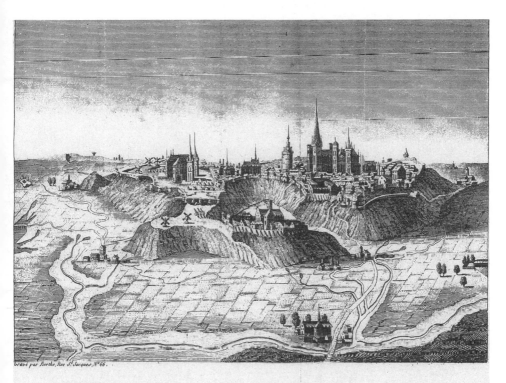

VUE DE LA VILLE DE LAON DESSINÉE SOUS LOUIS XIII.

Fig. 6. Early seventeenth-century drawing of Laon, seen from the southwest. The Bibrax, or "twin-spurs," of the mountain of Laon (see 161n.98) are clearly visible. The cathedral of Notre-Dame and the abbey of Saint-Jean are on the right spur, and the abbey of Saint-Vincent is on the spur opposite. From J.F.L. Devisme, *Histoire de la ville de Laon* (1822).

cannot be kept if the masters demand his return."[108] The archbishop concluded by saying that he had often talked about these things at the king's court, and even more often in other assemblies.

I have reported these events out of anticipation. Now let us return to a more orderly narrative.

108. Like Guibert "reconciling" the cathedral of Laon after Gérard's murder, Raoul uses the occasion of the burial of Gaudry to preach to the serfs a message of submission and a restoration of the status quo.

Fig. 7. Upper city of Laon, as it looks today, from the towers of the cathedral of Notre-Dame. The Bibrax is visible, curving to the left. Photo by Marianna M. Archambault.

11
Thomas de Marle. The sacking of Laon

When the wicked citizens of Laon began to weigh the enormity of the crime they had committed, they quivered with fear and greatly dreaded the retribution that the king would inflict. Nevertheless they continued piling injury upon injury when they should have been looking for a remedy. They appealed to Thomas, hoping that he would defend them against an attack by the king. Thomas, who was presumed to be the son of Enguerrand de Coucy and who himself owned the castle of Marle had, since his early adolescence, been robbing poor people and pilgrims on their way to Jerusalem.[109] He had enriched himself through incestuous marriages[110] and had attained considerable power by destroying a great number of people. His cruelty surpassed anything that our times had ever heard of; in fact some people with a reputation for cruelty seem gentler in killing cattle than Thomas was in killing people. He would not simply put to the sword, as is the custom, those who had committed a crime, but he would first put them through the most excruciating torture. To force certain prisoners to pay ransom he would hang them by the testicles, sometimes by his own hand; and often the body's weight would rip off the victim's parts, and the guts would spill to the ground. He would hang other prisoners by the organ itself or by the thumbs, and tie a large stone to their shoulders. Then Thomas would walk around, and if he was not able to get what he wanted from them he would beat them with sticks until they either gave in or died under the blows. How many people died in his dungeons—of starvation, disease, or torture—is impossible to tell.

No more than two years ago, as he was coming to someone's aid against some peasants in the Mountain of Soissons, three of the peasants hid in a cave. Thomas came up to the front of the cave with a spear and struck one of the peasants in the mouth, pressing so hard that the tip of the lance pierced clear through the man's bowels and came out his anus. Need I go on anymore? Thomas killed the other two on the spot.

One time Thomas had a wounded prisoner who could no longer march. He asked the prisoner why he didn't walk any faster, and the man answered that he couldn't. "Wait a minute," Thomas said, "I'll see to it that you really have a hard time walking," and getting off his horse he pulled out his sword and hacked off both of the man's feet, killing him instantly. It would be pointless to keep recounting the heinous crimes he committed; besides, we'll have an opportunity—and not an insignificant one—to tell about some of his other horrors. Now back to my story.

For a long time Thomas, who befriended none but the worst crimi-

---

109. Thomas, lord of Coucy in 1116. Known to history as an unscrupulous marauder and brigand, he was excommunicated from the church. Guibert has previously referred to him (3.7) as "virum omnium quos novimus hac aetate nequissimum."

110. An "incestuous" marriage in Guibert's time (and until the year 1215) was any marriage that violated church prohibitions on consanguinity. These problems could go so far as considering a marriage to a third or fourth cousin as "incestuous" (Labande, *Guibert de Nogent*, 363n.2; cf. Duby, *Love and Marriage*, 13).

nals, gave shelter and protection to Gérard's killers, who had been ex-communicated. To him, more than to Catiline, might have been applied Sallust's saying: "He was spontaneously evil and cruel."[111] To make matters worse the city leaders came up to him and begged him to come and protect them against the king, and they subsequently received him in the city. Thomas listened to their requests, then consulted with his own people about what to do. They unanimously answered that he did not have enough strength to hold the city of Laon against the king. So long as he was within the walls of the city Thomas did not dare communicate that reply to these madmen, so he told them to come out to the open country where he would give his advice. They had withdrawn about a mile from the city when Thomas said to them: "Since this city is the capital of the realm, I cannot hold it against the king. However, if you are afraid of the king's army, follow me into my territory and consider me your protector and friend."[112] When they heard this the citizens of Laon were speechless, but being at their wits' end because of the crime they had committed and fearing that the king would soon be at their throats, a countless mob of them ran away with Thomas.

Meanwhile Theudegaud, the slayer of the bishop, had his sword un-sheathed while searching through every vault and ceiling and nook and cranny of the monastery of Saint-Vincent to find escapees to kill. Wearing the bishop's ring on his finger as if to prove himself their head, he did not dare go back to the city with his accomplices, so he followed Thomas, almost empty-handed. While he was at Laon, Thomas had freed Guillaume, the son of Audouin, as well as other captives, for Guillaume was innocent of Gérard's murder.

With the speed of Pegasus, Fame spread the news to the people of the neighboring towns and cities that the city of Laon had been emptied of its citizens. So each and every peasant headed for the deserted city and took possession of its houses, which were full of things and without defense. Indeed, the citizens of Laon were rich while trying to appear poor, for they did not want to attract the envious attention of the nobles.

While this was going on, Enguerrand de Boves's unlawful, incestuous wife—I have mentioned her earlier—ceased having relations with her

111. Guibert is quoting, with a slight modification, Sallust's description of Catiline in *The War with Catiline*: "gratuito potius malus atque crudelis erat" (trans. Rolfe, 26).

112. However "evil and cruel," Thomas de Marle respected the fact that Laon was a royal city; and in keeping with an old Carolingian code he did not want to make an enemy of his monarch.

husband. She pretended she was doing it for the sake of continence, but in fact she was disgusted by her spouse's age and weight. Since she was not in the habit of doing without a lover, she began fancying a bright young prospect for that role. Enguerrand tried to prevent them from ever meeting, but his wife would then drive the man wild by suddenly playing the seductress. So Enguerrand invited the young man to their home, and made him a guest in his own house; then he betrothed her very young daughter to the young man so as to conceal the latter's scandalous affair with his wife, and made him the defender of his lands against Thomas, whose father he was said to be, a man whom he unstintingly hated and had every intention of disinheriting.[113] This young man, then, was residing at Coucy during this period and proclaiming for all to hear that he would take on Thomas of Marle by whatever means; but he lacked the funds to embark on such an undertaking. Fortune came to his aid in the way I am about to tell.

Enguerrand and Guy (for such was the young man's name) heard that Thomas had left the city with the people following him; so they headed for Laon, where they found houses deserted by their dwellers but overflowing with a tremendous abundance of wealth. The previous inhabitants had guarded it carefully to prevent its being wasted or taken by parasites and robbers; but no one now could prevent this young man from taking what he wanted. Indeed never again in his life would he suffer deprivation, for what he found there in the way of money, clothes, and victuals of all kinds simply defies description and credibility. Before the people of Coucy arrived, others had already been there—bands of peasants and other people from outlying towns, then people from Montaigu, Pierrepont, and La Fère.[114] It is difficult to tell what the first ones had found or taken away, but when our people got there later on they boasted that they had found everything clean and almost intact. But is it realistic to expect fools and barbarians to exercise prudence and moderation? They had no way of measuring the value of the wine and grain they found there almost by happenstance. Having no wagons to cart

113. Guibert is not casting doubt on Thomas's legitimacy, or casting aspersions on Enguerrand's first marriage to Ade de Marle, Thomas's mother, when he states: "contra Thomam, quem irremediabiliter ipse, qui dicebatur pater, oderat." He is showing, rather, how unnatural Enguerrand's sentiments have become toward Thomas de Marle, whom both he and his second wife, Sibylle, intend to disinherit.

114. Pierrepont is about twelve miles northeast of Laon, La Fère about twenty-five miles northwest.

things away they laid everything waste with a shameful recklessness. Quarrels arose among them, moreover, as to what to do with the things they had pillaged. Whatever had been taken by weaker looters was soon in the hands of the stronger. Any looter walking between two others was soon stripped of his booty. The city of Laon lay in a lamentable state. Those who had fled the city had set fire to the houses of the clerics and the nobles, both of whom they hated. Now the nobles who were still in the city were pillaging the houses of those who had fled, emptying them of all content, all furniture, taking even hinges, locks, and bolts.

Not even monks were able to enter or leave the city unmolested. Any who tried to do so were either stripped naked or robbed of their horses.[115] Innocent and guilty people alike had come to seek refuge at Saint-Vincent's abbey, taking a lot of money with them. Good Lord! how many swords were suspended over the monks' heads by assailants who had it in more for the attackers than for the money! It was here that Guillaume, Audouin's son, forgot how God had granted him his own freedom.[116] He allowed serfs belonging to Guimar and Rainier (who had been killed) to arrest a fellow noble, to whom he had guaranteed immunity of life and limb on his honor, and abandoned him to his fate. Guillaume's son, Audouin, tied the man by his feet to a horse's tail, and it wasn't long before his brains were gushing out. Then the man was hanged. His name was Robert, surnamed Le Mangeur, a good, decent man. As for the *Vidame*'s steward whom we have mentioned earlier (Evrard by name, if I'm not mistaken), this serf who had killed a master whose table he had shared that very same day was also hoisted up.[117] Others were despatched in the same way. The number of insurgents or counterinsurgents who suffered punishment in one form or other is beyond counting.

In any case it should be noted that Thomas came into the city the day after the bishop's murder—on Friday, that is—and left on Saturday. On Sunday, God brought punishment on them for their great crime. These

115. Guibert's description of the situation in Laon is consciously worded in terms similar to those he used to describe the events that led to the creation of the commune (3.7).

116. How this Guillaume had managed to avoid being killed by divine ordinance is narrated above (3.9). Perhaps it is because he had not consented to the assassination of Gérard: "qui non consenserat civibus in morte Gerardi." Cf. Luke 23.51, on Joseph of Arimathea: "non consenserat consilio et actibus eorum."

117. Guibert's phrase is ironic: "evectus est in sublime."

events occurred in the year of Our Lord 1112, on the Friday after Easter, the 26th of April.[118]

This bishop Gaudry had been an extraordinarily shallow man. However absurd or mundane his thoughts were they easily slipped off his tongue. In my very presence I have seen him mistreat my cousin (whom I have mentioned earlier as recently married at Laon and who behaved with consummate modesty), lash out at her and call her a shitty peasant, only because she shied away from seeing or talking to others, and because she didn't seek his company the way other women did.[119] In another instance he very much wanted to see a book I had written on the crusade to Jerusalem. When it was brought to him he was so incensed to see that I had dedicated the preface to my lord Lisiard, the bishop of Soissons, that he immediately refused to read it;[120] and yet he gave my other lesser works far more praise than they deserved. Finally, though he proved very successful in accumulating money, he immediately spent it all on useless things.

These evil things came to fruition during Gaudry's time as bishop, although one should add that is wasn't Gaudry's iniquity alone but that of a whole population that contributed to the accumulation of these crimes, which were greater in Laon than anywhere in all of France. A very short time before these events, a priest was sitting before the fire in his own house when he was stabbed in the back by a young servant boy, with whom he had been too familiar. The boy took the body and concealed it in a secret room that he locked from the outside. When the neighbors, who had not seen the priest for several days, asked the servant where he was the boy lied and said the man had gone off on some business. But the stench became intolerable and the body could no longer be hidden in the house; so the boy took his master's whole fortune, placed the body face downward on the ashes in the hearth, and let an instrument called a dryer, which was suspended above him, fall on him

118. Thomas of Marle's entrance into Laon took place on 26 April. Gaudry must have been killed on 25 April. Benton's translation reads: "from the Friday of Easter week to April 29th" (*Self and Society*, 188).

119. This self-effacing "consobrina" of Guibert's has been mentioned twice before. She had married Rainier, who became one of the first victims of the Laon commune.

120. Guibert had dedicated his *Gesta Dei per Francos* to Lisiard, bishop of Crépy, preceded with a letter (*epistula*) filled with effulgent praise for Lisiard's learning (*PL* 156.679–80). Lisiard was bishop of Soissons from 1108 to 1126.

so that people would think the priest had been killed by the instrument's falling on him. Then the boy made off with what he had stolen.

Shortly before the start of each month the church deans would hear cases concerning priests in each of their dioceses. When a certain priest named Burgund, a very chatty and impulsive man, brought some trivial accusation against a neighboring priest, the dean fined the latter six *denarii*. But the priest who had paid the fine did not take the matter well, so he lay in wait for Burgund as he was returning home one night. As Burgund was mounting the steps leading to his house holding a lantern, the priest came out from behind and clubbed him over the head. Burgund died on the spot without having made a will.

Another man, also a priest, ordered one of his servants to shoot another priest whom he despised with an arrow while he was at the altar celebrating Mass. The priest was struck but not killed, but the instigator and author of the crime was nonetheless guilty of intending to kill; he was accused of homicide and desecration, a crime that until then was unheard of among Christians.

Other crimes were reported during this same period and in this same area. Visions were also seen, heralding the crime that we have recounted. Someone thought he saw an orb like the moon come crashing down on Laon, signifying the city's rapid decline in the future. In the church of Notre-Dame, one of our monks saw three enormous beams placed in parallel position before the knees of the Crucified; and the spot where Gérard was murdered was covered with blood. The crucifix signified a particularly important church personality; and the three beams standing in his way obviously represented the enormous stumbling block that brought about his end: his criminal entry into office, his crime against Gérard, and finally his crime against the people. And if the place where Gérard was murdered was covered with blood because this perverse crime had not yet been atoned for by penance.[121]

I also learned from the monks of Saint-Vincent that an enormous commotion was heard in the city during the night hours (thought by some to be caused by evil spirits) and that the sky seemed ablaze with fires. A few days before these dire events, a child was born double from the waist up. That is, down to the kidneys there were two heads and two

---

121. For Guibert the murder of Gérard de Quierzy is the recurrent leitmotif that seems to hold all of Book 3 together. All the events narrated seem to to lead up to the murder or be a consequence of it.

bodies, each with its arms: double above, single below. It was baptized and lived three days. In short, many strange things occurred or were seen that predicted beyond the shadow of a doubt the great evils that were to come.[122]

12
The canons of Laon organize a money-raising tour with relics

The storm subsided for a time; and thanks to the zeal of the clergy the church began to be restored gradually. The intensity of the fire had weakened the wall next to which Gérard had been murdered, so at great cost the canons constructed several arches between the middle part of that wall, which had been more damaged by the fire, and the outer wall. One night there was an enormous clap of thunder, and the lightning struck and severed the arches sustaining the wall. Consequently the wall began to lean again and it became necessary to tear it down to its foundations. How wondrous is the judgment of God! How severe will your judgment be, Lord, of those who murdered a man standing in prayer before you, if you did not even allow the very wall next to which these events occurred, a wall incapable of feeling, to remain standing? And by no means, O Lord, is it wrong for you to find such wrong intolerable. For surely, if an enemy of mine were to throw himself at my knees begging my forgiveness and were struck dead in my presence by one of his enemies, all my animosity toward the first would immediately vanish because of the affront done to me by the second. So it is for us mortals,

122. In the best tradition of medieval chronicle writing, Guibert closes a chapter with a litany of great portents, telling of things rotten in the state of the world and anticipating worse things to come: "Multa denique et visa sunt et contigere portenta." Cf. Ordericus Vitalis's *Ecclesiastical History*, 4.20: "The calamities which threaten the sons of earth are endless, and if they were all carefully committed to writing would fill large volumes. It is now winter, and I am suffering from the severity of the cold (ed. Forester, 2.110; cf. ed. and trans. Marjorie Chibnall [Oxford: Clarendon Press, 1969], 2.361).

and you, Lord, are the very source of all mercy! If at the time of King Herod you gave the crown of glory to little children who did not know you at all, simply because you had been the cause of their undoing, is it even thinkable that you would have been harsh in your judgment of this man Gérard, undeserving sinner that he was, who was murdered in total disregard of your name? That is not your way, O source of infinite goodness.

Meanwhile, in keeping with the customary way, such as it is, of raising money, the canons began carrying round the relics of saints as well as their reliquaries. As a result the great Judge, who chastises with one hand but shows mercy with the other, accomplished miracles everywhere the relics passed. Now they were carrying, along with some box that is barely memorable, a magnificent reliquary containing parts of the robe of the Virgin Mother, of the sponge that was presented to the Savior's lips, and of his cross. (Whether it really contained some of the hair of Our Lady I don't know.)[123] This reliquary is made of gold and decorated with precious stones; and it has a verse inscription engraved in the gold that praises the wonderful things inside.[124]

On their second trip with the relics they came to a town in the district of Tours called Buzançais, which is held by a robber baron. There our clerics spoke to the people about, among other things, the sorry state of their church. Soon they began to realize that the baron and his townspeople were listening to them with evil in their hearts and planning to attack them whenever they would try to leave town. So the cleric whose mission it was to speak to the crowd found himself in a predicament; and though

123. Guibert showed such a detached, ironic skepticism toward the contemporary claims made for relics (for example, in De pignoribus sanctorum [PL 156.611–79]), that Abel Lefranc dubbed him a "rationalist" (Benton, Self and Society, 8). Yet Guibert had a great devotion to the Virgin; and he does relate, in the pages that follow, seven instances during the monks' tour when the relics proved successful. He seems more intent, however, upon giving a pragmatic account of the tour's success than upon proving the inherently miraculous nature of the relics.

124. Another account of this money-raising tour of relics by the canons of Laon is that of Hermann of Laon, written shortly after 1145 and entitled De miraculis beatae Mariae Laudunensis (PL 156.963–1018). According to Hermann, the gold-engraved inscription in the reliquary read: SPONGIA CRUX DOMINI CUM SINDONE CUM FACIALI / ME SACRAT ATQUE TUI GENITRIX ET VIRGO CAPILLI ("The sponge and cross of Our Lord, with the facial cloth, consecrate me, as well as the hair of your Virgin Mother") (Labande, Guibert de Nogent, 380n.1).

he did not believe in what he was promising he said to the people standing there: "If there is someone sick among you let him come up to these
holy relics and drink the water they have touched, and he will surely be
cured." The baron and the townspeople were delighted by the possibility
of proving our clerics were lying by taking them at their word, so they
brought forward a boy of about twenty who was deaf and dumb. The
danger that our clerics were exposing themselves to, and the anxiety they
felt at that moment, is impossible to describe. They prayed with heavy
sighs to the Lady known to all of us, and her only Son, Jesus. The deaf-
mute drank the holy water and was then asked some question or other
by the trembling cleric. The boy responded immediately, not exactly by
answering the question but by repeating the cleric's very words (since he
had never heard anything said to him he was ignorant of everything
except what had just been said). To make a long story short: in this poor
town, the hearts of the townspeople suddenly became larger than ever
before. The baron, who was lord of the town, immediately gave the
clerics his only horse, while the generosity of the townspeople went well
beyond their means. They became the defenders of those whom they had
wanted to attack, and shedding abundant tears, they praised God for the
help received. As to the boy who had been cured he was made keeper in
perpetuity of the holy relics. I have seen the boy in our church at Nogent: he was a simple-witted boy, clumsy in speech and slow in compre-
hension. He faithfully kept relating the great miracle, and he died not
long afterward discharging his function.

In the city of Angers there was a woman who had married as a young
girl. Day and night since that tender age she had kept her wedding ring
on her finger—one might almost say "irretractably." As the years went
by the young girl put on weight to such an extent that the flesh sticking
out around the ring covered it almost entirely; there was no longer any
hope of removing the ring from the finger. Now when the holy relics
came to Angers, the woman in question came forward after the sermon,
along with other women, to make her offering. When she stretched her
hand toward the relics to leave the money she was carrying, the ring
snapped and fell off her hand before the very relics. When the people,
especially the women, saw what a grace the Virgin Mother had bestowed
on the woman (who did not even dare ask for it herself), the amount of
money contributed by the people, and especially the number of rings and
necklaces contributed by the women, were beyond my description. The

whole Touraine area bathed in the fragrance of the graces poured upon it by the great Lady; but Anjou now could boast it had the Mother of God within a hand's reach, as it were.

Elsewhere in the same diocese (but I am unable to say in which town) the clerics brought the relics to an honorable lady who had for a very long time been in the grip of a desperate illness and who had requested them urgently. Once she had paid the humblest veneration to the relics and drunk the water in which they had been immersed, she was cured immediately, through Mary's intercession. She had honored these gifts of God with offerings of her own, as was expected, and the bearer of the sacred relics was about to leave her home when a young boy came up, sitting on a horse drawing a wagon, and blocked the middle of the narrow street by which the procession of clerics was to pass. The relic-bearer said to him: "Stay where you are until the relics go by." When the bearer had gone past, the boy began to urge his horse forward but was unable to continue his journey. Seeing this the relic-bearer said: "Go, in the name of the Lord," and with these words both the horse and the wagon started forward again. See what Mary can do and the kind of respect she demands!

There was a third trip during which the relics were brought to the castle of Nesle. Raoul, the lord of this castle, had in his house a young man, a deaf-mute, who was said to know the art of divination—picked up from devils no doubt—and whom Raoul was said to love dearly for this reason. So the sacred relics were brought to this castle, but the inhabitants honored them with very meager offerings. The young deaf-mute, however, who had learned through sign language about the healing of the other deaf mute (previously mentioned) and even saw him present, gave his shoes to a poor man, and with bare feet and a penitent heart he followed the sacred relics all the way to the monastery of Lihons. At one point he lay down under the reliquary just at the lunch hour, while most of the clerics went off to eat. A small number of them stayed behind to guard the relics, but even they went off for a short walk outside the church. When they came back they found the young man stretched out on the ground and in great pain, while blood flowed out of his mouth and ears, causing a great stench. When they saw this the clerics hastened to call those of their companions who had gone off to dinner back to the scene of this great miracle. When the young man came out of his convulsion the clerics tried to see whether he was able to speak, by asking him some question or other. He immediately answered by repeating the words he had just heard. The clerics then offered infinite praise to God on high, and their elation was beyond description. Then at everybody's urging the clerics returned to the castle of Nesle so as to make up for the insufficient donations that had been made to the relics the first time around; they succeeded magnificently. It was here, then, that the Lady glorified herself: Her divine Son completed the natural gifts that until then he had refrained from giving.

13
The tour of relics in England.
Curious events at Laon

From here the relic bearers headed for lands overseas.[125] While they were sailing in the Mediterranean, they found themselves on the same ship as some wealthy merchants. They were enjoying favorable winds and a calm sea when suddenly they saw, coming straight toward them, galleys filled with fearsome pirates. They were terrified. As the pirates' oars chopped through the water, the galleys' prows barged through the masses of waves. Soon they were no more than two hundred yards' distance from us, and the relic bearers were as terrified as the crew of their ship. At that moment one of our priests stood up in their midst, and raising the box that contained the relics of the Queen of Heaven, in the name of Christ and his Mother he forbade the pirates to come any closer. At this command the galleys turned around and headed away as speedily as they had approached. You can imagine the shouts of praise and glory that were raised among those who had just been delivered. As a token of gratitude the merchants offered many gifts to the gracious Mary.

The relic bearers made their way safely to England and came to the city of Winchester, where they worked a great number of miracles. The same thing happened at Exeter, which also produced an abundance of gifts. Let us pass over the ordinary healings of the sick and speak of the exceptional cases. For we are not recording their itinerary—they can

125. According to Hermann of Laon, they embarked at Wissant on 25 April 1113.

write that themselves — nor considering each individual fact, but are picking out examples useful for sermons.

They were received almost everywhere with the reverence they deserved; but in one village they were refused admittance by the priest in his church, and by the peasants in their homes. Finding two uninhabited houses they stored all their baggage in one and used it for their lodgings, while the other was used to shelter the holy relics. The loathsome peasants persisted, however, in their obstinate refusal of things divine, and the clerics left the village the very next day. As they were leaving, suddenly, with a terrific clap of thunder, a bolt of lightning burst out of the clouds and struck the village, reducing all of its houses to ashes. And — a sign of God's marvelous sense of discrimination! — those two houses, which were situated in the midst of the others that were on fire, were spared. God wanted to give a very clear sign that if these wretches had been afflicted with fire it was because of their irreverence toward the Mother of God.[126] As for the wicked priest, who had merely increased the cruelty of these barbarians he was supposed to educate, he gathered up household goods that he was delighted to think had escaped heaven's fire, and came to the edge of a river (or of the sea, I'm not sure which) hoping to get across. But there everything he had collected to move elsewhere was annihilated on the spot by lightning. Thus, this savage band of rustics who were uninstructed in the mysteries of God were taught to understand through their sufferings.

They came to another town where the evidence of the miracles and the faith of the observers elicited many fervent donations to the holy relics. It happened that one Englishman, standing in front of the church where the relics were venerated, said to a companion: "Let's go have a drink." "I have no money," said the other. "I'll get some," said the first. "How will you do that?" asked his friend. "Well," said the first, "I've noticed that these clerics have been pumping all kinds of money from these clods with their lies and tricks. I'm going to find some way of siphoning some of that money for my own entertainment." Then he entered the church, walked right up to the platform where the relics had been placed, and giving the impression that he was bending over to venerate them with a kiss, he drew his lips close to some coins that had

---

126. This is not the first time that Guibert has interpreted fire caused by lightning bolts as a sign of divine wrath. Cf. the successive fires inflicted on the monastery of Saint-Germer de Fly as punishment for the avarice of certain monks (3.23).

been left there as offerings and sucked them into his mouth. Then he turned to his friend and said, "Now let's go and drink; I'm sure we have enough money for that now." His friend said: "Where did you get that money? You had nothing a while ago." "I sucked it with my mouth out of the offerings that are given to these impostors in the church." "You have done an evil thing," said the friend, "because you've taken what belongs to the saints." "Shut up," said the first, "and let's go into this nearby tavern."

To make a long story short they drank until the sun went down. Then at nightfall the one who had stolen the money from the holy altar got on his mare and wanted to head home; but when he reached a nearby wood, he made a noose and hanged himself to a tree, thereby expiating his sacrilegious act with a shameful death. I believe these few instances suffice to show the many miracles the powerful Virgin performed among the English.

After the relic bearers had returned to Laon from their campaign, a cleric with a good character, who had been charged with supervising the transportation of materials to repair the roof of the cathedral, told me that one of the oxen had collapsed going up the mountain. The cleric was then quite exasperated, not being able to find a fresh ox to replace the first one, when suddenly another ox ran up to offer his services as if he were deliberately volunteering his help. This ox deployed great energy in helping the others pull the wagon up to the cathedral; but the cleric then became concerned about finding this mysterious ox's owner to give him back. But when the ox was unyoked he did not wait for a driver or an oxherd but headed swiftly in the direction from whence he had come.[127]

The cleric who told me this story also recounted the following story. On the day Bishop Gaudry set off for Rome after arranging for Gérard's assassination, this man was standing behind the priest at Mass (for he was a deacon) when suddenly, though it was a beautiful day and no wind was blowing, an eagle fell out of the gildings above the chest that contained the saints' relics, and fell as if it had been violently thrown. This event led some people to the following conclusion; namely, that the chief element in this place, that is, the bishop—was going to die. In fact, I feel that this conclusion may have been justified, but I also think that what was being symbolized was the ruin of a city which had been the

---

127. The dedicated oxen that were used to transport building materials up the mountain of Laon have been immortalized by the sculptors of the Laon cathedral.

Fig. 8. Sculpted oxen from the cathedral of Notre-Dame de Laon today (see 179n.127). Photo by Marianna M. Archambault.

most royal of all the cities of France and which was to fall into even greater ruin. During that critical phase of the city's history, which I have already recounted, the king, whose greed had contributed to it, did not come back to visit the city. As for the royal provost, when he realized what evils were about to be perpetrated there, he sent his concubine and children on ahead and left town just a few hours before the uprising was to paralyze the city. He was no more than three or four miles away when he saw the city in flames.

14

Laon has a new bishop.
Thomas de Marle's maneuvers

Once Bishop Gaudry was eliminated, the clergy began clamoring for the king's ear about the choice of a successor. Without any election, the king gave them the dean of Orléans.[128] This happened because the king's chancellor, a certain Etienne,[129] who could not himself be bishop, was eyeing the dean's office at Orléans, so when Etienne obtained the bishop's seat for the dean he acquired the deanship. When this new bishop appeared for his consecration and they searched the book for a prophecy they fell upon a blank page. It was as if the book were saying: "I will prophecy nothing about this man, because he will hardly do anything." Indeed, he died a few months later, although he did have time to rebuild some of the episcopal houses.

After his death the present bishop[130] was elected, lawfully though with reluctance. I say "lawfully," in that his election had nothing corrupt about it, nor was his behavior motivated by anything like simony. The Gospel verse that served as a prophecy, however, had a harsh resonance

128. Hugh, dean of the cathedral of Orléans, was consecrated 4 August 1112. He died a few months later.

129. Etienne de Garlande, chancellor to Louis VI from 1108 to 1127.

130. Barthélemy de Jux, who was related to both Saint Bernard de Clairvaux and Thomas de Marle.

to it, being the same as Gaudry's prophecy: "A sword will pierce your—meaning his—soul." Whatever misfortune awaits him God only knows.

Before we proceed to other matters I must tell you that Theudegaud, who had betrayed and killed Bishop Gaudry, was captured two years later by Enguerrand's soldiers, and taken to the gallows. He was arrested during Lent after eating and drinking to the point of vomiting. He boasted in the presence of several witnesses—this is the most impious part—that he was full of God's glory, and as he said this he stuck out his belly and rubbed it with his hand. Once arrested he was thrown into a dungeon, where he asked forgiveness neither of God nor of men; and when he was led to his execution he spoke to no one. In death he showed the same indifference to God as in life. But let us return to a few things I have omitted.

Thomas de Marle had allied himself, as we have said, with this perverse commune and had supported those horrid men who had killed first Gérard, then the bishop, his lord and kinsman.[131] His viciousness having grown unspeakably worse, he was repeatedly struck with anathemas by all the bishops and archbishops throughout France, not only in councils, synods, and assemblies of the king's court, but, as time went on, regularly every Sunday in every parish and cathedral. Now his stepmother, that woman whom Enguerrand was wickedly consorting with, was more cruel than any she-wolf;[132] and seeing that Thomas was slowly emerging as a rival she forced Enguerrand to forswear all fatherly love toward Thomas, and even the name of father. With his wife's instigation, then, Enguerrand began to deprive Thomas of his rights and to treat him openly as an enemy: in short, if I may borrow the words of a comic writer, he began "driving a crazy man insane."[133] Day by day Thomas endured the measures that were being taken against him until his mind was driven to

131. Guibert has already accused Thomas de Marle of having supported Gérard's assassins (3.11); but in view of the fact that they also enjoyed the support of Enguerrand de Boves, at a time when Enguerrand and Thomas were bitter enemies, the accusation seems unfounded.

132. Guibert literally accuses Sibylle de Porcien of having "a soul more cruel than a wild she-bear" ("crudeliorem ursa fera gereret animum"). I have translated freely.

133. In Terence's *Eunuch* (P. Terenti Afri Comoediae [Leipzig: Teubner, 1848], 2.2.1.254), Parmeno the slave says of Gnatho the parasite" "What a man! He takes imbeciles and turns them right into fools" ("Scitum hercle hominem! Hic homines prorsum ex stultis insanos facit"). Since both Parmeno and Gnathos are low-class types in Terence's comedy, Guibert is perhaps implying that Enguerrand, Sibylle, and Thomas, in spite of their aristocratic origins, are essentially low class in their brutality.

such a pitch of fury that he thought it entirely right and proper to treat people as little more than beasts. Because he was being unjustly disinherited by that wretched woman (which was the case), he thought it justified for himself and his companions to gorge themselves with massacres. Every day that vicious woman would devise new strategies to raise up enemies who could overthrow Thomas; and he in turn wasted no effort in using pillage, fire, and murder to even the score with Enguerrand.

I have never in my time seen two persons come together and by their common action produce so much evil. If Thomas was the fire, one might say his stepmother was the oil. Their morals were such that after indulging in their promiscuous sexual acts they could still be just as cruel, even more so, when the opportunity presented itself. Just as the laws of marriage never held her back, so also neither of Thomas's wives could ever deter him from consorting with prostitutes or indulging in extramarital affairs. Need I say more? Every day this woman would try to think of new ways to do Thomas harm; and he in turn was unable to appease his rage in spite of murdering many an innocent person. It reached a point where one day Thomas gouged out the eyes of ten men, who died immediately. Out of sheer exhaustion, Enguerrand and Thomas would sometimes make peace for a while; but very soon that woman would rub the old sores, and slaughter would once again break out on both sides.

While the province of Laon was plagued by the malicious acts of these two, God in his justice allowed the calamity to pass to the diocese of Amiens. For after the tragic event that was the destruction of Laon, the citizens of Amiens, having bribed the king with money, created a commune to which the bishop, who was not under any violent coercion, should never have agreed, especially since he was not being pressured by anyone; and he was not in ignorance of the miserable end his fellow bishop had met with, as well as the violent conflicts between the citizens.[134] When Enguerrand, who was the count of Amiens, saw that the

134. Godfrey had been Guibert's predecessor as abbot of Nogent before becoming bishop of Amiens. Guibert adopts a judgmental tone toward him for having agreed to the creation of a commune at Amiens, by a peaceful agreement between the burghers and the bishop. Guibert has, by this time, adopted an entirely negative attitude toward communes as something inherently evil ("post funestum excidio Laudunensis eventum"). He therefore condemns the creation of a commune in Amiens without fully understanding its complex political picture. The chief resistance to the creation of a commune came from Enguerrand, who felt he was losing his ancient feudal rights without sufficient compensation.

association of burghers being formed threatened his ancient rights, he attacked the rebels with as much force as he could muster. He was aided in his effort by a certain Adam—for that was his name—who was personally in charge of a tower.[135] Having been driven from the city, Enguerrand hid himself in the tower. There he was subjected to relentless attacks by the burghers, who called upon Thomas to swear allegiance to their commune, as if he were the lord who loved them most, and they thereby stirred up the son against his presumed father. Thomas had a disgraceful mother[136] and was always deprived of fatherly affection. Meanwhile Enguerrand, who pondered the meaning of being ridiculed for his age and girth by tavern-keepers and butchers, sent for Thomas and made a pact with him. Even Thomas's stepmother was included in this renewal of friendship, which was sealed with innumerable oaths. This woman, who had an extraordinary sense of where her own interests lay, did not fail to demand considerable sums of money from Thomas for this restoration of peace.

When Thomas had fully depleted the treasury he had accumulated, he offered his support to Enguerrand against the Amiens burghers, who in turn were being supported by the bishop and the *Vidame*.[137] Thomas and Adam, the tower guardian, began a very bitter struggle against the *Vidame* and the burghers; and as both were hostile to the alliance that the bishop and his clergy had made with his burghers, Thomas was soon invading church property. He established his garrison in one of the church manors, and from there he managed to destroy the others through fire and pillage. From one of these manors he took a large company of prisoners and large sums of money; as to the large crowd of remaining refugees of both sexes and of various ages who had sought refuge in the church, Thomas burned them to death by setting fire to the church. Among the prisoners was a hermit who had come to the manor to buy bread. He had been arrested and brought before Thomas. The feast of Saint Martin was close; in fact it was coming the next day.[138] The hermit told Thomas his state in life, told him his purpose in coming, and tearfully begged for mercy for the sake of Saint Martin. Thomas pulled a dagger from his sheath and ran it through the hermit's chest and belly. "Take this," he said, "for Saint Martin."

135. Adam was the castellan of Amiens, and his tower was called Le Castillon.
136. Ada de Marle, Enguerrand's first wife.
137. Guermond de Picquigny.
138. 11 November 1113.

Thomas had also thrown a leper into prison. When an assemblage of lepers from that province heard about it they came clamoring at the tyrant's doors asking him to set their companion free.[139] Thomas threatened to burn them alive if they did not go away, and they fled in terror. Having reassembled in safety, coming from all the outlying parts of the region, they called upon God to avenge them, and shouting to the heavens with one voice they cursed him. The leper died that very day in the prison into which Thomas had thrown him. Likewise, a pregnant woman who had been thrown into a dungeon also died there.

A few of his prisoners happened to be walking too slowly for Thomas's tastes, so he ordered his men to pierce their throats in the place called the "windpipe," and had cords inserted into five or six of them, if I am not mistaken, and made them march in terrible pain.[140] Soon afterward they perished in captivity. Need I add more? On this occasion alone Thomas himself put thirty prisoners to the sword.

His stepmother, seeing that Thomas was braving many dangers and anxious to see him killed, ordered the *Vidame* to keep a secret watch over his comings and goings. One night, as Thomas was on his way somewhere—I don't know where, exactly—the *Vidame* laid an ambush for him and riddled his body with wounds: one enemy footsoldier struck him in the leg with his lance. Seriously wounded in the knee and in other places, Thomas had to call off his enterprise.

Before his church suffered its tragic destruction, the bishop of Amiens was getting ready to celebrate Mass on a feast day. One priest, who appeared truly religious, had unwittingly celebrated Mass right before the bishop while consecrating nothing but water. The same thing happened to the bishop. Having drunk out of the chalice and realized that

139. It is interesting to note the sense of solidarity that existed among lepers at this time, comparable to the bonding felt by members of the same guild or association.

140. Guibert's text clearly reads: "quibus sub collo eas quas vocitant canolas praecipiens perforari." Benton (*Self and Society*, 201) and Labande (*Guibert de Nogent*, 404) both seem to doubt that Guibert could have been so cruel as to pierce the windpipes of his prisoners. Benton suggests that Thomas yoked them like cattle, the word *canole* meaning both "windpipe" and "cord" in old French. It seems entirely credible that Thomas might add the piercing of prisoners' windpipes to a list of cruelties that included the burning of a church containing innocent hostages, the fatal stabbing of a hermit, and the imprisonment of a leper and of a pregnant woman. And it seems doubtful that, as Benton suggests (*Self and Society*, 201n.10), Guibert was "unfamiliar with the technical terms of the peasantry" to the point of not knowing the two meanings of the word *canola*.

there was nothing but water in it he said: "Surely a great evil is going to befall this church." The misfortune that had befallen the priest earlier certainly confirmed this.

When the bishop realized that his presence was desirable neither to the clergy nor to the people, since he could please no one, he took one of our monks with him, and without consulting anybody he gave his clergy and the people what you might call a letter of annulment. He sent his ring and his sandals back to the archbishop of Reims and let everyone know that he was going into exile and that he would never be a bishop again. Once an ex-bishop, he set off for Cluny where he acted as a bishop once again of his own initiative and consecrated an altar. He then left Cluny to go to the Chartreuse, a place I have already spoken about at the start of this book.[141] There he lived in a cell away from the community, keeping for himself six marks of silver out of the provisions he had taken on the road. When two months had passed, he was called back, not by one of his own clergy but by the archbishop, and he was not slow to return, for he knew that the money he had brought with him would be useful for the return trip. It was not without regret that the clergy and the people received him back, for during his absence they had not managed to find a replacement for the man whom they had rejected with a certain contempt. The bishop himself was the one who had set forces in motion that he could no longer control.[142]

Back to Thomas. He was carried back to his home, his wounds having made it impossible for him to do anything. Now Adam's son, a very handsome lad named Alleaume, had become engaged to one of Thomas's daughters; and Enguerrand's foul concubine, now that she had neutralized Thomas, was getting ready to attack Adam and his tower. Until now Adam had remained loyal to Enguerrand against the Amiens burghers. With the help of the king, she lay siege to the tower. One should remember that Adam had paid homage to the king and had not broken his word. The king, in turn, had received him in fealty.[143]

141. Guibert has earlier discussed the founding of the Grande Chartreuse by Saint Bruno (1.11).

142. Godfrey notified the Council of Beauvais of his abdication sometime between November and December 1114. He was reinstated by the Council of Reims in late March 1115. In telling of Godfrey's resignation as bishop and of his subsequent reinstallation, Guibert uses a similar irony toward his coy predecessor as he used toward himself in admitting his naiveté toward the commune at Amiens.

143. Guibert is implying that King Louis VI should not have attacked Adam the

No one can say, not even those who were involved in its dangers, how many burghers were massacred by those in the tower, not only before the siege but even more so afterward. There was no activity among the townsmen, only passive suffering. At first, before the evil had spread, Bishop Godefroy could have calmed the situation, as everyone knows, had he not feared his *Vidame,* who had the utmost contempt for him. It is clearly the *Vidame*'s practice to revere or favor only those who speak ill of, or do ill to, the bishop; but when one is afraid of being bitten by someone else and begins knowingly trying to please this most treacherous person, God in his righteous judgments allows everybody to tear this person to pieces, starting with the one he fears most.

Thomas was unable to deliver the tower in which he had placed his daughter and some of his best soldiers. So evil were the deeds he had committed that the archbishops and the bishops had brought the complaints of their churches to the king and added that they would stop performing the divine services in his kingdom unless he punished Thomas.[144] At the time that stinking wretch was aiding the burghers of Laon against Enguerrand. Toward the middle of Lent, Gautier (who has been mentioned already), the only one of Gérard's betrayers still living, came with Guy, his fellow archdeacon, to meet with his uterine sister, Enguerrand's worthy companion.[145] Gautier had himself promoted this adulterous union. Thomas learned of his mission and swiftly despatched a delegation to a certain Robert—one of those thoroughly corrupt paid criminals such as Thomas likes to have in his service—ordering him to watch Gautier upon his return from Amiens and to kill him if possible. Robert waited on the mountain of Laon itself to spy the archdeacon's advance; then with his men he rode down in Gautier's direction, using the deep curve in the road where it comes down from the mountain. Gautier had sent his companions on ahead and was already approaching the city on his mule. Taking advantage of that moment when Gautier was alone, Robert's men attacked him and treacherously put him to the sword. Once he was dead, they returned to Thomas in a gay mood, bringing Gautier's mule with them.

News of these and other crimes, punctuated by loud, painful outcries

---

castellan because Adam "regi hominum fecerat, nec ab eo defecerat." Louis should have known better than to throw his support to the side of Sibylle de Porcien.

144. The Council of Beauvais made this statement to the king late in the year 1114.

145. Gautier was the son of Roger, count of Porcien, and the brother of Sibylle de Porcien.

from the churches, reached the king's ears. During Lent of the year following the archdeacon's assassination the king raised an army against Thomas and attacked the strongholds that Thomas had built in the manors of the abbey of Saint-Jean. Those in knightly order were not very hearty in their offer of help to the king, since few of them presented themselves; but the force of lightly-armed footmen was immense. When Thomas got word of the army that was being raised against him he could only chatter mockingly, confined as he was to his bed. The king summoned him to destroy those unlawful castles, but Thomas contemptuously refused; when many of his close associates offered him their assistance he spurned it. Then the archbishop and the bishops mounted high platforms that had been built for the purpose, assembled a large crowd of people, gave them their instructions for this purpose, absolved them of their sins,[146] and ordered them as a form of penance and as a means of assuring the salvation of their souls to storm the famous castle called Crécy.[147]

With admirable boldness, the crowd began its assault. Now this fortress was so extraordinarily massive that many people thought it ridiculous to attempt to take it. In spite of a vigorous defense by the castle's inhabitants the king captured the first moat, gained a footing under the great door of the castle, and summoned the defenders to surrender. When they refused to do so the king swore he would fast until the place was taken. The king nevertheless put off his assault that day; but the next day he returned and armed himself, although hardly any of the knights wanted to take up arms with him. Charging them with open treason the king grouped his infantry together and was the first to charge across the moat and to try to get inside the walls. Soon they had penetrated the castle's defenses, found a great abundance of food supplies, captured the defenders, and destroyed the castle.

A short distance away Thomas had established another fortress by the name of Nouvion. Its keys were brought to the king and its inhabitants fled. At Crécy some of the prisoners were hanged to instill terror

146. The attack on Crécy-sur-Serre, situated about ten miles north of Laon, took place in April 1115.

147. Thomas had "unlawfully" built strongholds at Crécy-sur-Serre and Nouvion-l'Abbesse, on land that belonged to the convent of Saint-Jean de Laon. It is interesting that the archbishop and the bishops are treating Thomas as an "infidel" and assuring the attackers the same benefits in attacking Crécy as they would be entitled to in going on a Crusade.

in the defenders; and others were killed in other ways. As for the attackers I am not sure whether they lost more than one soldier. As for Thomas he stayed in safety at Marle, paid a money ransom to the king and his courtiers, repaired the damages he had done to the churches, and procured peace on one side and a readmission to Holy Communion on the other. Thus, the proudest and most wicked of men was punished by the hand of the poorest people, whom he had so often punished and despised.

I must not fail to mention that when the king came to Laon with his army the bad weather made all military action impossible. Then the archbishop said to them: "Let us pray God to give us good weather if he wants us to accomplish our task." No sooner had he spoken when the weather turned fair.

On Palm Sunday[148] Bishop Godefroy returned from the Chartreuse and began preaching things far different from what he had learned there. He summoned the king and on that solemn and venerable feast he preached a sermon more Ciceronian in tone than divine, inciting the king and the people standing around him to action against those in the tower, promising the kingdom of heaven to those who should die in the attack.[149] On the next day enormous siege machines were brought up to the wall of the Castillon—for such was the tower's name—and knights were placed in them. The people in the tower had previously protected themselves with curtain walls so as to conceal their defenses. As for the bishop he had gone barefooted to Saint-Acheul, but his prayers were not to be heeded in this matter. The tower people, in the meantime, were allowing the enemy to draw close to their walls and to move the siege-towers into position. Once they were in place, a man by the name of Aleran, an expert in such matters, placed opposite them two catapults that he had built, and charged some eighty women with the task of jettisoning the large stones that he had placed in the catapults.[150] The defenders in the tower had now begun to fight the attackers with swords. And while the men defended their ramparts with a courage worthy of Achilles, the women, not to be outdone, hurled stones from the catapults

148. Palm Sunday, 11 April 1115.

149. Bishop Godfrey also treats the attack on the tower at Amiens as a holy crusade, promising the kingdom of heaven to the attackers.

150. Women—presumably wives of burghers who were favorable to the commune at Amiens—played a key role in the long siege of the tower of Le Castillon at Amiens, whose defenders were hostile to the commune.

and destroyed the two towers. As the shower of missiles intensified, however, all eighty women, it is reported, were wounded, and they even wounded the king with a shaft that pierced his mail-coated breast. Of all those who were pierced with arrows only one was saved. I have this information from a cleric named Rothard, a nephew of the bishop.

Seeing themselves overrun, the soldiers who were perched in the siege-machines began taking flight and were soon joined by the others. Once they were gone the defenders in the tower surged forward, smashed the siege-machines, and dragged the pieces of timber back inside, watched from afar by nearly three thousand men who had fought before but did not dare to attack now. The king now realized that the tower was impregnable and retreated, ordering the place blockaded until the defenders were starved into submission. The siege is still in effect today, and it is impossible to say the number of burghers alone who are perishing every day.[151] Adam is positioned outside the suburbs of the city and launches frequent attacks against Enguerrand and the *Vidame.* If vexation gives understanding to those who are willing to hear [Isa. 28.19], they might understand that, even though Thomas might have been defeated, not every cause is the same, nor are God's judgments so equal toward all as to give a bishop license to incite others to murder.[152]

15
Wicked crimes at Laon. The thief Anselm is tried and executed

Before going on to events in the surrounding regions—for we are going to say something about the people of Soissons—it should be known that of all the provinces of France the people of Laon are the most abominable in their conduct. For, besides killing priests, a bishop, and an archdeacon, most recently the abbess of Saint-Jean, an extraordinary woman

151. The siege had not ended at the time Guibert was writing, presumably later in the year 1115.
152. This is the last of Guibert's jibes against bishop Godfrey for having "incited others to murder" by agreeing to the creation of the Laon commune.

by the name of Rainsende, a native of Laon from an outstanding family
and a benefactor of the Church, was murdered by one of her serfs and
bore her suffering out of loyalty to the church.[153] Might we not say that
the church of Laon has had its share of sacrileges? Since the Queen of
the Universe did not leave these deeds unpunished, it is only proper that
we should enter into some detail.

Those whom we call sextons, who were charged with the safekeeping
of the church treasures, began stealing the sacred vessels and then putting the blame on the clerics who governed them, for these sextons were
simple laymen. At first just a few of them committed these crimes. Then,
in a second phase, Anselm, an uncouth barbarian who came from the
dregs of the city, made off with crosses, chalices and other gold objects
before matins one night after Christmas. Then some time later he
brought a small portion of the gold he had stolen to sell it to a Soissons
merchant; he admitted to having committed this sacrilegious theft but
made the merchant swear not to betray him. The merchant, however,
soon heard that those who had participated in the crime were being
excommunicated throughout the parishes of Soissons; and after thinking
the matter over he came to Laon and revealed everything to the clergy.
Need I say more? When he was summoned Anselm denied everything.
The merchant deposited money as a guarantee of his good faith and
challenged Anselm to a boxing match, which the latter could not avoid.
It was Sunday. The fight began, hurried on by some clerics, and the man
who had challenged the robber was beaten and fell to the ground. This
incident makes one of two things clear: either the merchant, in breaking
his oath and betraying the robber, had behaved unjustly, or—and this
seems much closer to the truth—the merchant fell victim to an absolutely invalid law. What is quite certain is that there is no canon to
legitimize such a law.[154]

Anselm felt safer after his victory and marched on to sacrilege number
three. By some incredible trick he managed to force his way into the
church treasury and to steal gold and jewels in abundance. After his
theft, when he submitted to the ordeal of the holy water and was thrown
in with the other sextons, he was convicted by staying afloat on the

153. Abbess Rainsende was murdered in August 1112, a few months after the uprising of the commune.

154. There had been some clerical resistance to laws or combats, or ordeals, to
prove the guilt or innocence of an accused person; but these were obviously still being
practiced.

surface, along with others who were party to his first theft. Some of these were hanged and others acquitted. When Anselm himself was dragged to the gallows he said he would talk; but once freed he changed his mind. When he was hoisted on the gallows a second time he swore to reveal everything. Once he was freed he said: "Without a reward I will do nothing." — "Well, you'll be hanged," they said. "And you," he replied, "will have nothing." In the meantime he was hurling insults of all kinds at the castellan Nicolas, son of Guimar, an outstanding young man who was in charge of the proceedings.[155] The bishop and Master Anselm of Laon were consulted as to what should be done. They answered: "It is better to give him some money rather than lose such a quantity of gold." It was agreed that he would be paid about five hundred sous,[156] and when that promise had been made, he gave back much of the gold, which he had hidden in his vineyard.

He had agreed to leave the country after the bishop agreed to grant him a three-day grace period to do so. Since he wanted to escape secretly within that time, he had already scouted each and every exit in the city. Then he saw great rivers appear before his eyes that seemed to bar his advance entirely. These floods of water present in his mind's eye, though invisible, compelled him openly to remain on the spot without being able to steal away with the fruit of his thefts. When he was approached he said, mumbling his words like a raving madman, that he would not leave. When the bishop urged him even more forcefully to do so, he began murmuring like someone quite beside himself, that he knew of other things that he had neglected to say. The bishop learned of this through his *Vidame* and, since the robber had already sworn that he knew nothing, the bishop seized the opportunity to take from this robber the money he had suggested the robber be given, and had him thrown into prison. After being tortured he admitted that he had on him some jewels from a broken vessel. Then he led his torturers to the hiding place and showed them these objects wrapped in a little cloth bag and hanging under a stone. With all these other things he had also stolen some holy reliquaries, but so long as he had them in his possession he had been unable to

155. Guimar, already mentioned in 3.8, was an important noble of Laon who fought for Bishop Gaudry during the uprising of the commune. He may have been in charge of the fortress of Laon and he seems to have survived the slaughter that followed the insurrection. See Benton, *Self and Society,* 174n.2.

156. About twenty pounds, enough to buy five good horses or a medium-sized vineyard (Benton, *Self and Society,* 208n.4).

sleep: the saints kept beating his savage spirit, which was quite overcome by the horror of such a blasphemous deed. Finally he too was hoisted on a scaffold and went off to join his fathers, who were surely devils.

16
Count Jean of Soissons and his many crimes

Now turning my pen to what I had promised: Jean, count of Soissons, was a man skilled in the military arts and eager to make peace, yet his only real concern was looking after his own interests. From his father and grandfather he had inherited a wicked character that led to the ruin of Mother Church.[157] Moreover, his mother, among other marvelous signs of her power, had ordered a deacon's tongue pulled out of his throat and his eyes gouged out. No doubt the daring of a parricide pushed her to commit extraordinary deeds, for once with the help of a Jew she had poisoned her own brother just because she coveted his county; and for this deed the Jew was burned at the stake. After dining to excess on the eve of the first day of Lent, she herself suffered a paralyzing stroke a few hours after falling asleep that night, incurring loss of speech, and total incapacitation of her body. Worst of all she never thereafter had the slightest taste for anything pertaining to God and lived like a pig. By the just judgment of God, her tongue was almost cut out in an attempt to cure her. She remained this way from the beginning of Lent until the octave of Easter, when she died. Between her and her sons — this Count Jean and Bishop Manasses[158] — there were not merely rivalries, but deep, deadly hatreds; for in that family they all hate one another. As she was being led to her place of burial and was being interred, Count Jean himself told me some of the things I have just

157. Jean was the son of Guillaume Busac and Alais, daughter of Count Renaud of Soissons. He is mentioned as count of Soissons as early as 1082.

158. Manasses, bishop of Soissons, mentions Guibert in a charter of 1107. Guibert seems to have been on familiar terms with both Manasses and John. He relies on John for some of his information ("inter sepeliendum mihi comes isdem de ea quae sunt superius relata narrabat").

related and added: "Why should I lavish money on her when she was unwilling to do so for the salvation of her own soul?"

In sum Count Jean, of whom it might have been said: "Your father was an Amorite and your mother a Hittite,"[159] not only duplicated his parents' wickedness; he did things far worse. He regarded the false beliefs of Jews and heretics so highly that he personally uttered blasphemies against the Savior, something the Jews out of fear of the faithful never dared to do. The evil with which he set his mouth against heaven might be understood from a little book I wrote against him at the request of Dean Bernard.[160] Since these are words that cannot be pronounced in the mouth of a Christian, and that the ears of the pious can only abhor, I have omitted them. In spite of his high regard for Jews, the Jews themselves thought him insane, for while he said he approved of their practices he publicly followed ours.

At Christmas and during Passiontide and on other holy days he exhibited such humility that one would scarcely think him a heretic. On one Easter eve he had made his way into a church for the vigil, having begged a pious cleric to tell him something about the mystery of those days. When the cleric had explained to him how the Lord had suffered, and how he had risen from the dead, the count hissed and said: "That's all fable and wind!" The cleric replied: "If it's all fable and wind, why are you here keeping vigil?" "Because," he said, "I enjoy watching the beautiful women who spend the night here."[161] This was a man who could spurn his young and lovely wife to cavort with a wrinkled old hag. He would often have a bed prepared for himself and this old woman in the house of a Jew; but he could not restrict his lust to a mere cot. Such was the fury of his lust that he would throw himself upon this squalid woman in some dirty old corner or in some closet. Once he even ordered a miserable parasite to sleep with his own wife and to impersonate him in

159. Cf. Ezek. 16.3: "And say, Thus says the Lord God to Jerusalem: Your origin and your birth are of the land of the Canaanites; your father was an Amorite, and your mother a Hittite." Like Ezekiel speaking of Jerusalem, Guibert is implying that Jean of Soissons should have taken no false pride in his "barbaric" origins.

160. *Tractatus de Incarnatione contra Judeos* (*PL* 156.489–528). Guibert wrote the *Tractatus* about the year 1111, at the request of Bernard, dean of Soissons. He mentions it earlier in the *Monodiae* (2.5) as the book he sent to Guillaume, the Jew who converted to the monastic life, at Saint-Germer.

161. "Pulchras . . . mulieres, quae istic coexcubant, libenter attendo." The verb *coexcubare* can mean to "keep vigil" and to "sleep out."

his own bed with the lights out, so that he might accuse her of adultery. His wife immediately sensed from the feel of the man's body that this was not the count—her husband's skin was covered with pustular boils—and she began striking this rascal with all her strength, with the help of her women-in-waiting. Need I say more? His sexual abuses spared neither dedicated women nor cloistered nuns, nor did he ever abjure open rivalry with the holy brothers.

At last the Virgin Mother, who is queen of all, could no longer put up with the blasphemies of this foul, stinking man. One day, as he was coming back from an expedition in the king's company, an enormous swarm of fellow devils appeared to him as he was approaching the city. When he got home his hair was standing on end and he was out of his wits. That night he rejected his wife and slept with the old hag, and later he fell ill with a deadly disease. He was now beginning to panic, and he asked the cleric with whom he had spent the Easter vigil to examine his urine. The cleric began talking to him about death, about his soul, and about his debaucheries. The count interjected: "Do you think I'm going to hand out my money to some ass-licking priests?[162] No, I tell you, not a penny. I have learned from many people far cleverer than you that all women should be in common and that this is a sin of no consequence." This is what he said; and from then on there was nothing other than rage in his words and in his gestures. His wife was standing next to him, and he tried to kick her with his foot, but instead he struck a soldier so hard that he knocked him to the ground. The man was now totally insane, and those around him had to tie his hands to prevent him from clawing at himself or others. Finally he fell back exhausted, and the devils could then wrench his iniquitous soul from the hands of the Virgin Mother and of her divine Son.[163]

17

The trial and punishment of some Soissons heretics

Since we have in mind the heretics whom this impious Count of Soissons loved, we might mention a certain peasant by the name of Clement, who

162. "Vis . . . ut leccatoribus, scilicet presbyteris, mea erogem?"
163. John of Soissons died late in September of 1115.

with his brother Evrard lived at Bucy,[164] a village in the vicinity of Soissons. It was commonly reported that he was one of the leaders of a heresy. The infamous count used to go around saying that a wiser man than this Clement was nowhere to be found.

This is not the type of heresy whose teaching is openly defended by its holders; rather, it crawls clandestinely like a serpent and reveals itself only through its perpetual slitherings. In a nutshell it might be summed up as follows: they declare that the incarnation of the Virgin's Son is a delusion; they reject the baptism of children before the age of reason whoever the godparents may be; they call their own discourse the word of God, which comes about through a long recitation of words; they so abhor the mystery that we perform upon our altars that they call the mouth of any priest the mouth of hell. If in order to hide their heresy from others they ever receive our sacraments, on that day they consider themselves bound to fast and take no more food that day. They make no distinction for cemeteries between sacred ground and any other type of ground. They condemn marriage and the procreation of offspring; and indeed, wherever they are scattered throughout the Latin world one might see men living with women without taking the name of husband and wife. Nor do men and women confine themselves to the same partner: men are known to sleep with other men, women with women, for they hold the intercourse of man and woman to be a crime. They eliminate any offspring issuing from their intercourse.

They hold their meetings in underground vaults or hidden cellars, without distinction of sex. Then they light candles and come forward to present them from behind to a young girl who, it is reported, lies in a prone position having bared her buttocks for all to see. Soon the candles are extinguished, they shout "Chaos!" from all sides and everyone has intercourse with the first person who happens to be at hand. If a woman becomes pregnant in the process, they come back to the same spot after she has given birth. A large fire is lit, and those sitting around toss the baby from one hand to another through the flames until the child is dead. When the child's body has been reduced to ashes they make bread with these ashes and a part is distributed to everyone as a kind of sacrament, and once it is taken no one ever recovers from that heresy. If one rereads the list of heresies compiled by Augustine one realizes that this one is

164. Bucy-le-Long, about three miles east of Soissons.

most like that of the Manicheans.[165] Originally started by well-educated people, this heresy filtered down to the peasants who, claiming to be leading the apostolic life, have read the "Acts" of the Apostles and little else.

So bishop Lisiard of Soissons, a most illustrious man, summoned before him for the purposes of an inquiry these two heretics we have mentioned. The bishop began by charging them with holding meetings outside the church and with being known as heretics by those around them. To which Clement replied: "My lord, have you not read in the gospel where it says, "Beati eritis"? ["You shall be happy?"][166] Since he was illiterate he thought the word *eritis* meant "heretics," and moreover he thought "heretics" was to be understood in the sense of "heirs," though not of God to be sure. When they were interrogated about their beliefs, they answered in a most Christian fashion, yet did not deny holding meetings. But since such people typically deny all charges and then seduce the hearts of simple-minded people in secret, they were sentenced to the ordeal of exorcised water. While the preparations for this ordeal were taking place the bishop asked me to draw their opinions out of them in private. When I brought up the question of infant baptism they answered: "Whoever believes and is baptized shall be saved."[167] As I was aware that such a good answer could, in their case, conceal the most subtle perversity I asked them what they thought about those who are baptized according to another faith. They answered: "For God's sake, do not expect us to search so deeply!" And to each of the questions they added: "We believe everything you say." Then I remembered one of those sayings that all of the Priscillianists used to assent to: "Swear, perjure yourself, but don't give away the secret."[168] So I turned to the

---

165. See Augustine, *Liber de haeresibus ad Quodvultdeum* (*PL* 42.34–38). Most descriptions of heresy in France in the eleventh and twelfth centuries refer to variants of Manicheanism such as those listed by Augustine. The Manichean revulsion against marriage, especially for purposes of procreation, is described (42.33): "et si utuntur conjugibus, conceptum tamen generationemque devitent, ne divina substantia quae in eos per alimenta ingreditur, vinculis carneis ligetur in prole." In spite of his own austere view of sexuality, Augustine condemned the Manichean teaching that the body is the creation of an evil deity, and the consequent Manichean dissociation of sexuality from procreation.

166. John 13.17: "If you know these things, blessed are you if you do them."

167. Guibert is quoting Mark 16.16: "qui crediderit et baptizatus fuerit salvus erit."

168. This is a direct quotation from Saint Augustine's *Liber de haeresibus* (*PL* 42.44). Speaking of the Priscillianists' tendency to indulge in secrecy even at the cost of per-

bishop and said: "Since the witnesses who heard them profess this doctrine are not here, lead them to the judgment that has been prepared." The witnesses were a certain lady, whom Clement had been driving mad during the past year, and a deacon who had heard Clement say the most perverse things.

So the bishop celebrated Mass, and the heretics received the sacrament from his hand as he said: "May the body and blood of the Lord try you this day." Afterward, this most holy bishop headed for the waters, along with Peter the archdeacon, a man of unshakable faith who had rejected the heretics' request not to be submitted to the ordeal. With many tears the bishop recited the litany and then proceeded to the exorcism, after which the accused swore they had never believed or taught anything contrary to our faith. Thrown into the vat of water, Clement stayed afloat like a piece of straw. Seeing this the whole assembly went rapturous with joy. It should be added that this test had drawn such a crowd, of both sexes, that no one present could remember ever having seen anything like it. Clement's companion confessed his error but without expressing any compunction; and with his convicted brother he was thrown into chains. Two other avowed heretics from the village of Dormans[169] had come to the spectacle, and likewise they were arrested.

We then went on to the Council of Beauvais to consult with the bishops about what should be done. But in the meantime the faithful people, fearing the weakness of the clergy, ran to the prison, forced it open, and burned the heretics on a large pyre they had lit outside the city. Thus the people of God, fearing the spread of this cancer, took the matter of justice into their own zealous hands.[170]

---

jury, Augustine says of this "perverse" Manichean sect: "Propter occultandas autem contaminationes et turpitudines suas habent in suis dogmatibus et haec verba: Jura, perjura, secretum prodere noli."

169. A village on the Marne belonging to the count of Champagne.

170. Guibert approves the fanaticism of the mob toward the (presumed) heretics, comparing it to a preventive surgical operation on a cancer ("Quorum ne propagaretur carcinus"). As in the case of the simoniacal distribution of church prebends (1.7), the *populus* often preceded, and exceeded the clergy in both its zeal and its violence.

18

Demonstrations of the Virgin's miraculous power in northern France

At Noyon there is a parish church that Hardouin, a former bishop, had dedicated in honor of Saint Nicaise. When the saint's relics were translated to this place by the people of Reims, they lay in repository here for a while: not in the church itself but in the city. About five years before, as the feast of the martyr drew near, the parish priest had ordered that it be celebrated on the appropriate date. On that very day a poor young girl who lived alone with her mother had dared to do a small piece of needlework.[171] While she was preparing the work with her hands she stretched the thread between her tongue and her lips, as is usually done in such cases; but a very large knot of thread lodged itself into the tip of her tongue as if it had been very sharp. It was impossible to remove it, and anyone who tried to do so merely provoked intolerable pain in the poor girl. In the company of her mother and a great crowd the unlucky girl made her way toward the cathedral to invoke the mercy of the Queen of martyrs—but not with words. Indeed, she could hardly speak at all, since the thread had pierced her tongue and was left hanging from it. Why say more? After witnessing the poor girl's long struggle with pain, the weeping crowd of spectators went home. The girl herself, with her mother beside her, persevered in prayer that whole day and the following night. On the following day, they both implored the Queen of heaven with the most intensely heartfelt prayers (so it was reported to me by Anselm the priest, who was the sacristan of that church), the mother reciting litanies and the daughter responding in a low voice, all of this in admirable alternation as if they both knew Latin. After this, the daughter approached the altar of the Virgin Mother and tearfully embraced it. And all of a sudden, amid her repeated embraces, the thread fell off.

The clergy and the people rushed to the scene of such a great miracle and rendered unending praise to God and to the Virgin mother. In this matter she had indeed proved herself the Queen of martyrs, for while avenging herself of a fault that had been committed against a martyr,[172]

171. All manual work was forbidden on Sundays and feast days, under the pain of mortal sin.
172. Against Saint Nicaise, whose feast it was.

she had also calmed her need for revenge after she had received satisfaction. The martyr's excellence, in turn, was also made abundantly clear, for it was obvious that if he had punished a poor humble girl, how much harsher he would be in punishing the proud who strive against him? This story was related to me in the very church in which it occurred; and the priest I have just mentioned showed me the extraordinarily large thread, with the knot still covered with blood! Closer to our day a similar case occurred on the feast of the Annunciation of the Blessed Mary. It was recorded in writing by Radbod, bishop of Noyon.

On the lands belonging to this very church of Nogent, which we serve by the grace of God, a knight had committed robbery by carrying off oxen belonging to the brothers. When he reached the castle of Chauny[173] he cooked one of the oxen with the intention of eating it along with his accomplices. As he was about to put the first piece of meat into his mouth, he was struck down by God's might. As he was preparing to chew, both his eyes flew out of their sockets, and his tongue flew from his mouth. Thus condemned, the man was forced to give back what he had stolen, whether he liked it or not.

Another knight attempted to annex to his fishing property a segment of the neighboring river, called the Ailette, which had belonged to the brothers of this abbey of Nogent since ancient times. The knight drove away from this part of the stream one of the brothers trying to fish and brought many suits against the church of Nogent on this matter; but one day the powerful Lady struck him down by paralyzing him in several parts of his body. The knight ascribed this mishap to chance, not to divine vengeance, so the most holy Virgin came up to him as he lay sleeping and gave him several not very gentle slaps on the face.[174] This woke him up and brought him to his senses. The man immediately came barefooted to me to ask my forgiveness, showing me what Blessed Mary had done to him in her anger, and restored what he had usurped. If I have learned one thing, it is this: no one is hostile to the church and perseveres in his hostility without clearly inflicting damage on himself.

At Compiègne some royal provost kept harassing the church of the Blessed Mary and of the blessed Corneille and Cyprien. The clergy as-

173. About twelve miles north of Nogent, on the Oise.
174. It must have been consoling for Guibert to know that the fishing rights of his abbey were protected by a Lady as powerful and swift in her interventions as any of the Olympian goddesses.

sembled in the middle of the marketplace and in the name of that great
Lady and of so many patron saints called upon him to put an end to his
harassment. The provost showed no respect for any of these holy names
but, rather, hurled the most vile accusations to the faces of his suppliants.
Sitting on his horse as he screamed, he suddenly fell to the ground, and
his bowels gave way beneath him, so that at once he found his breeches
as messy as can be.

Since we have started speaking about the respect that should be shown
to the saints, there is in that same region a town by the name of Saint-
Just, which belongs to the bishop of Beauvais. There was an insurrection
in the town, and a few lower class types, fed by incredible arrogance,
mounted a vicious attack against the town burghers. To calm the popu-
lace some clerics bore in the feretory relics of Saint Just the child and
martyr. One individual who had placed himself in a more advantageous
position than the others came out and blocked the procession and irrev-
erently struck the most sacred reliquary with his sword. Faster than it
takes to say the words, he fell to the ground and, like the man just
mentioned, there issued from him the stink of his own excrement.

In the same district of Beauvais there lived in one of the manors a
priest who had charge of a church. A peasant from the same area showed
great hatred for him, and the situation grew so serious that the priest
was in danger of being killed. Since he could do nothing openly, the
peasant attempted to poison the priest. He therefore cut up a toad into
little pieces and poured them into an earthen jar that the priest used to
keep his mass wine. The vessels made for this purpose usually have
protruding bellies and a long, narrow neck. When the priest came to
celebrate his mass, he performed the sacred mysteries with that poisoned
wine. He had hardly finished when he began to feel deathly ill, to be
disgusted at the sight of food, to vomit everything he had eaten and
drunk, and to waste away completely. After being bedridden a long time
he managed painfully to get up and made his way to the church. He held
up the vase that he now knew to be at the root of his illness, broke open
its neck with a knife and poured onto the floor all the liquid it contained.
It was as if the wine used for the consecration at the Mass was full of
spawn teeming with tadpoles. Now the priest realized that his insides
were mortally afflicted; but while in the deepest despair and awaiting his
fate as something inevitable, someone gave him this piece of advice: "If
you want to throw up all the poisonous matter you have swallowed ask
someone to bring you dust from the tomb of Marcel, the bishop of Paris,

or from his altar.[175] You must take it with water, and then you can be sure you will immediately get better." The priest hastened to carry out this advice, and with a deep devotion toward the saint he drank the sacred dust. Immediately he began to vomit globs of countless reptiles, with all the infectious stuff in which they were imbedded. His illness disappeared entirely, and he got his health back. It is not surprising that Marcel, now in God's presence, is able to do these things, for even earlier, when his body kept him at a distance from God, he had accomplished things no less wonderful in a similar case.[176]

19

Other marvelous occurrences.
The Devil remains active

The story I am about to relate, which is without precedent in our time, I learned from a monk both humble and pious named Geoffroy. Formerly Geoffroy had been lord of Saumur as well as other castles in Burgundy. Because his life was distinguished by a commitment to truth, I think this story should be told in his own words. Here it is. On the neighboring lands right above his there lived a young man bonded to a woman not in the proper, that is, matrimonial, manner, but, if I may speak like Solinus, in a mercenary, that is, improper, manner. Having at long last regained his wits for a while he played with the idea of going on a pilgrimage to Saint-James in Galicia.[177] But he introduced a bit of leaven into the

175. Saint Marcel was bishop of Paris in the early fifth century.

176. The "marvelous" occurrences narrated in this and other chapters have several related, underlying motifs in common: (1) the power of Mary (and the saints) to intervene, or avenge, is similar to God's own power; (2) immanent retribution awaits any act, big or small, committed against God, the saints, or the church; (3) all temporal rights and possessions of the church fall irrevocably under this protection.

177. The pilgrimage to the church of Saint James of Compostela, in northwestern Spain, which, according to ancient traditions, was evangelized by the apostle Saint James the Major, was perhaps the most famous in medieval Europe. See William Melczer, *The Pilgrim's Guide to Santiago de Compostela* (New York: Italica Press, 1993), 7–23.

dough of his good intention, for he was bringing the woman's sash with him and using it improperly as a memento of her; and so what had begun as a proper offering was now being used for an improper, divided purpose.[178] In the course of the trip, the Devil made it a point to run into the man, disguised as Saint James the Apostle, and said to him: "Where are you headed?" "To Saint-James," replied the other. "It's not worth the effort," said the Devil, "I am James whom you are going out to see, but you are carrying on you an object that is totally unworthy of my dignity. For until now you have wallowed in the mire of your own fornication, and suddenly you wish to appear like a penitent, and like anyone who would like to reap the fruits of a good initiative, you claim to be going to visit my shrine. Yet you're still wearing the sash of that obscene whore of yours!" The man blushed at hearing this, and thinking he was dealing with the holy apostle he said: "I know, my lord, that then, and even now, I have behaved most shamefully. Tell me, please, what advice you would give to one who was about to appeal to your mercy." "If you wish," said the other, "to produce penitential fruits that are worthy of the turpitudes you have committed, cut off that member by which you have sinned—your penis, that is—as a sign of fidelity to God and to me. After that, do away with your own life, which you have conducted so badly, by slitting your throat." After saying this the devil vanished from the man's eyes, leaving his mind in the greatest upheaval.[179]

Returning to his inn that night he made preparations to heed the advice not of the apostle (as he believed) but of the Devil. When his companions were asleep he began by cutting off his penis, then he plunged the knife into his throat. But his companions were roused from their sleep by the dying man's cries of agony and by the gurgling sound of his blood as it rushed out. Bringing torches, they saw what had happened to him; and they were stricken with grief in seeing the horrendous end their friend had brought upon himself, without realizing that he had

178. A pilgrim must go forth on pilgrimage with a complete purity of heart in order to expect remission of sin. By bringing his mistress's sash with him the young man remains in a state of sin.

179. Guibert's disclaimer for using Geoffroy's "own words" to tell this story is perhaps merely a disguise for his own prurience here. Benton notes (*Self and Society*, 218n.2) that this story first appears as a poem by Guaiferius of Salerno, an eleventh-century monk of Monte Cassino, entitled *De miraculo illius qui seipsum occidit* (*PL* 147.1285–88).

been counseled by the Devil. Being unaware of the causes that underlay this event they did not refuse him the rites of burial, which in such a case he should not have been entitled to; rather, they arranged for the celebration of a Mass in honor of one whom they took for their companion in pilgrimage. As these prayers were addressed to God in faith, it pleased God to heal the wound in the dead man's throat and to revive him through the intercession of his apostle. The man sat up and, amid a consternation that is beyond all telling, he began to speak. When his companions inquired about his motives for wanting to kill himself he admitted that the Devil had appeared to him in the guise of the apostle. They asked him what judgment he had incurred after he had killed himself. He answered: "I was carried before the throne of God, in the presence of our Lady the Virgin Mary, Mother of God. My patron, the Apostle Saint James, was there also. There followed a debate in God's presence about what should happen to me. The blessed apostle remembered my intention, however sinful and corrupt it had been until now, implored the blessed mother in my favor. And from that sweetest of mouths there issued my sentence: to a man as unlucky as I, who had run into the wiles of the Devil cloaked in saintly garb, indulgence was to be granted. Thus, with God's permission, I have been allowed to return to this world, to amend my life, and to denounce these devils."

The old man who told me this story said he had heard it from someone who had seen this man after his resurrection from the dead. It was reported that a large scar was still quite visible on his throat, giving the miracle wide publicity; and where the severed penis had been there was some sort of small orifice, so to speak, for passing urine.

There is another famous story, which I am not sure has ever been committed to writing. It concerns a man who had exchanged his status of layman for the religious life, if I am not mistaken, and entered a monastery, where he had professed his religious vows. Realizing that the observance of the rule was not as strict as he had hoped, he obtained permission from his abbot to enter another house reputed to be stricter in its observance, and there he lived a life of great devotion. Some time later he fell sick, and then died of his illness. But as he took leave of the world he immediately became the target of opposing forces. In the face of the accusing spirits who tried to condemn him by arguing that he had broken his original vow, the spirits of light, who based themselves on the testimony of his good actions, pleaded strenuously on the other side.

The question was referred to Peter, the keeper of the heavenly gate, but he immediately referred the case to the divine presence. When the facts had been laid out before Him, the Lord said: "Go and see Judge Richard, and do whatever he decides." Now this Richard had been an extraordinarily powerful man in his earthly possessions, but he was even more powerful for the quality of his sense of equity and justice.[180] So Richard was sounded out, the case was laid before him, and he pronounced his sentence: "Since the accused has been found guilty of breaking an earlier vow, he has clearly incurred the accusation of perjury. The devils' case, therefore, is not unfounded, although the man's many just actions are clearly an argument against them. My verdict, in God's name, will be that the accused return to the world to expiate his perjury." Returning to the world the day before his funeral he called upon his abbot, told him what he had seen, made public penance for his sin of desertion and perjury, and went back to his former monastery. Let every monk know, then, wherever he may be, that if he has vowed before God to remain stable, he must keep his promise made to God and the saints. He must not change monasteries unless he is forced to do wrong by those in charge there.[181]

It is useful at times to speak of the character of those who are dying. There was a man from Laon who practiced usury everywhere he went, and his end showed itself to be perfectly in keeping with the way he had lived. As he lay at the threshold of death he still demanded of a poor woman, whose debt had been paid off, that she pay the usurious interests. The woman implored him, in view of his impending death, to absolve her of the interest, but he emphatically refused. Being in a bind, the poor woman managed to borrow the money needed for the interest and brought it to the usurer, minus one farthing. For this one farthing she asked to be absolved, but he swore that he would never grant her a thing. Let me be brief. The woman went about begging for the farthing and had a hard time finding one, and she brought it to the usurer whose screams clearly showed him to be in his final agony. The dying man took the farthing into his mouth and swallowed it almost like a viaticum; then

---

180. Richard was duke of Burgundy from 877 to 921.

181. Stability was an important aspect of the monastic life. The Rule of Saint Benedict warned against wandering monks, called *gyrovagi*, whom Benedict called "servants to the seduction of their own will and appetites." As a Benedictine monk, Guibert himself had taken a vow of "stabilitas," which he had broken once. He was dissuaded from doing so on another occasion only by his mother's dream.

he gave up the ghost and, with this sort of protection, went off to the Devil. He was buried outside consecrated ground, and rightly so.

I will add a story about a man of similar character at Arras. For a long time this man had fattened his purse with ill-gotten gains. Finally, having amassed mountains of metal coins he approached his final hour. Suddenly, the Devil appeared to him disguised as a man leading a black ox before him. He approached the dying man's bed and said: "My lord is sending you this ox." The sick man answered: "I am grateful to my lord for the gift." And turning to his wife he said: "Go prepare something to eat for this man who brought the ox; as for the ox, bring him inside the house and take good care of him." After saying these words he expired immediately.

The man's dinner was prepared for him and fodder was brought for the ox; but neither one nor the other was anywhere to be found. Everyone considered this with dismay and horror, and it escaped no one that this sort of gift bode nothing but ill. The funeral was prepared, the body placed on a bier, and clerics came in procession to the man's house so as to perform the customary ceremonies for the dead; but the devils, who were already celebrating the last rites for their servant, raised such a turbulence in the air as the clergy approached that, while it was a perfectly sunny day, a whirlwind tore off the front part of the house, which is called the gable, and even lifted a part of the bier placed in the middle of the house. I believe I have now said enough about these usurers who gnaw away at the poor.[182]

No one should be surprised in our day by the power these maleficent spirits have, whether it be to trick or to hurt people, especially because what they do they do it like beasts and not in the Lords name. For instance, we have heard that just a few years ago in the district of the Vexin some of the nobles from that area were out hunting somewhere in the neighboring area. They caught a badger that had not managed to escape to its hole; at least they thought it was a badger, for it was really a demon that they had thrown into their bag before taking it away. It took them the greatest effort to carry him away, for they felt that he weighed far more than the animal they presumed to have caught. They had already begun to carry him as night was falling when a voice echoed from a neighboring hill right into the middle of the forest: "Listen," it cried, "listen." Then many other voices, coming from elsewhere, cried

182. Guibert never loses sight of the underlying moral intention of his *Monodiae*, which he illustrates with *exempla*.

out behind these: "What is it?" The first voice replied: "They are taking Caduceus away." (Not without reason was he given this name, for he had brought about the *de-cadence* of many!)[183] When these words were uttered, innumerable flocks of demons roared out from every direction as if to rescue their fellow demon; and the whole forest seemed overrun with them. The hunters, now almost gone mad, tossed the Devil they were carrying—and it was not a badger—as far from them as they could and ran away. Within a very short time after reaching their homes they were dead.

In this same province, one Saturday evening at dusk, a peasant returning from work had sat down on the bank of a stream, his legs uncovered, his feet naked, so as to wash his feet. Suddenly from the bottom of the water in which his legs were soaking a devil came out and grabbed his feet. Feeling himself trapped the peasant cried to his neighbors for help. They carried him back to his own home, where in their typical gruff manner they tried by every means to free his feet. They struggled for a long time in this useless round of efforts but all their attempts to free the man were vain. Spiritual things can only be counteracted by spiritual things. Finally, after they had gone around in circles for a long time, a pilgrim joined them who pounced on the man's fettered feet while they looked on and freed them within seconds. After this he vanished before anyone could even ask who he was.

Everywhere one also hears of demons' love for women and even of demons seeking to sleep with women. We could say much about these matters if shame did not deter us from doing so. There are also demons who inflict the most cruel tortures on others, while others are content merely to play tricks on humans. Perhaps it were better if my pen turned to lighter matters.[184]

The story I am now about to tell I heard quite recently from a monk of Monte Cassino. An abbot of that monastery by the name of Desiderius became a candidate for the papacy after the death of Hildebrand, who was known as Gregory VII. Desiderius was one of the cardinals of the Roman church, and he obtained the pontificate for himself with money gotten from the vast store of things he had stolen from the church of our lord Benedict. While he was celebrating his first Mass after being

183. Guibert puns on the words "caduceum" and "cadere," meaning "to fall."

184. Before turning to "lighter" matters Guibert cannot refrain from telling three more anecdotes, two of them involving simony: like a good storyteller with a few afterthoughts.

raised to the Apostolic See, he turned toward the people to pronounce the words "Pax vobis," when suddenly he collapsed. He was seriously wounded when his head hit the pavement, and was taken away. One night as he was sleeping Saint Benedict appeared to him and said: "You simoniac, how did you dare raise yourself to such a great office? You have committed a detestable sacrilege by robbing me of what belongs to me, and you have usurped a position that far surpasses your merits! Renounce it, then, and do penance for this shameful fall of yours; for if you ever choose to persevere in your present undertaking you will suffer the most damaging retribution." Hearing this, Desiderius feared that he would incur multiple punishments for his double sin, particularly the punishment that such a noble and powerful authority as Benedict was threatening against him. So he resigned his undeserved office and returned to his former monastery, where for a full year this arrogant man, now turned humble, expiated for his excesses by serving as a porter. Having demonstrated his humility—indeed he had made himself very useful—he was worthy to be elected abbot a second time.

Things turned out quite differently, I've often heard it said, for a certain monk of Fleury. After promising money to the king of France, he snatched away this same church of Saint Benedict from the abbot Abbon, a man as deeply holy as he was deeply learned. Abbon then pursued this man like a sheep gone astray to arrest him and bring him to custody. It so happened that he found him at Orléans. When the simoniac heard that the abbot was in the city, finding no place to run to, he took refuge in the latrines, as if the weight of his bowels were forcing him to go there. When Abbon arrived he looked for the monk, but he was nowhere to be found. Nothing but his cowl was found suspended on a hook, for the man had vanished and the only respect due him was due to his sacred habit.

I also saw Véran, a nobleman and a relative of mine, devoted to such injustice and villainy that he was expelled from his abbot's post in spite of the king's interventions in his behalf. God usually chastises more severely those leaders who turn to crime. I have heard that these same monks of Fleury quite some years ago strayed so far from their rule that the most holy Father condemned several of them to shameful deaths.

20
Miracles of the saints

The English have a most blessed martyr in the person of King Edmund,[185] who continues to be a source of miraculous events now as he was formerly. I shall not even mention his body, which has remained free of corruption, with its skin pigmentations not human but heavenly; one is still amazed to find his nails and hair continuing to grow. What should be added, however, is that though King Edmund's body is clearly in miraculous condition it does not tolerate being examined by anyone. In our own day one of the abbots of the abbey of Bury Saint-Edmunds wanted to find out by himself whether the saint's head, which had been cut off during his martyrdom, was still joined to his body, as was popularly alleged.[186] He began by fasting, along with his chaplain; then he uncovered the body and saw what we have already related: the flesh was in no way withered, and it seemed as if the saint were sleeping. The abbot continued his investigation through sight and touch, but to his own peril. Thus he and his companion stood, one at the saint's head, the other at the feet and they both pulled to see what condition the body was in, and were convinced that it was one piece. Soon afterward, however, both of them suffered permanent paralysis of their hands.

I will tell you other astonishing things. In this same monastery the monks have nourished a he-goat since the time it was a kid. The animal would frolic about in his kid-like way through the buildings and even into the church, until one day he broke a leg. Limping on three legs he kept ambling about as best he could throughout the monastery, when one day he made his way into the church and headed for the martyr's tomb. Hardly had he indulged his animal's curiosity when the leg was cured. One can imagine how much more the blessed martyr would do if a prayer were addressed to him in faith by a human creature, when he showed such instinctive generosity or, I should rather say, a royal benevolence to a beast.

In the city of Winchester, Saint Swithin has proved himself a great

185. Edmund, king of East Anglia, was decapitated by the Danes in 870. The monastery of Bury Saint-Edmunds was built around his shrine.

186. Saint Edmund's head was said to have been reunited to his body in the tomb. Guibert may be repeating stories about Saint Edmund and Saint Swithin told him by the canons of Laon during their money-raising tour of England.

doer of miracles to this very day.[187] Not so long ago there was a monk whose hands were both covered with the ugliest sores. His condition was so bad that he seemed more afflicted than any leper and totally unfit for any kind of work. Saint Swithin took offense when the monk did not attend the night office on the eve of his feast, so he appeared to him inquiring why he had been absent from the community office. The monk immediately replied that the pain and festering of his hands were his reason for not going. "Stretch forth your hands," Saint Swithin said. Hardly had the monk extended his hands when the Saint squeezed them both very tightly and pulled off the entire coating of leprous skin like a pair of gloves, leaving in its place a skin more tender than a baby's.

In the castle town I come from was preserved an arm of the blessed martyr Arnoul.[188] Someone had brought it to this place, but the townspeople had been very skeptical as to its authenticity, so as a test it was thrown into the fire, from which it immediately leaped out. A short time later one of my cousins, one of the nobles of the castle, was stricken with a very serious illness. When the blessed martyr's arm was applied and came in contact with the painful area, this area would switch to another part of the body. The painful area would keep changing places, and the martyr's arms would keep pursuing it; finally, after a long chase that covered the patient's face and bodily members, the illness concentrated itself in full virulence in the area between the neck and the shoulders. The skin was raised as if a little mouse had crept under it, making it look like a little ball. Finally the ball vanished, painlessly. For this reason every year the noble gave a generous banquet to all the clergy every year so long as he lived on Saint Arnoul's feast day; and his successors have never failed to do the same. The arm was entirely covered with fine gold and precious stones by a woman from my grandfather's household, not his wife but one of the women who was familiar with such matters and skilled in worldly things.

An arm of Saint Arnoul is also said to be at Guise, a castle in the

---

187. Saint Swithin's day is celebrated 15 July. Saint Swithin (or Swithun) was consecrated bishop of Winchester in 852. He died 2 July 862. His relics were translated to Winchester 15 July 964 and became a popular place of pilgrimage. William of Malmesbury described the patron saint of Winchester as "a rich treasure of all virtues." See Alban Butler, *The Lives of the Fathers, Martyrs, and Other Principle Saints*, 2 vols. (London: Henry & Co., n.d.), 2.61.

188. The relic of Saint Arnoul of Clermont, about forty miles southwest of Nogent, the birthplace of Guibert.

Laon area. Some robbers, who had already taken the church treasure, also wanted to carry away the relic, but it kept slipping out of their hands, and they were unable to carry it anywhere. The robbers themselves confessed to this after they were arrested with the rest of their booty, at the very moment they were being led to the gallows. We might add that in the gold covering in which this arm is encased there is a spot where no precious stone can be kept inserted by any skill of any gemsetter. Whenever a stone is set, it immediately falls out. The workmen change, but neither the workman nor the work is in any way improved.

We also know, of course, of Saint Léger's power in working miracles, and his swiftness in bringing aid. In my case, how well I remember the time when I was a little boy in my mother's care, and during one Easter season I was suffering from a daily, debilitating fever. At the foot of our castle there was a church dedicated to Saints Léger and Maclou where my mother in her humble faith kept an oil lamp perpetually burning. I had reached the point where the very thought of food made me sick, so my mother put me under the care of two clerics, her house chaplain and my tutor, and ordered them to lead me to that church. I should add that in keeping with the deplorable customs of those days the church was under my mother's jurisdiction. The clerics went to the church and prepared beds before the altar where I would sleep that night in their company. In the middle of the night it seemed to us that the ground within the church itself was being struck with hammers, that the locks of the chests were being torn off with a loud noise, and that the chests themselves were being beaten with rods. The clerics were awakened by these noises and were immediately afraid that fear would worsen my condition.

What more do I need to say? I could hear them whispering, but I wasn't terribly afraid, given how close they were to me, and the lamp nearby giving off a fine light. We made it through the night, and I went back to my mother in perfect health as if I had never been sick. Before my illness I could not stand the sight of the finest foods; now I was quick to eat even the most ordinary fare, and they even found me anxious to play ball.

King William I of England had a tower built at his own expense in the church of the magnificent Saint-Denis.[189] How high that tower would have been if construction had continued and if it were still standing! But

189. The tower of King William at the basilica of Saint-Denis was discovered only in 1946.

since the church's engineers had not planned it carefully, it seemed every day to be in danger of collapsing. Yves, who was the abbot at the time, and his monks were most concerned that the collapse of the new edifice would seriously damage the old basilica, where stood Saint Edmund's altar and the altar of so many other saints. The abbot had the following vision. He saw a lady of very honorable appearance standing in the middle of the church of Saint-Denis; like a priest she was performing the ceremony of exorcism by water. The abbot was astounded by the authority that flowed from this woman's most unusual behavior, and he noticed that after blessing the water she walked about the church performing aspersions and making the sign of the cross on the spots that she had aspersed.

Within a short time the tower collapsed, but it did no damage to any part of the church. For She who is the most blessed among women—blessed is the fruit of Her womb!—had in fact protected the church with Her benediction, as the abbot had seen in his vision. But right next to the church the tower's collapse killed a man passing by. When it became clear to all that there was a man buried under the rubble, sheer humanitarian impulse made them want to remove the pile under which he lay buried. When they had finally removed the mountains of cement and rocks and reached the man, they found him—this is simply incredible—unhurt and cheerful, as if he had been sitting at home. The square stones had wedged themselves into one another and created some kind of little shelter for him; so although he had been trapped in there for who knows how many days, this isolated man had suffered neither hunger nor fear nor the acrid smell of mortar.

Let us now place the most excellent Mary, patroness of heaven and earth, together with Denis, the lord of all of France, as a conclusion to this book.[190]

---

190. Having dedicated the two previous chapters to illustrating the power of Mary and the saints in avenging human sin, Guibert consciously ends his Monodies illustrating the power of saints' relics to cure, aid, protect, and save. The book ends on the happier ("laetiora") note Guibert had promised in the previous chapter.

Bibliography

Augustine, Saint. *The City of God against the Pagans.* Trans. David S. Wisen. Loeb Classical Library. Cambridge, Mass.: Harvard University Press, 1968. Books 8–11.

———. *Confessions.* 2 vols. Cambridge, Mass.: Harvard University Press; London: W. Heinemann, 1931–42

———. *De doctrina christiana.* Ed. J. Martin. *Corpus Christianorum. Series Latina* [*CCSL*] 32. Turnholt: Brepols, 1972.

———. *Epistolae.* In *Patrologiae Cursus Completus. Series Latina* [*PL*]. Ed. J. P. Migne. Paris: Montrouge, 1848

———. *Liber de haeresibus ad Quoduvultdeum.* In *Patrologiae Cursus Completus. Series Latina* [*PL*]. Ed. J. P. Migne. Paris: Montrouge, 1841.

Ausonius. *Ausonius.* 2 vols. Trans. Hugh G. Evelyn White. Cambridge, Mass.: Harvard University Press; London: W. Heinemann, 1919–49.

Baron, Salo Wittmayer. *A Social and Religious History of the Jews.* 2d. ed. 8 vols. New York: Columbia University Press, 1957.

Benton, John F. *Self and Society in Medieval France.* New York: Harper & Row, 1970; rpt. University of Toronto Press, in association with the Medieval Academy of America, 1984.

———. "The Personality of Guibert de Nogent." *Psychoanalytic Review* 57 (1970–71): 563–86.

Bede. *The Ecclesiastical History of the English Nation.* Trans. Vida D. Scudder. New York: E. P. Dutton, 1919; rpt., 1930. Everyman's Library no. 479.

Biblia Sacra iuxta vulgatam versionem. Ed. Bonifatio Fischer et al. Stuttgart: Deutsche Bibelgesellschaft, 1983.

The Holy Bible. Revised Standard Version. New York: Thomas Nelson & Sons, 1952.

Benedict of Nursia. *The Rule of Saint Benedict.* Ed. and trans. Abbot Justin McCann. London: Burns Oates, 1952.

Bloch, R. Howard. *Etymologies and Genealogies: A Literary Anthropology of the French Middle Ages.* Chicago: University of Chicago Press, 1983.

————. *God's Plagiarist: Being an Account of the Fabulous Industry and Irregular Commerce of the Abbé Migne.* Chicago: University of Chicago Press, 1994.

Boethius. *The Consolation of Philosophy.* Rev. Trans. H. F. Stewart. Cambridge, Mass.: Harvard University Press, 1966.

Bourgin, Georges. *Guibert de Nogent. Histoire de sa vie (1053–1124).* Paris: A Picard et fils, 1907.

Butler, Alban. *The Lives of the Fathers, Martyrs, and Other Principal Saints.* 2 vols. London: Henry and Co., n.d.

Chazan, Robert. *Medieval Jewry in Northern France.* Baltimore: The Johns Hopkins University Press, 1973.

Cicero. *De Lege agraria. M. Tulli Ciceronis Scripta Quae Manserunt Omnia.* Leipzig: Teubner, 1885.

Corpus Christianorum. Series Latina [CCSL]. Vols. 30–32. Turnholt: Brepols, 1972.

Courcelle, Pierre. *Les Confessions de Saint Augustin dans la tradition littéraire.* Paris: Etudes Augustiniennes, 1963.

Crossley, Ceri. *French Historians and Romanticism.* New York: Routledge, 1993.

Dictionnaire de droit canonique. 6 vols. Ed. A Naz et al. Paris: Letouzey & Ané, 1935–57.

Duby, Georges. *The Chivalrous Society.* Trans. Cynthia Postan. Berkeley: University of California Press, 1972.

————. *The Knight, the Lady, and the Priest.* Trans. Barbara Bray. New York: Pantheon Books, 1983.

————. *Love and Marriage in the Middle Ages.* Trans. Jane Dunnett. Chicago: University of Chicago Press, 1994.

Dwyer, John C. *Twenty Centuries of Catholic Christianity.* New York: Paulist Press, 1985.

Fawtier, Robert. *The Capetian Kings of France.* Trans. Lionel Butler and R. J. Adam. New York: St. Martin's Press, 1966.

Freud, Sigmund. *The Future of an Illusion.* Trans. James Strachey. New York: W. W. Norton, 1961.

Flandrin, Jean-Louis. *Le Sexe et l'occident.* Paris: Seuil, 1981.

————. *Un Temps pour embrasser. Aux origines de la morale sexuelle occidentale. VIe–XIe siècle.* Paris: Seuil, 1983.

Gratianus. *Decretum Gratiani.* In *Patrologiae Cursus Completus. Series Latina* [PL]. Ed. J. P. Migne. Paris: Montrouge, 1891.

Gregory of Tours. *The History of the Franks.* 2 vols. Trans. O. M. Dalton. Oxford: Clarendon Press, 1977.

Gregory the Great. *Dialogues.* Ed. Henry James Coleridge. London: Burns and Oates, 1874.

Guizot, M. (François). *Collection des Mémoires pour servir à l'histoire de France.*

Vol. 9: *Histoire des croisades, par Guibert de Nogent—Vie de Guibert de Nogent, par lui-même*; Vol. 10: *Vie de Saint Bernard, Guillaume de Saint-Thierri*. Paris: J.L.G. Brière, 1825.

Hallam, Elizabeth M. *Capetian France 987–1328*. New York: Longmans, 1980.

Horace (Quintus Horatius Flaccus). *Satires, Epistles, and Ars Poetica*. Trans. H. Rushton Fairclough. Cambridge, Mass.: Harvard University Press, 1961.

Jotischky, Andrew. *The Perfection of Solitude: Hermits and Monks in the Crusader States*. University Park: The Pennsylvania State University Press, 1995.

Kantor, Jonathan. "A Psychological Source: 'The Memoirs' of Abbot Guibert of Nogent." *Journal of Mediaeval History* 2 (1976): 281–303.

Labande, Edmond-René. *Guibert de Nogent: Autobiographie*. Paris: Les Belles Lettres, 1981.

Le Goff, Jacques. *La Naissance du purgatoire*. Paris: Seuil, 1981.

Lubac, Henri de. *L'Exégèse médiévale*. 4 vols. Paris: Seuil, 1968.

Lucan (M. A. Lucanus). *M. Annae Lucani belli civilis libri decem*. Ed. A. E. Housman. Oxford: Basil Blackwell, 1958.

———. *Pharsalia*. Trans. Jane Wilson Joyce. Ithaca: Cornell University Press, 1993.

Luchaire, Achille. *Louis VI le Gros. Annales de sa vie et de son règne (1081–1137)*. Paris, 1890; rpt. Brussels: Culture et Civilisation, 1964.

Melczer, William. *The Pilgrim's Guide to Santiago de Compostela*. New York: Italica Press, 1993.

Migne, Abbé J. P., ed. *Patrologiae Cursus Completus. Series Latina* [PL]. 227 vols. Paris: Éd. d'Amboise, 1864–84.

Misch, Georg. *Geschichte der Autobiographie. Das Mittelalter*. Frankfurt am Main: G. Schulte-Bulmke, 1959.

Monod, Bernard. *Le Moine Guibert et son temps (1053–1124)*. Paris: Hachette, 1905.

———. *Essai sur les rapports de Pascal II avec Philippe Ier (1099–1108)*. Paris: Champion, 1907.

Montaigne. Michel de. *Essais*. 2 vols. Paris: Garnier, 1962.

Mourret, Rev. Fernand. *A History of the Catholic Church*. Vol. 4: *Period of the Later Middle Ages*. Trans. Rev. Newton Thompson, S.T.D. London: B. Herder, 1947.

New Catholic Encyclopedia. 15 vols. Washington, D.C.: Catholic University of America; New York: McGraw-Hill, 1967.

Ovid. *Metamorphoses*. 2 vols. Trans. Frank Justus Miller. Cambridge, Mass.: Harvard University Press, 1977.

Quintilian. *Institutio oratoria*. 4 vols. Trans. H. E. Butler. New York: G. B. Putnam's Sons, 1933.

Richer. *Richeri Historiarum libri quatuor.* Ed. and trans. A. M. Poinsignon. Reims: P. Régnier, 1855.

Sallust. *The War with Catiline.* Trans. J. C. Rolfe. New York: G. B. Putnam's Sons, 1920.

Sidonius Apollinaris. *Poems and Letters.* Trans. W. B. Anderson. 2 vols. Cambridge, Mass.: Harvard University Press, 1936.

Seneca, Lucius Annaeus. *Ad Lucilium epistulae morales.* 2 vols. Trans. Richard M. Gummere. New York: G. B. Putnam's Sons, 1930.

Southern, Richard W. *Saint Anselm and His Biographer.* Cambridge: Cambridge University Press, 1963.

Suger, Abbot. *The Deeds of Louis the Fat.* Trans. and notes by R. Cusimano and J. Moorhead. Washington, D.C.: Catholic University of America Press, 1992.

Terentius, P. Afer. *Eunuchus. P. Terenti Afri Comoediae.* Ed. A. Fleckeisen. Leipzig: Teubner, 1848.

Thierry, Augustin. *Lettres sur l'histoire de France.* Paris: Garnier, 1828.

Vergil (P. Vergilius Maro). *Aeneid.* 2 vols. Trans. H. Rushton Fairclough. Cambridge, Mass.: Harvard University Press, 1966.

Vitalis, Ordericus. *The Ecclesiastical History of England and Normandy.* 4 vols. Ed. G. Forrester. London: Henry G. Bohn; rpt., New York: AMS Press, 1968.

————. *The Ecclesiastical History of Orderic Vitalis.* Ed. and trans. Marjorie Chibnall. 2 vols. Oxford: Clarendon Press, 1969; rpt., 1983.

Ward, Sister Benedicta, trans. *The Prayers and Meditations of Saint Anselm.* Harmondsworth: Penguin Books, 1973.

Index